COLLECTIBLE *Vernon* KILNS

IDENTIFICATION AND VALUE GUIDE

SECOND EDITION

MAXINE FEEK NELSON

COLLECTOR BOOKS

A Division of Schroeder Publishing Co., Inc.

❧ *Dedication* ❧

In Memory of Jane Bennison Howell, daughter of Vernon Kilns founder Faye Bennison and an artist in her own right, whose work will be her legacy, and Edward J. Fischer, the last president of Vernon Kilns, who in his nineties was still actively interested in the company and the products that he helped to create.

Cover design by Beth Summers
Book design by Lisa Henderson

Front Cover: Statue of Liberty 10½" plate, Aquarium 6½" plate by Don Blanding, *Sari*, 14½" tall, by May and Vieve Hamilton, Vernonware display sign, Early California 2-cup coffee pot.
Back Cover: Pierced Pedestal, 12" diameter, by Jane Bennison.

This book makes reference to various Disney copyrighted characters, trademarks, marks and registered marks owned by *The Walt Disney Company* and *Disney Enterprises, Inc.*

The current values in this book should be used only as a guide. They are not intended to set prices, which vary from one section of the country to another. Auction prices as well as dealer prices vary greatly and are affected by condition as well as demand. Neither the Author nor the Publisher assumes responsibility for any losses that might be incurred as a result of consulting this guide.

Searching For A Publisher?

We are always looking for people knowledgeable within their fields. If you feel that there is a real need for a book on your collectible subject and have a large comprehensive collection, contact Collector Books.

❧ Contents ❧

✎ Acknowledgments ✎

Some ten years have passed since *Collectible Vernon Kilns* was first published in 1994. Since then, I have done a great deal of research, and the internet (eBay) has played an important role in my ability to uncover scarce examples of Vernon Kilns pottery. Many more photos of rarities, and some unknown items that were not seen in either my last book *(Collectible Vernon Kilns)* or in my previous two books *(Versatile Vernon Kilns; Versatile Vernon Kilns, Book II)* are now pictured and described in this edition. Our knowledge of Vernon Kilns has truly evolved over the years, thanks mostly to all those whom I have acknowledged previously; I now again thank many of those same people, plus others who have been most helpful, for lending me photos and offering their knowledge and suggestions.

Those to be thanked, especially for research information and the pictures that were so generously shared with me for this book, are Michael Pratt, author of *Mid-Century Modern Dinnerware: Ak-Sar-Ben Pottery, Denwar Ceramics, Iroquois China Company, Laurel Potteries of California, Royal China Company,* and *Stetson China Company;* Steve and Debra Soukup (Steve is the author of an upcoming book covering Poxon tiles, entitled *California Tile — The Golden Era 1910 to 1940)*; and Pat Faux, editor of *Vernon Views,* who was an invaluable source with her albums of material from twenty-two years of publication and who also generously updated the index of this edition. A special word of thanks to Dan Trueblood, for his words of encouragement and, again, for the shared research information and the many photos from his collection. John and Joanne Barrett, Tim and Linda Colling, Dennis Donnal, Harvey Duke, Carol House (Elliott House's widow), Bob Hutchins, Bill Stern, and Ray Vlach are also to be given special thanks. I am grateful to Jean Fischer Volner for the added information regarding her father, Edward Fischer, the last president of Vernon Kilns. Al Alberts deserves special mention for his previous contribution of an index to the 1994 book and his continued support and information for this book. Cindy Anderson, Jim Burrett, Sara Bell, Kay Bernhard, Vernon and Mary Carrens, Nancy Franz, Linda and Jerry Lakomek, Padraig MacRauiri, Sean Meredith (Track 16), Brent and Sandra Purdom, Philip Shurley, Mark Smith, and anyone I may have inadvertently overlooked, all shared and are contributors to this edition. My heartfelt thanks to all.

To the many who have contributed to the three previous books, once again my thanks. These include Judi Thompson, Dave Thompson, Nancy and Bill Schadeberg, Manuel Palazuelos, Alex and Katherine Shaner, Floyd Hathaway, Carolyn Lee, and David R. Smith, a Walt Disney archivist. Others are Bif and Mike of Laguna, James Bloesser, Willard Burkhardt, Virginia Carpenter, Carole Chapman, Jack Chipman, Bess Christensen, Thomas and Marisa Craig, Marily Erickson, Lois Finnerty, Doris Frizzell, Tom and Jan Fuelling, Anne Gallagher, Carl Gibbs, Bill Harmon, Cathie Heather, Sandy and John Hockaday, Tamara Hodge of Ceramics Care Unit, Bill and Bette Lallas, Linda Lease, Harold and Theresa Matthews, Glen Minert, Josephine Morse, Donna Obwald, Malinda Pretz (granddaughter of Faye Bennison), Robert Rightmire, Veronica Sanford, Warren and Elizabeth Scott, Doug Smith, Gladys Spector (widow of George Spector), Georgette Stock, Frank and Seville Tosto, Betty Truro, Billie Nelson Tyrell, Marina Gerwig Walton, Norvelle Weeks, and Margaret and Fred Wilhelm.

Early in my research and several years prior to publication (in 1978) of my first book, *Versatile Vernon Kilns,* several personal interviews enabled me to later relate firsthand the stories of Vernon Kilns and Poxon. Faye G. Bennison, founder of Vernon Kilns, graciously furnished most of the background about his company in several interviews prior to his death on August 31, 1974, at the age of 91. The late Edward J. Fischer, last president and general manger, filled in many gaps. Mr. Fischer passed away on November 19, 2002, at 97 years of age.

My first meeting with Jane Bennison Howell was during interviews with her father. I was fortunate to remain in personal contact with her during the years following. A talented artist in her own right, she was a foremost art ware designer at Vernon Kilns. Her career ended when she married her college sweetheart, B. N. "Bud" Howell. Jane passed away on January 15, 2001, in San Pedro, CA, at the age of 88. In the years before her death, she had shared her memories, which are recalled in this book, and her art ware, which is photographed.

Other former Vernon people who were helpful are Doug Bothwell, Mr. Bennison's son-in-law and former vice president of sales; Zepha Boget, former advertising manager who provided several 1950 company price lists; James Cox, and Ollie Bunyard.

For the Poxon story, credit is given to the sons and daughters of the late George and Judith Furlong Poxon: Dr. Leon Poxon, Mrs. Roberta Moore, Sister Judith Poxon, and daughters-in-law Mrs. Vincent Poxon and Mrs. John Poxon.

I would also like to thank the staff of St. Martha's church for providing helpful informaton about its location, and Ms. Dolores Petullo of the Vernon Chamber of Commerce for providing information about the old Vernon Kilns site.

For providing Rockwell Kentiana, I thank the late John F.H. Gorton, husband of Sally Kent Gorton (Rockwell Kent's widow), who had been director of the Rockwell Kent Legacies before his death in February of 1980. I also wish to thank George Spector, who was the editor of the *Kent Collector* until his passing in July of 1987.

Photos in the two prior books are credited to Vincent Ivicevic (of Vincent's Commercial Studio in Huntington Beach, CA) and C. L. McClanahan. Individual photos are noted. Mark renderings and original line drawings are credited to Chuck Steers.

Not to be overlooked is my daughter, Pamela Renard, who helped with computer problems and was always available with loving support, advice, and editing.

My association with the two Mr. Schroeders began in 1983, with Bill senior, when my book *Versatile Vernon Kilns* was published. In 1994, Mr. Schroeder agreed to publish an expanded version, entitled *Collectible Vernon Kilns*. I want to express my deep appreciation for their continued confidence in publishing my books, ending with this second edition. Also, my thanks to Gail Ashburn and Amy Sullivan, editor and assistant editor, and to their staff for their expertise, guidance, and invaluable assistance.

To repeat words from my last book, though I had not expected to ever do another book on Vernon Kilns, "With the support of collectors and many others, the story of this mid-century pace-setting California pottery company is told."

❧ *Preface* ❧

During the past twenty years, a new generation of collectors has emerged, and some truly wonderful Vernon Kilns pottery is found in major collections today. In the past, hundreds of pieces of pottery that were loaned to me by collectors and dealers everywhere and were not in previous books, were sent to me for photographing, and those pictures remain in this revision. In addition, much information previously undocumented and scores of photographs of pottery (much of it rare) were sent by collectors and dealers for use in this revision.

My interest in Vernon Kilns traces back to 1946, just after the close of World War II. I was a newlywed arriving with my husband in Southern California, where we planned to make our home. One of our first gifts was a starter set from my family in Seattle of Vernon's Brown Eyed Susan, purchased at the Marshall Field's store Frederick & Nelson's (now closed). Looking back, I was completely oblivious to the fact that the pottery had been made in the nearby industrial city of Vernon that bordered South Central Los Angeles. Nevertheless, the day came when the pottery, and its proximity, led to my intensive research.

Twelve years passed, and I was disappointed when my open stock Susan pattern was no longer available because the pottery company had gone out of business. So what was left of my set was simply packed away and forgotten. In the early 1960s, I caught the collecting bug and would occasionally spot a piece of my Susan at local flea markets. I became aware of the many Vernon Kilns picture plates. Before long, I had managed to accumulate quite a collection of the plates, including ones for my home state of Washington, the city of Seattle, and my alma mater, the University of Washington. Definitely a high point was the day when at a Los Angeles antique show, I found a Timothy Mouse figure for $7.50. I was surprised to find it marked "Vernon Kilns" along with the Walt Disney copyright and date.

The purchase of a Memento plate signed by Faye G. Bennison, founder and president of Vernon Kilns, ultimately led to my first visit, on October 13, 1971, with this impressive elderly gentleman. It was fascinating to hear the story of his company firsthand. The memory of my last visit will always remain vivid. Mr. Bennison was in his nineties by then, yet remained remarkably alert and active. He ushered me into the kitchen of his spacious home, mounted a stepladder, and reached up to the top shelf of a cupboard. Taking them down piece by piece, he proudly showed me a 12 place settings of Kent's Salamina, including egg cups and tumblers, and the additional matching serving pieces.

In 1978, my first book, *Versatile Vernon Kilns,* was published. It documented Vernon Kilns history as learned from Mr. Bennison and other former employees, and pictured examples of known Vernon Kilns pottery. Interviews with members of the Poxon family also provided historical information and pottery examples of the predecessor company, Poxon/Vernon China. This little book seemed to open the floodgates; before long, the need for another book became apparent, leading to *Book II* in 1983, which led to an even more comprehensive book in 1994. All books have long been out of print, and because of the interest and apparent need for information about Vernon Kilns pottery, I was encouraged by my publisher to compile this updated revision. This edition features examples of rare art ware and newly documented patterns and products. Also included is new Poxon information and pictures of Poxon art ware.

Values in this price guide are averages, based upon prices observed in leading national trade publications, California and western state shops, and pottery shows among dealers who specialize in pottery and American dinnerware. The prices are for pieces in their original condition having no wear, chips, cracks, scratches, or defective glazes. This is meant to serve as a guide only. Prices will vary from area to area and will be determined by popularity and availability. In the cases of those rare pieces whose prices are not determined, price is shown as PND. Some prices will be indicated with a plus sign ($400+), which indicates that the piece is worth at least this amount in the seller's market.

❧ Introduction ❧

In the early depression years of the 1930s, there were many potteries in Southern California busily producing colorful, inexpensive pottery. The region had long been a mecca for artists from all over the world. Many of these talented artists were at work designing and decorating these wares, the production of which became a kind of panacea for them during those hard times.

Vernon Kilns was among these California potteries and a successor to an earlier company, Poxon China, which traced its roots to both the '49 Gold Rush and to England. Poxon China (later called Vernon China) was founded in Vernon, California, in about 1912 by a brilliant young Englishman, ceramist, and chemist, George J. W. (Wade) Poxon, a member of the Wade family. (Wade is a well-known English pottery, which today is a subsidiary of Royal Doulton.)

In 1931, the company's ownership passed to Faye G. Bennison. Under his dynamic leadership, the pottery company now called Vernon Potteries, Ltd., remained at the original site in Vernon, California. Despite depression, earthquake, fire, and war years, the company survived and flourished, ultimately becoming a leader in the pottery industry and internationally famous for the quality and versatility of its wares. Pottery included movie star figurines, Walt Disney–designed figures, vases, and dinnerware, as well as Coca-Cola and other types of advertising wares. Political, fraternal, religious, and patriotic themes, and famous people and places were subjects of the historical and commemorative specialties. Scores of dinnerware patterns were designed by celebrated artists. The pottery was available in better department stores, jewelry stores, and gift stores throughout the United States and Canada and through sales offices in all major cities.

But like many of its American pottery and glass contemporaries, the company was unable to survive the flood of foreign imports; this was further complicated by domestic labor disputes of the postwar era. In January of 1958, the company reluctantly announced its decision to cease operations. Later that year, it closed its doors forever.

Metlox Potteries of Manhattan Beach, California, bought the Vernon tradename, goodwill, molds, and some remaining stock, and continued producing several dinnerware patterns for a very short time (see Dinnerware section). Metlox continued to use one set of molds (the San Fernando shape) for its Vernon Ware line until its demise in 1989.

Vernon Kilns was not destined for obscurity. Today, almost a century after it was founded, its pottery is sought by collectors everywhere.

∾ Evolution of Marks ∾

Poxon China (also known as Vernon China), marks 1912 – 1931:

Mark 1, 101 Incised

Mark 2, Embossed

Mark 3

Mark 4

Vernon Kilns marks (also known as Vernon Potteries, Ltd. – see mark 5), 1930s:

Mark 5, Paper label brown & gold Rare!

Mark 6, Mission Bell #1

Mark 7, Sometimes Multicolor

Mark 8, Mission Bell #2 – Montecito

Mark 9

Mark 10, Embossed

Mark 11*

Mark 12

1930 – into early 1940s:

Mark 13*

Mark 14*

Mark 15*

Mark 16*

Mark 17*

Mark 18*

Mark 19*

Mark 20*

Mark 21*

Mark 22

*Pattern identity

Note: In mark 7, the overlaid letters in the square are *VPL* ; these are the initials of Vernon Potteries, Ltd.

1955:

Mark 23

Mark 24*

Mark 25*

Mark 26*

Transitional Marks, 27 also a Metlox mark with the added, "By Metlox," and 28 is a Metlox Vernon Ware mark, used 1956 – 1960:

Mark 27*

Mark 28

Designer-Artist and Special Marks:

Mark 29

Mark 30

Mark 31

Mark 32

Mark 33

Mark 34*

Mark 35*

Mark 36*

Mark 37*

Mark 38, Bisque base

Mark 39

Mark 40*

Mark 41*

Mark 42*

Mark 43*

Mark 44*

Mark 45*

Mark 46*

Mark 47*

Mark 48*

Mark 49*

*Pattern identity is given in mark.

Note: Marks were underglaze and usually in the color of the predominant pattern color. There were many variations to some marks; e.g., marks 12 through 22 and 33.

❧ Poxon China (Vernon China) ❧
1912 – 1931

In about 1848, a relatively common event of the time occurred. Two brothers left their native Ireland, each to seek his fortune and go his separate way in the New World. This event culminated in a series of uncommon events that resulted in the founding of a pottery in Vernon, California, at the turn of the century and indirectly led to a major industrial center in Southern California.

The two brothers, Robert and James Furlong, left Wexford, Ireland; Robert went to Nova Scotia and James to Australia. When gold was discovered in California in 1849, each brother, without the other's knowledge, set out for California to join the search for gold. Robert walked across the Isthmus from Nova Scotia via Panama (where he contracted malaria) and boarded a boat for San Francisco. James took a boat from Australia, likewise bound for San Francisco. Amidst thousands of gold seekers flocking to California, the two brothers met, by an extremely remote chance, in San Francisco. There they joined forces and left for Nevada City to work in the gold fields.

Striking it rich, the two brothers settled in the Bakersfield area as ranchers. They brought their wives-to-be over from Ireland; the women traveled across the United States on the transcontinental train. In about 1880, some years after they married, Robert and his wife Martha moved to Southern California. For eleven hundred gold coins they bought a ranch in Vernon, a town on the southeast perimeter of Los Angeles. They had four children: Tom, James, Annie, and Judith (1881 – 1967), the youngest, who was to play an important role in this story. In 1883 Robert died, leaving his wife Martha and his son Tom (at nine years of age, the eldest) to run the ranch and raise the children.

By 1900, Vernon had a population of a few hundred, mostly farmers. Tom and James Furlong were by now young men, leading citizens, and large landholders. They, along with another rancher, John Leonis, acted as trustees of the City of Vernon and were responsible, in 1905, for the decision to incorporate and develop the farming community into a manufacturing center. They encouraged large eastern manufacturers, such as American Can and the Aluminum Company of America, to locate in Vernon, and were instrumental in having the railroads lay their track into the city, facilitating easy access to and from points of shipping for the manufacturers. The Los Angeles stock yards were also located here. Thus, this industrial center was born indirectly of the Gold Rush fifty years before. Because of the tremendous growth of industry, the population to this day has remained static, and today there are only a handful of residents. The Furlongs, influential in its shaping, were still active in the city government as late as 1978.

Meanwhile, about 1910 in Stoke-on-Trent, England, another young man, George J. W. (Wade) Poxon (1887 – 1950), a pottery chemist, graduated with honors, first in his class, from Staffordshire Technical College. He was about to embark on a career that brings us to the theme of his story. George, related to the Wade family of Wade Pottery in England, along with his uncle, William Wade, left for America about 1911. Nothing is known of their path between England and California, but it is surmised that they may have journeyed through Ohio, where many early potteries were in business. Nor has it been learned why they eventually settled in Vernon, California. Some mention by the family has been made of American Encaustic Tile, and it is thought that at one time George was employed by them. In his journal, he mentioned various Ohio pottery companies.

The earliest record of George Poxon in California, according to the family, was in 1912, when he leased land adjacent to their ranch house from the Furlong family. He founded Poxon Pottery, a small tile factory with two large beehives and one small glost kiln. The address of the pottery was 2310 East 52nd Street, Vernon, California.

Pottery Factory under construction, May 12, 1912.

Poxon China building and kilns after completion, circa 1912.

George and Judith Poxon's wedding photo.

Here in Vernon, young George Poxon, a "delightful, fun-loving, charming man, soft spoken easy going" (in the words of a family member), met and wooed Judith, a school teacher, the youngest daughter of Robert (deceased) and Martha Furlong. On August 29, 1913, George, at age 26, married Judith in St. Martha's church. The small church, named for Judith's mother, had been built largely through the efforts of Judith and her sister Annie as a mission church of the St. Matthias Parish. It is now situated in nearby Huntington Park.

First pottery, 1916.

The new Poxon company imported workers from George's native England, and from East Liverpool, Ohio. Eventually a work force existed of around 65 employees, including a number of Mexican girls. Very little information is available about the early days of the factory.

The first Poxon products were small hexagonal-shaped tiles, the type used on bathroom floors.

At the onset of World War I, the company became known as Poxon China and shifted from producing tile to producing earthenware dishes and heavy hotel and restaurant-type ware.

At some point during the years, Poxon produced art pottery. Examples are pictured on pages to follow.

Pottery workers, 1925.

After pottery fire, 1927.

A page from George Poxon's journal showing preparation procedures.

Another page from George Poxon's journal,
showing cost of glaze, October 1924.

James Cox, who was employed at Poxon soon after finishing high school, gave the following account of Poxon production in the late 1920s:

"The plant superintendent was Otto Hupp; Eddie Fischer, accountant, and Emma Aley were the only office help. [Both Hupp and Fischer later affiliated with Vernon Kilns.] *Others were Mr. Hall, chief dipper; Frankie Mann, assistant clay shop foreman; Bill Trembly, cup turner; Jessie Hupp* [Otto's wife], *caster; Simit Owens, George Sass man, and Fred Thorley, kiln men* [James Cox was a kiln man, too]; *Harvey Walker, jiggerman; Gene Barnard, decorator kiln; Charlie Durkee and Fred Daniels, saggermakers; Bob Furlong (son of Tom Furlong) engineer and maintenance man; Bill Graves, shipping clerk; Hutch Hutchinson, packer (pottery was packed in carload lots with straw); Mike (last name unknown), decorator shop foreman; Mr. Hoyt and his son Arnold, liners; and Frank Bad dley, who later taught school in Pasadena.*

Most of the clay was from nearby Alberhill, near Lake Elsinore. Some of the ball clay came from Ohio and Kentucky. All of the kilns in the George Poxon era were beehive type kilns, heated with gas to cone 10. There were two large beehive kilns (14 ft. high by 15 ft. diameter) and one small glost kiln. It took one and a half days to fire the two large kilns and the small decorator kiln about a day to place and fire. The methods and equipment in the early Poxon days were rather primitive in comparison to the equipment and methods used in later days at Vernon Kilns, and were the same as had been used in England.

In the clay shop things were the most primitive in comparison with modern manufacturing. There a jigger crew consisted of jiggerman, a batter out, a mold runner, and finisher. Pugged clay in six-inch wads about two feet long was brought in, stacking it next to the jiggerman. The mold runner would go into a heated room, bring out the molds with the formed ware sticking to it. The finisher would strip the molds; the batter out would take a plaster mall, flatten a wad of clay much like a pancake, throwing it over the mold. The jiggerman would place the mold with the batter clay on a jigger wheel forming the piece as it turned. A jiggerman and crew could make as many as three hundred dozen to five hundred dozen plates a day. I remember dish jiggerman Harvey Walker, who made oval platters and bakers. All the dishes he made were oval in shape. When he jiggered the ware, his head bobbed back and forth, the same as the shape of the ware.

Most of the pottery was decorated with European decals [often the same used by other dinnerware manufacturers] *and border lines. The decorating girls would cut the decals to size before placing them, then size the plates, stick on the decals, and place the ware in tubs of water, rubbing off the paper, leaving the decals. From there it went to the liners, who would put gold lines or bands around the ware. Then it was placed in the kiln and fired to decorating fire, approximately cone .010.*

They filled the bisque kiln with green ware placing the dishes in saggers, a container made of clay in which to fire the dishes. The kiln 'placer' used special hats with a roll in it. It looked rather odd to see the kilnman walk into the kiln balancing a sagger filled with ware on his head and carrying another in his arms. He would go up ladders in the kiln when it got too high to reach. Cups were carried in on ware boards, five dozen cups to a board in two layers, two and a half dozen on top of each other in stacked fashion.

The glost saggers were made in various shapes. One sagger was called a double banjo. There were pins of clay in the sides of the sagger. These were placed from the bottoms up. You could get about 18 plates in each sagger. Each sagger was made in shapes that would accommodate the ware that was to be fired.

There was some handpainted semi-vitreous ware [as seen in the picture of the peacock plate on page 19]. *The wares were mostly sold to stores in the West."*

James Cox stayed on for awhile after the company changed hands, leaving Vernon Kilns in order to start a short-lived pottery in San Pedro, California. In 1943 he opened a retail pottery shop, California China Company, at 17th and Wilshire in Santa Monica, where the author interviewed him in the late 1970s. Incidentally, his shop shelves still held Vernon Kilns pottery for sale.

George Poxon, whose talent lay also in research, was to move on to new opportunity. Around 1928 he branched out into other ventures, leaving the company in the capable hands of his wife Judith and her brother James Furlong, who was then mayor of Vernon. At this point in time, the company was renamed Vernon China. The same dish patterns might be marked Poxon China or Vernon China (marks 3 and 4 respectively, as illustrated in Evolution of Marks on page 7).

The bell, undoubtedly a symbol of the California missions, is believed to have been used on dealer signs for Poxon's Vernon China line. This mission bell symbol was later adopted by Poxon's successor, Vernon Kilns, as one of its first trademarks.

When the Great Depression hit and hard times befell the Poxon/Vernon China company, the family decided to sell, and in 1931 the company was bought by Faye G. Bennison.

An article in the October 23, 1932 edition of the *San Jose Morning Herald* reported that George Poxon had become the third partner with Al Solon and Frank Schemmel in a new company, a separate business of Solon and

Schemmel Tile Company. The company manufactured colored restaurant ware and a brand new crack-proof oven ware called Sainte Claire. George Poxon was the partner credited with the idea and with the formula for producing the non-cracking restaurant oven ware, which used a mineral found in Death Valley. Al Solon — a master potter whose family had run a pottery in Toulouse, France, for 200 years — and George Poxon were both natives of Stoke-on-Trent, England, and had been apprentices of their trade about the same time.

According to an account given by the Poxon family, in the 1930s George went on to organize the Electric Tile Company in Whittier, California. He wanted to use electric power, but it was unavailable. Being an inventive man, he bought a World War I Liberty airplane engine, hooked it up to a generator, rigged a natural gas carburetor onto it, and he was in business. He later joined Wallace China on Soto Street in Los Angeles, again successfully setting up the pottery manufacturing system and then leaving. Wallace mostly manufactured heavy restaurant ware; this western cowboy motif is also popular today. It is believed that Poxon was also linked with the organization of Catalina Clay Products, located on Catalina Island off the coast of Southern California.

In his later years (about 1948), George Poxon worked in Trona, California, as a chemist for a borax company. He also held a claim for a mine that produced material for a red glaze. Here in Trona, he researched and taught pottery making and glazing. He made periodic visits to England, and was in England in 1939 when war broke out.

George Poxon died of leukemia in 1950. His wife Judith passed away in 1967, at the age of 86, having spent her entire life on the ranch adjacent to the pottery company.

George and Judith Poxon had seven children, and four were still living in Southern California communities adjacent to the Los Angeles area in 1978. All were most helpful in providing pictures and history of their family and the pottery company.

Through the years, the Poxon and Furlong families continued to be active in the city government of industrial Vernon. Mrs. Judith Poxon was city councilwoman for many years, acted as city treasurer, and held police and fire commission posts. Her brother James, Vernon's second mayor, continued as mayor for many years. Her brother Tom was city clerk for a year, and Tom's son, Robert, was mayor until he died in 1973.

On the land where two family houses had been built, little remains of the original ranch, and a textile factory is housed in the large complex that now stands on the old Vernon Kilns factory site.

A later-date photo of George Poxon.

∽ *Poxon Art Ware* ∽

Some art pottery was made, such as the El Camino Real 10" vase, decorated with a lamp post and a mission bell. The embossed design represents the light standards that once dotted California's El Camino Real — "The King's Highway" — and the mission bell represents the chain of 21 missions linked by the early highway. (The first missions appeared in the late 1700s and were built from adobe, by Indians under the direction of Franciscan missionaries led by Father Junipero Serra.) A few of the light standards are still standing along today's modern El Camino Real. One of the vases has been reported to be housed in the Smithsonian, in Washington, D.C.

George Poxon's specialty was glazing, and his talent is displayed in the bowls in the pictures to follow. Bowls from No. 100 through No. 106, except for Nos. 102 and 105, are pictured. The collection belongs to Steve and Debra Soukup; they have graciously provided the photos.

Both bowls are No. 103 and have a script mark. The bowl on the left is in mottled shades of mauve and brown, 8⅞" x 2⅜". On the right, the bowl is in mottled brown and green, 9" x 2½".

Both bowls have mottled blue and green glaze and have mark 1. Small bowl (No. 104) is 5¾" x 2⅜", and larger bowl (No. 100) is 10⅞" x 1⅞".

Bowl No. 106 (script mark). Mottled mauve and green, 10" x 3".

An unmarked bowl, number not known, possibly No. 105; purple, mauve, and green drip glaze, 8½" x 2⅜".

LEFT TO RIGHT: 4½" dark blue bowl, mark 2, has intact paper label on bottom which reads "Shape #1, Size 4, $6.00, Color C" (believed to be a salesman's sample.) Brown clay is highlighted under the glaze, $75.00; 10" bowl No. 101 with interesting glaze (mark 1), $135.00. El Camino Real 10" vase, mark 1, hexagonal sided, stoneware bisque finish, high glaze light green interior, $195.00.

Further research, provided by Steve Soukup, has revealed that along with pottery and porcelain, the Poxon Tile Company made colored tiles. Four examples of six-inch tea tiles are pictured that are currently recognized and credited to Poxon's factory. These feature designs which depict the California missions San Luis Rey, San Gabriel, and Santa Barbara. Only one of these has a thickset celadon matte glaze; the remaining round tiles are buff-colored bisque. Two are concisely impressed "Poxon" on the backs in block letters (mark 1 — Evolution of Marks); two are unmarked. The glazed tile example bears a circular mark featuring a mission bell and the word "ANGELUS" above "LOS ANGELES, CAL." The mission bell was also used on a figural dealer sign (see page 7 for example).

Poxon tea tiles and bowls are from Steve and Debra Soukup's collection. $75.00+ each tile.

Mission San Luis Rey (Poxon mark).

Mission San Gabriel (unmarked).

Mission Santa Barbara (unmarked).

Mission Santa Barbara, glazed (Angelus mark).

Poxon Porcelains — Vernon China

The following information from an August 1926 trade publication was supplied by Harvey Duke (author of the *Official Price Guide to Pottery and Porcelain, Eighth Edition*). The article was entitled "Poxon Pottery New Los Angeles Venture," and the information was as follows:

"Heretofore all the vitrified hotel china used on the Pacific coast has been manufactured in the east and shipped from there. However, when the second plant of the Poxon Pottery Mfg. Co., of Los Angeles, Cal., is completed in about two months, part of the $3,000,000 annual Pacific coast business in vitrified hotel china will go to a local firm. It will be a pioneer project in every sense of the word, being the first plant on the coast to manufacture and distribute the product.

The older plant, located at 2300 East 52nd Street, in the Vernon industrial district of Los Angeles, has been manufacturing a full line of semi-porcelain products, but will discontinue this line on the completion of plant No. 2, and devote itself exclusively to vitrified china.

Three acres in the Vernon industrial district, served by a spur track of the Union Pacific railroad, and located at 56th and Miles Avenue, have been purchased as a site for the plant. $100,000 will be expended on the 400 x 50 foot main building of the latest modern fireproof construction equipped with four carloads of Patterson machinery. The machinery is of the latest type, and each machine is individually driven and controlled by electric motors. Three kilns, two glost and one biscuit, will be built and the products will be decorated by under glaze. The demand for the product is large enough to insure the success of the project."

Examples of Poxon and Vernon China wares are seen in the pictures that follow.

This 9" plate is an example of "POXON VIT-RIFIED CHINA," as indicated in the back-stamp. May have been restaurant ware. $12.00.
Bill Stern photo.

Poxon/Vernon China dishes with decals. Unless otherwise noted, all have mark 4.
TOP: Child's mug, $35.00; 9" plate, $12.00; gravy boat, $18.00; 9½" plate (mark 3), $10.00.
CENTER: Two children's mugs, $30.00 – 45.00 each; hotel-type mug (mark 3), $15.00; 7" soup, $12.00; 9" oval vegetable bowl, $15.00.
BOTTOM: 4½" purple bell embossed "Vernon China," dealer display sign, $150.00.

13" game plate, decal, artist signed R.K. Beck, mark 4, $95.00.

9½" handpainted peacock plate, mark 3, $75.00.

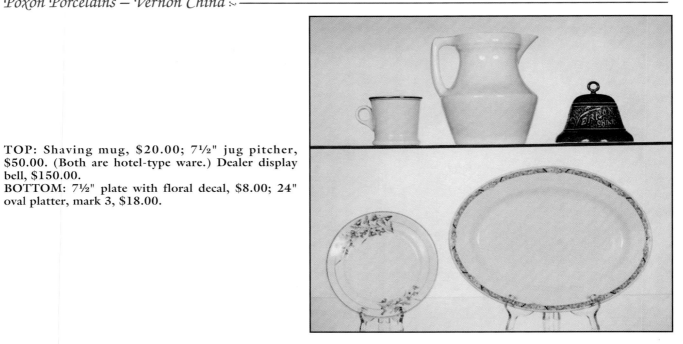

TOP: Shaving mug, $20.00; 7½" jug pitcher, $50.00. (Both are hotel-type ware.) Dealer display bell, $150.00.
BOTTOM: 7½" plate with floral decal, $8.00; 24" oval platter, mark 3, $18.00.

Vernon China bell, dealer display sign; "Mr. Jumbo's School" 7½" child's plate, mark 4, $45.00. Not shown is the "Golliwog's Joy Ride" child's bowl, picturing a golliwog on a cart pulled by a harnessed pink pig, mark 3.

Child's bowl, mark 3, 6¾" diameter, 1½" deep. Colorful decal of pigs on bicycles, gold rimmed. $45.00. *John and Joanne Barrett photo.*

The Founding of Vernon Kilns
✍ (Vernon Potteries, LTD.) ✍
1931

Poxon China set the stage for Vernon Kilns, founded by Faye G. Bennison. In his privately published *Our Family*, Mr. Bennison said, "Some people seem to have little curiosity or a desire to know from whence they came, but I do believe that the vast majority of this family will not only be interested but will carry on the family records for generations to come." Vernon Kilns pictorial pottery itself is evidence of his belief in documenting American historical events, people, and places for future generations of American people.

Born in Creston, Iowa, on March 6, 1883, Faye Bennison learned merchandising early; his hardworking father owned a small chain of prosperous mercantile stores. Educated at Morgan Park Academy in Illinois and the Bond Institute of Mercantile Training in New York City,* Mr. Bennison opened a dry goods store in Cedar Falls in 1908. He sold the store when hard times hit the Iowa farmlands, and in 1921 he moved his family — a wife and three small daughters — to California. In California, he invested in a glass factory that made bottles and jars, going in as secretary-treasurer and eventually becoming general manager and vice-president. The company flourished and was bought by Owens-Illinois Glass. It was at this time that Mr. Bennison crossed paths with the Poxons, who were looking for a buyer for their pottery. In July of 1931, he acquired the company, became president and general manager and, in his own words, "immediately changed the name to Vernon Kilns."

*At that time, the Bond Institute was affiliated with Columbia University. Today, examples of Vernon's Rockwell Kent china can be found in the University museum.

Early pottery company.

The former owners maintained a lively interest in the company, which remained on their ranch land. As part of the mortgage agreement, members of the Poxon and Furlong families were promised two complete dinnerware sets of their choosing every year, for as long as they desired.

Despite prevailing economic depression, Mr. Bennison instigated major changes upon assuming ownership of the pottery. Between 85 and 100 competent people were hired, including some employees from the Poxon Company. Otto Hupp joined on as plant superintendent, the same position he had held with the former company. Another employee was Ralph Martin, who in 1933 worked in the laboratory with the body clays. Hupp left the same year, which was also the year of the earthquake, to start his own pottery. Martin was promoted to assistant to the plant superintendent, Armand Schreiber. In the late 1930s, Martin became superintendent and remained in that position until the pottery closed. Our last report stated that Mr. Martin was retired and living in Prescott, Arizona.

Edward J. Fischer, an accountant for Poxon, joined the new company, Vernon Kilns, at the time of the transfer of ownership. Eventually he succeeded Faye Bennison as president, and he remained a close, loyal friend to Mr. Bennison even after the doors of the pottery closed. Mr. Fischer was born in Madison County, Nebraska, on March 1, 1905. He and his wife moved to California in 1926. He attended Loyola University in Los Angeles, and after graduating in 1930, went to work for Poxon. Mr. Fischer passed away on November 19, 2002. Mr. Fischer is seen in the picture on page 123, standing in front of a giant United States map created from commemorative plates.

James Cox, a Poxon employee who stayed on as kiln man, said "Mr. Bennison came in during the bad years, the Depression, yet he saw that nobody earned less than $10.00 a week and kept our morale high. He told us to go along with him, and we'd come out of this. Maybe not eating steak, but you'll be eating." Thomas Cosgrove, who went to work as a time study engineer and headed up the payroll department, also stayed till the end. Robert Wrightson invented some equipment for the factory and was responsible for maintaining it. There Bob met his wife Helen, a decorator; they named their son Vernon. There was a strong bond of loyalty among the people who worked at Vernon. When Bob Wrightson retired, Mr. Bennison presented him with a plate personalized especially for him.

For awhile, the company continued with remaining Poxon stock, producing a variety of ware with decals. An example of this ware is one with a Mexican motif pattern that Mr. Fischer had described as "Romeo and Juliet" and is also referred to by some authors as "Mexican Serenade." This ware is reported to have been premium ware in sacks of tortilla flour. A collector has also alleged that in the 1930s, the ware was given away with each ticket purchased at the San Carlos theater in Los Angeles.

The Poxon blanks were fairly heavy, and the shapes had embossed and scalloped rims. A variety of patterns, including the Mexican motif and the Autumn Leaf decal, are pictured and described. Though no doubt scarce, place settings and serving pieces might be found in these early Vernon Kilns patterns that used Poxon blanks.

The first Mission Bell mark, number 6, and the script "Vernon," mark 7, are the backstamps most often found on the pottery of this early period. Note the monogram "VPL" within the square overlaying the letter *V* of the Vernon mark in number 7. This probably signified the initials of Vernon Potteries, Ltd., the less commonly used name of Vernon Kilns. In *Versatile Vernon Kilns*, I stated that these marks were believed to be Poxon's, but all evidence now indicates they are the first marks of Vernon Kilns.

Partial sets of the Wild Rose pattern have been found on both Vernon Kilns' Montecito and Poxon's scalloped shapes, pictured on pages 24 and 26. A variety of backstamps on the Poxon shapes include marks 6 and 7 and variations of later marks 13, 14, and 15.

An early paper label having gold lettering and a mission arch on a dark brown background, mark 5, is rarely found. After seventy years, a remarkably intact label of this kind is still affixed to an early tab-handled bowl, found along with some unmarked Early California grill plates at an estate sale in Pennsylvania. A scarce carafe-type pitcher with an applied pottery handle was also found with the early paper label, in Oregon. Both are pictured in the Montecito dinnerware listing on page 145.

It is presumed that the initial period of production ended with the destructive earthquake that hit Southern California in 1933. Most of the pottery stock was shattered as it fell to the concrete floor of the factory. Truckloads of broken pieces had to be hauled away, and extensive repairs were made to the beehive kilns. This probably prompted the decision to design new molds. As a result, the disaster was followed by an era of unparalleled success because the company had been forced to start anew.

The next photos show Vernon Kilns' gradual transition from Poxon/Vernon China ware with decals to the same decals on the first and earliest Vernon Kilns shape, Montecito.* The Poxon/Vernon China flatware most commonly seen has rims of embossed scallops, fans, and flowers, and is referred to as the "Scallop and Flower" shape; cup handles are pointed at the top, and the cups have scalloped base rims. Generally, the former china company shapes had plain flat rims.

*Montecito shape is described in the Dinnerware section.

Examples of Vernon Kilns dinnerware all executed on Vernon China/Poxon shapes.
TOP: Scenic 9½" plate , mark 7, $15.00; square 9½" plate, Spanish tile illusion, mark 7, $20.00; Cactus decor on cup and saucer and 9½" plate, mark 6, cup and saucer $12.00, plate $10.00.
BOTTOM: 9" plate, mark 6, handpainted, $8.00; 5½" fruit, $5.00, and 6½" plate, $7.00, both Cactus, mark 6; 9½" scenic plate, mark 7, $18.00.

The cactus was a popular motif with other china manufacturers. Hall China used the same decal in 1937, Limoges Pottery had the similar Posey Shop pattern, and a Japanese pottery did an excellent copy of Cactus.

More examples of Vernon Kilns' use of old Poxon China ware are seen here. All have mark 6 unless otherwise indicated.
TOP: Three ewers, far left is different shape than the other two, middle one is decorated, $35.00 – 45.00.
BOTTOM: All over floral 9½" plate $15.00; matching cup (unmarked), and saucer, an elegant pattern richly spattered with 22 K gold, as indicated in stamped mark, $12.00; pretty 10" plate with floral-ringed border (mark 7), $12.00.
  Other companies manufactured ewers identical to the ones pictured center and right. Vernon ewers, although not necessarily marked, are distinguishable from other versions because they are noticeably lighter in weight.

The next pictures show the changeover, with the same decals on both the predecessor's ware and Vernon Kilns' Montecito shape. In these groups are two popular motifs, Autumn Leaf and the Mexican Romeo and Juliet scene (sometimes referred to as Mexican Serenade). During this period of time, pottery was sold to ten-cent stores but was also given as premiums by local grocery stores or by theaters on "dish nights." Mr. Fischer recalled that the Romeo and Juliet dishes were premium-type ware.

All items bear mark 7, with exceptions noted.

TOP: Cup and saucer (mark 8), Spanish tile illusion (sometimes referred to as Spanish Courtyard), matches plate on page 23 (top row, second from left), $15.00; Mariposa Ivory 7½" plate, $12.00 (Butterfly mark by Vernon Potteries, see photograph top of page 25); creamer, not typical Vernon China shape, pattern design similar to the artwork of mark 7, possibly by the same artist, $20.00; Rock-A-Bye Baby 7½" plate,* $45.00; demitasse cup and saucer (mark 8), also found with green and yellow color bands, $12.00.

CENTER: Cup and saucer (mark 6), poppy decor, $12.00; demitasse cup, unmarked, and saucer, unmarked, flower basket motif (matches 9½" plate on page 19 and platter on page 25), $15.00; 5½" fruit (mark 6), $5.00, and cup, unmarked, $5.00, both have Wild Rose motif; 6" plate (mark 8), floral, $5.00; 7½" plate, $7.00, and 6½" plate (mark 6), $5.00, both Wild Rose.

BOTTOM: Autumn Leaf 10½" plate, $35.00; 12½" platter, same as Santa Fe RR California Poppy decal, $25.00.

*A child's Goldilocks bowl with verse has also been reported (with mark 7).

Close-up view of Mariposa Ivory platter. $18.00.
Barbara Erickson photo.

Mariposa Ivory backstamp.

All have mark 6 unless otherwise noted.
TOP: 9" floral plate, $10.00; saucer, basket of flowers, silver-spattered rim, backstamped "Pure Sterling Silver," $6.00; 12" platter (mark 7), identical to plate pictured on page 19, $18.00; 8½" vegetable bowl, $12.00.
BOTTOM: 5½" fruit, $6.00 and 11½" platter, marked "18 Karat Gold," $25.00, both are the Mexican Romeo and Juliet pattern on former company's shape; creamer, $10.00, and sugar, $12.00, creamer and sugar unmarked except for "22 Karat Gold" on sugar; both Romeo and Juliet on Vernon's Coronado* cubist shape, substantiates the theory that Vernon Kilns did continue with former company's stock and patterns; Vernon's Autumn Leaf 5½" fruit (mark 7), scarce, $20.00; 5½" fruit, color band design, $5.00.

*Coronado shape is described in the Dinnerware section.

Pictured are examples of mostly Montecito decal-decorated ware.

TOP: 9½" plate, mark 8, dainty floral border, $10.00; sugar bowl, 5" diameter, mark 8, floral bouquet, $15.00; 9½" plate, mark 9, scenic, $15.00; 8½" plate, mark 8, floral matches sugar, $8.00.

CENTER: 7½" plate, mark 9, Wild Rose, $7.00; 6" plate, mark 6, Poxon shape, marked "Nasco, Pure Silver and Platinum decoration,"* $6.00; 10" oval vegetable, mark 9, Wild Rose, $15.00; 9" round vegetable, mark 13, floral, yellow ground, $12.00.

BOTTOM: Creamer, unmarked, $8.00; cup, unmarked, and saucer, mark 9, Wild Rose, $10.00; sauce boat, mark 10, hand-painted striped ring border, $12.00.

*Nasco is a name often found on Japanese ware, which would indicate that some dinnerware was jobbed. Another dinnerware pattern executed on Montecito shape has been found having Vernon's mark 9 and backstamped "Pacific China Company."

Joshua Tree, another early decal on Montecito shape. 10" oval serving bowl, $12.00; cup and saucer, $10.00; 10½" and 8½" plates, mark unknown, $10.00 and $8.00 respectively.

❧ Art Ware ❧

Originally known as Art Moderne, today this style is referred to as Art Deco. Beginning in 1910, it reached its height of popularity between 1925 and 1935. It is a complete change from the Art Nouveau style. Rooted in Europe, the influence of the Art Deco movement was not felt in the United States until the 1920s. Art Deco designs were cubist and angular in shape. Some Art Deco pieces were decorated with florals, birds, or animals, and others with rounded female figures. Small sculpted human and animal figures were produced during this historic art period. Dishware also reflected the new style, with stepped shapes and rounded handles.

During a 1993 visit with Jane Bennison Howell, she recalled that after her father acquired Vernon Potteries, he and five others from the company made a trip to Ohio. The purpose was to tour the potteries and to learn firsthand their techniques. Later he toured Europe, again for the same reason, and returned with many ideas for design. The groundwork was laid for hiring artists of the Art Deco school of design such as Gale Turnbull, who had studied in France; Harry Bird, with his naturalistic designs; Jane Bennison, a student of art design; and May and Vieve Hamilton, sisters who had already achieved international recognition for their pottery and sculptures.

In the mid-thirties the art ware department was established, but it lasted for only a brief period. Jane Bennison and Harry Bird shared the desire to continue the art line, but it was ended in about 1937, due to the economy.

In this book, art ware values are averages based upon those reported by collectors and advertised by dealers throughout the country. Nevertheless, these may not reflect much higher values seen in shops and antique shows in some areas of the country. When uncertain, prices have not been determined (PND).

Bennison Art Ware ❧

Jane Bennison, the talented daughter of Vernon Kilns' owner, worked summers from 1931 to 1935, while a student at the University of Southern California. After obtaining her art degree, she joined the company as a full-time artist and stayed on for two years, creating many pottery vases, bowls, candlesticks, and figures. She was also responsible for the design of the distinctive "upside-down" handles applied to the Ultra hollowware of Gale Turnbull's design. Her personal trademark was an anchor riding the waves, mark 29, an anchor being her college sorority emblem. Examples of Jane Bennison art ware all bear mark 29. These were made in various colors, and some were produced in graduated numbered sizes, No. 1 being the largest. Both Kent and Blanding patterns are found decorating Bennison bowls and candlesticks (see pages 231, 239, 240, and 242).

Pieced Pedestal comport in blue. 12" diameter, 6½" high, $350.00.

TOP: Moon Bowl No. 1, 7½" high, $100.00; 12" console bowl, backstamped Salad Bowl No. 1, (diameter of Salad Bowl No. 33 is 9½"), $150.00; pair of 4½" hexagonal candlesticks (matching hexagonal bowl in next picture), $100.00; fluted 10" pedestal bowl (see page 240 for Kent-decorated bowl), $150.00.

BOTTOM: Dayrae No. 3 11½" bowl (Dayrae No. 1 measures 15½", see page 231 for Blanding-decorated Dayrae and page 240 for Rockwell Kent's Moby Dick in yellow), $100.00; 10" x 4" rectangular bowl, not numbered (a larger bowl is pictured on page 29), $125.00; Pine Cone No. 2, 5½" high (also pictured in four sizes on page 29), $150.00; 11" Walnut bowl, features embossed walnut halves around outside rim and walnut shell handle, also found in pastel colors and orange, $250.00.

Group of bowls.

TOP: Aqua Pierced Base bowl, 10½" diameter, 4½" high, $175.00; Ivory Pierced Pedestal comport, 12" diameter, 6½" high, $350.00; cobalt blue hexagonal bowl, 10" diameter, 4½" high (matches candlesticks in preceding picture), $150.00.

BOTTOM: Ring Bowl No. 2, 10" diameter, $100.00 (see page 23 for Blanding-decorated Ring bowl).

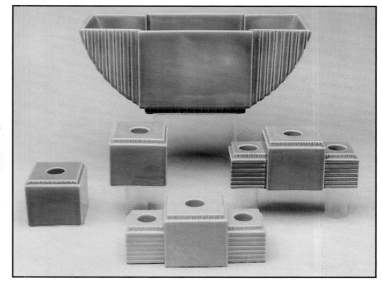

Rectangular group.
TOP: Bowl, 13" lengthwise, 5½" high, $175.00.
CENTER: Pair of single candlesticks (Kent decorated, see page 239), $150.00; triple candlestick, 6½", $150.00.
BOTTOM: Triple candlestick, marked only "Made in U.S.A.," $150.00. (This has been found decorated with Blanding's Hawaiian Flowers.)

Miss Jane Bennison, artist-designer of the Vernon staff.

THE BENNISON BOWLS

These designs by Miss Bennison are refreshingly new and modern and decorative. You can get them in all the seven "Early California" and the six "Modern California" colors—enabling you to match centerpiece with dinnerware exactly. Shown are: Dayrae bowl, $2.50 to $4.00; Phoenix bowl, $10.00; Pine Cone bowl, $1.50 to $4.00; Moon bowl, $1.00 to $3.50; Candlestick, 75c; Fluted bowls, $3.00 to $5.00; Oblong center bowl, $5.00.

Pine Cone bowls, showing four sizes and colors.
No. 1 is 7½" x 10", No. 2 is 5" x 8", No. 3 is 4¼" x 6½", No. 4 is 3½" x 5½".
TOP: No. 1, $200.00.
CENTER: Both No. 2, $150.00.
BOTTOM: Nos. 4, 3, 4. No. 3, $100.00; No. 4, $125.00.

A page from a mid-1930s company brochure showing the Bennison Bowls.

Sphere candlesticks, 3" high, not always marked, rings are discernable at base, $100.00 a pair. (See page 231 for Blanding-decorated example.)

Picture shows the great detail of the Phoenix Bird planter, 18" long and 10" high. Hand painted, $750.00+; solid color, $500.00+. Jane Bennison stated that there were candlesticks made to go with the Phoenix. The candlesticks were triple and the design was curved like the tail. Jane also said that she personally hand painted to order every piece that was made of her pottery. Most of her pottery was sold to floral shops and custom ordered.

In a company brochure, the Phoenix was pictured in a table setting alongside brightly-colored of Early California dinnerware. To quote from the brochure regarding Bennison art ware, "...in all seven Early California and the six Modern California colors — enabling you to match centerpiece with dinnerware exactly." The Early California colors were described as yellow, turquoise, green, blue, brown, ivory, and orange; the six Modern California pastels were Azure, Orchid, Mist, Pistachio, Sand, and Straw. Colors that are considered rare and have added premium are Orchid, Cobalt Blue, Chrome Yellow, and orange.

Prices in the brochure were as follows: Dayrae bowl, $2.50 – 4.00; Phoenix, $10.00; Pine Cone, $1.50 – 4.00; Moon bowl, $1.00 – 3.50; hexagonal candlestick, $0.75; fluted bowl, $3.00 – 5.00; oblong (rectangular) bowl, $5.00; and Walnut bowl, $3.00.

For the first edition of this book, Jane Bennison provided her personally-owned Toucan bird, which is seen in this photograph. Having a simpler design than the Phoenix, but equally colorful, the sculptured figural bowl measures 12½" long and 6" wide. An unmarked, unpainted solid color Toucan has been reported.

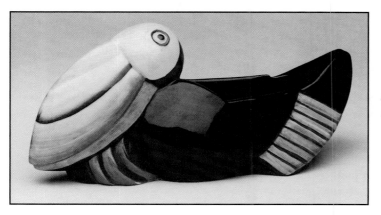

Toucan bird planter. Hand painted, $750.00+; solid color, $500.00+.

Two rare Bennison Hand Bowls, bowls which sit on hand-shaped pedestals modeled from Jane Bennison's own hand, are pictured. She sculpted this design while still a senior in college. It won an award from the Syracuse Museum; except for a few bowls, it never went into production.

An informal view was captured by the author in 1992, of Jane Bennison Howell holding her Hand Bowl. PND.

Multi-colored Hand Bowl, dry foot, mark 29 inside the base. Bill Stern reports two others, both white with the inside of the bowl glazed in Modern California blue: one with a glazed base and no mark, which came from the Bennison family, and the other with a dry foot that is inscribed "JANE F. BENNISON 5/1/37." *Bill Stern photo.*

Hamilton Art Ware ⚬

Accomplished artists Diane May Hamilton de Causse and Genevieve Bartlett Hamilton Montgomery were sisters who worked together in 1936 and 1937 at Vernon Kilns creating a line of vases, figurines, plaques, and two dinnerware lines. According to Jane Bennison, she knew the Hamilton sisters and had worked with them in the Pasadena studio. She introduced them to her father, who was impressed with their talent and hired them. They had previously worked with Gale Turnbull, probably at Leigh Potteries in Alliance, Ohio. Their pottery was generally produced in solid pastels with a doeskin-like finish. Their trademark was a Pekingese dog inside a circle and over the name Vernon Kilns (mark 32).

The sisters were natives of Missouri; May was born in January of 1886, and Genevieve in June of 1887.* They were said to have complementing personalities May was the calm one, Vieve the feisty one. May was married to James F. de Causse, the designer of the Franklin car. Both women studied extensively at renowned art centers in the United States and abroad. Genevieve studied at the Chouinard Art Institute and Mark Hopkins University in California; May at the Otis Art Institute, New York Art Students League and American School of Sculpture in New York City, and at the Fontainebleau School in Paris. They designed pottery and sculpture owned by Metro-Goldwyn-Mayer, Fox, and other studios and used as set dressing in films. Academy Award–winning art director Cedric Gibbons of MGM owned the Hamilton Head with Hand (page 47). Incidentally, he was the second husband of film star Dolores Del Rio, who was responsible for commissioning Harry Bird's Olinala Aztec dinnerware.

May was involved in research, museums, and potteries in France, Italy, Spain, England, and the United States. In *Pottery in the United States* (Helen E. Stiles, 1941), it was mentioned that a line of art ware was created by the two sisters and glazed in the same colors as the Vernon dinnerware sets, which made it possible to match dinnerware and art ware.

The sisters' exhibits and prizes were identical and included the Los Angeles Museum Award 1924 – 1925 and the Third Annual Robineau Memorial Ceramic Exhibit, Syracuse Museum of Fine Art Award 1933 – 1934.**

In October of 1936, the Fifth National Ceramic Exhibition (Robineau Memorial) opened at the Syracuse Museum of Art in New York. Over 600 entries were submitted by outstanding ceramic artists from 26 states, and from this group May and Vieve Hamilton were selected by the Jury of Selection for their pottery, which was characteristic of American ceramic art. Other renowned artists selected were Arthur E. Baggs, Sorcha Boru, Paul Bogatay, Guy Cowan, Waylande Gregory, Glen Lukens, Marie Martinez, Viktor Schreckengost, and Leon Volkmar. The exhibit was later circulated to seven American museums.

* 1900 Federal census

** Adelaide Alsop Robineau of Syracuse was a pioneer American ceramist and had been awarded 2nd Prize and a "Diploma di Benemerenza" in 1911, at the exposition of Turin. National ceramic exhibitions were arranged annually in Robineau's memory, concentrating exclusively upon ceramic art.

Black and white picture of Hamilton Gift Pieces from a mid-1930s company brochure.

Listed in the exhibition catalogue under each sister's name was "May and Vieve Hamilton Pottery, Vernon Kilns." The pottery selected for the exhibit was May's *Tropical Bowl* and carved *Monkey Vase* in white and Vieve's *Carved Ovoid* vase, *Pierced Plate* in white, *Way-Shower* in white and a *Rythmic Bowl* in white. (The Hamiltons spelled *rhythmic* as *rythmic*. See the Rythmic mark on page 55.)

Early in 1937, the first exhibit of Contemporary American Ceramics, under the auspices of the American Ceramic Society, was assembled for travel on invitation from European countries. The European Circuit appeared in Copenhagen, Denmark; Gothenburg, Sweden; Stockholm, Sweden; and Helsingfors, Finland. Listed in the Contemporary American Ceramics catalogue were individual ceramists' names and the ceramics selected for the exhibit. Again Hamilton ceramics were chosen. Shown for May Hamilton de Causse of May and Vieve Hamilton Pottery, Vernon Kilns, were *Neckers* (giraffes) and *Carved Monkey Vase*, white. For Vieve Hamilton, May and Vieve Hamilton Pottery, Vernon Kilns, ceramics shown were *Pierced Plate*, white; *Tropical Bowl*, white; *Rythmic Table Service* of cup, saucer, and plate, white; and *Torso*, small green nude.

It may be noted that in the 1936 exhibit, credit for *Tropical* was given to May whereas in the 1937 exhibit, credit was given to Vieve.

The Hamiltons achieved international recognition, as did Vernon Kilns. Today, there is a renewed interest in Hamilton pottery, and it is eagerly sought. It has been said that in their late years the sisters were virtually penniless. Their last known address was the one they shared in 1957, 455 South Santa Anita Avenue, Pasadena. May's death occurred in January of 1971, and Vieve's five years later, in April of 1976.*

Examples of their pottery are shown in the following photographs. Most pieces were done in different colors, especially pastels, and often in several sizes. All marked pottery will have the Hamilton mark (32), and some will be found with one or the other sister's name inscribed at the base of the sculpture.

Color is the key to Hamilton ware values, with an added 20 to 25% for premium colors. Colors considered premium are orange, chrome yellow, and orchid. Mid-range colors: white, Azure, pistachio, and Ultra California Blue. Low range colors: Mist Gray, pink, beige, and light yellow. In the company brochures, orange was always slightly higher priced.

*Federal Social Security Death Records.

Group of May and Vieve Hamilton pottery giving perspective of sizes.
LEFT TO RIGHT: Milady Vase, 7"; 12" Petunia bowl; Cylinders No. 3, 8"; Godey Lady, unpainted, 10"; Rose bowl No. 4, 5"; Pierced Plate, 16½" plaque; Cocotti, 7½". See close-up views of these following.

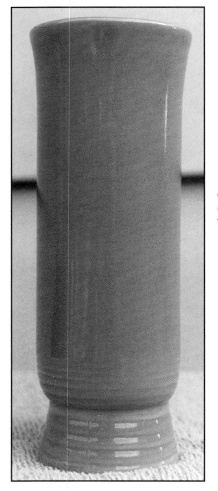

Cylinders No. 4, 7" tall. There are 4 sizes of Cylinders: Nos. 1 (12"), $350.00; 2 (10"), $300.00; 3 (8"), $250.00; 4 (7"), $200.00. Note: There is sometimes a ¼" variation in size. *Daniel J. Trueblood photo.*

Pictured is Cylinders No. 3. Hand painted under glaze. Artist signature appears to be K. Ewell. $275.00. *John and Joanne Barrett photo.*

Spheres/Rose Bowls in 4 sizes.
LEFT TO RIGHT: No. 1 (8"), $350.00; No. 2 (7"), $300.00; No. 3 (6"), $250.00; No. 4 (5"), $200.00. Generally speaking, the larger the vase, the higher the value. In the company brochures, orange was always priced slightly higher. Spheres and Rose Bowl are identical in shape. It is a mystery why some pieces were marked "Rose Bowl" and others were marked "Spheres." *Daniel J. Trueblood photo.*

Close-up view of No. 3 Spheres. Note the concentric rings encircling the neck and midway. Another vase is seen in the group picture above — as a Rose Bowl No. 3. *Daniel J. Trueblood photo.*

Petunia, 12" diameter bowl, engraved abstract leaf and ruffled flower petal in center. $300.00. *Daniel J. Trueblood photo.*

Cocotti, 7½", stately bird, tail forms tray. $250.00.
Daniel J. Trueblood photo.

Pierced Plate, striking 16½" plaque, reticulated 4½" rim. Engraved Art Moderne design of palm tree and nude female. Designed by Vieve Hamilton. Colors known are chartreuse, orange, pink, white, and blue. Selected for 1937 European circuit tour by the American Ceramic Society. Exhibited in 1939 Golden Gate Exposition, San Francisco. Whitney Museum Exhibit in 1937. $1,000.00.

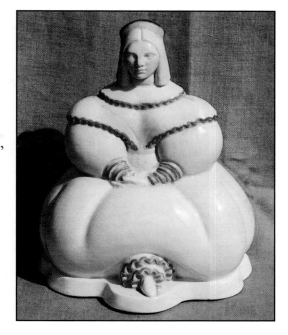

Godey Lady, 10" period-costumed figure. Rare hand painted, $500.00. Unpainted, $350.00+. *Sara Bell photo.*

Back view.

Mark within hollow base.

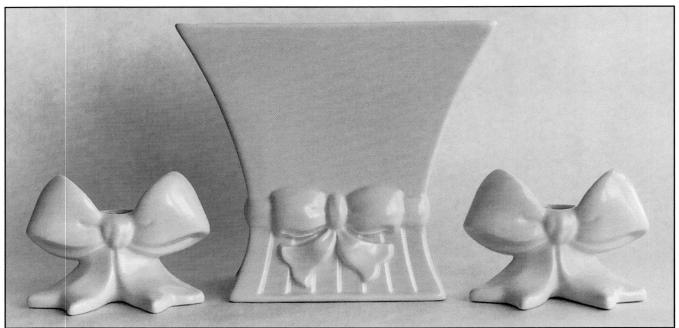

Milady vase, 7½" with matching 3½" tall Milady candlesticks. Light yellow. Vase, $200.00. Pair of candlesticks (marked "Made in USA"), $200.00.

No. 3 (10½") and No. 1 (14½" x 6⅛") Milady bowls. Regardless of size, these are all in the same price range, $175.00. Not pictured is the No. 2 bowl (12½" x 6¼"). *Daniel J. Trueblood photo.*

Milady figural planter, 11" tall, 8½" wide. Sculptured head with long wavy hair flowing into 3½" deep open flower bowl at back. Figural pictured is an unmarked piece. Uncommon. $500.00 – 750.00.
Daniel J. Trueblood photo.

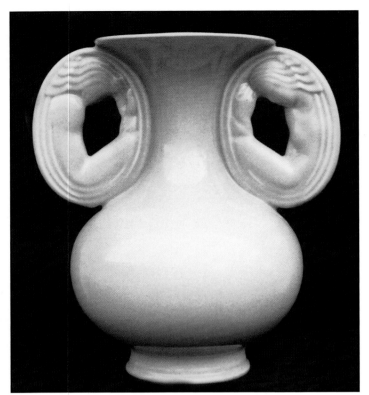

Carved Handles vase, 12". Difficult to find today. $1,100.00.
Daniel J. Trueblood photo.

Carved Ovoid vase, 13". Shown in two different colors. Also found in pink. Designed by Vieve Hamilton. Considered by many to be the finest example of Art Deco design created by the Hamilton sisters. Sought after by collectors. 1936 National prize winner. Winning design — Robineau Memorial Ceramic Exhibit. Selected for 1937 European Circuit Tour by American Ceramic Society. Was pictured in *Better Homes and Gardens* magazine's December 1937 issue. Rare, $2,000.00+.
Daniel J. Trueblood photo.

The large plaque pictured below was an exciting find. Signed in mold, lower right corner, by M. H. deCausse (May Hamilton). In very high art deco style and glazed in bright turquoise, it depicts a pair of women.

Plaque measures 12¾" x 23¾", bright turquoise. PND.
Steve and Debra Soukup photo.

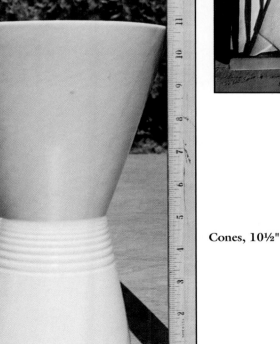

Cones, 10½" tall, $500.00. *Daniel J. Trueblood photo.*

Goblet, 8½" tall, $500.00. *Daniel J. Trueblood photo.*

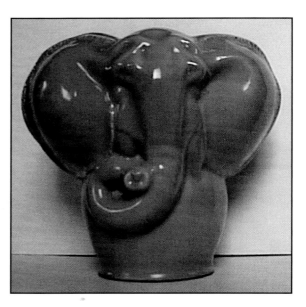

Elephant vase, 7½" tall. Scarce, $900.00.

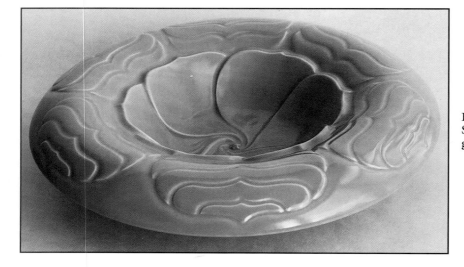

Flower Bowls, 12" diameter, blue. $400.00. Colors known: pink, white, green, yellow.

Kinetic, 12" tall, lower half has 15 narrow rings. Art Moderne design. The two sisters were both credited for Kinetic in the Official Catalog for the exhibit at the Decorative Arts display at the 2939 Golden Gate Exposition, San Francisco. Slight difference in size might be observed in photo, the white being the larger. Rare. $1,100.00+. *Daniel J. Trueblood photo.*

Chalice, 9½" tall, and its backstamp. $500.00. *Daniel J. Trueblood photo.*

Tropical, a large bowl, 14½" top diameter, 8" high, 7¾" diameter base, incised design of coconut palms. By May and Vieve Hamilton. This piece was also an exhibit piece. 1936 National Prize winning design. Robineau Memorial Ceramic Exhibit. Whitney Museum Exhibit. Selected for 1937 European Tour by American Ceramic Society. Very scarce. $2,000.00+. *Daniel J. Trueblood photo.*

Shown in the colors of yellow and white are Calas Nos. 1 (10¼"), $350.00; 2 (8½"), $300.00; 3 (6½"), $250.00; and 4 (5"), $175.00. Other colors known: Orchid, blue, Sand (tan). Generally speaking, the larger the vase, the higher the value. The larger sizes are less commonly found. Note: There may be slight variations in sizes.

Example of mark on Calas No. 1. *Daniel J. Trueblood photo.*

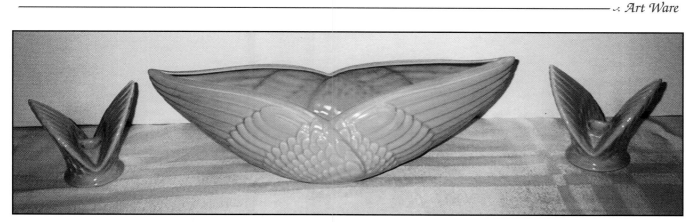

Wings bowl, 16½" x 8", $400.00. Candlesticks, 4½" tall, $300.00. Various backstamps have been reported. Pictured is a backstamped Wings bowl; other bowls may only have the Hamilton mark, candlesticks may be marked "Wings" or "Wings Candlesticks." *John and Joanne Barrett photo.*

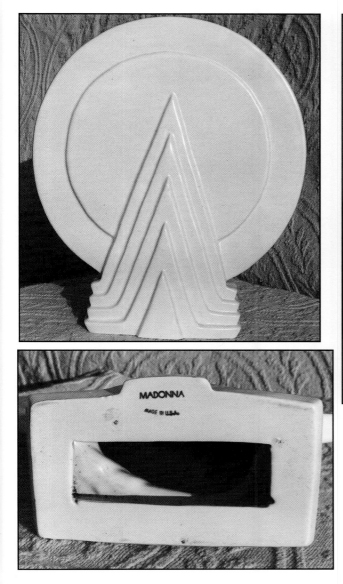

Madonna and Child sculpture with deco triangular design on obverse. 13" high. It was pictured and called "Madonna and Child" in *California Arts and Architecture*, December 1934, and attributed to "Diane May Hamilton deCausse, Courtesy of the Hamilton Pottery." The one pictured was marked (below) only with a blue stamp reading "Madonna, Made in USA." Difficult to find. Rare item. $2,000.00+. *Daniel J. Trueblood photo.*

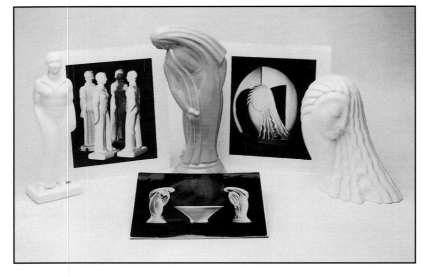

The photo at left features figurines against a backdrop of original photos of the same figures. (Photos are from the Hamilton estate.) LEFT TO RIGHT: *Hollywood Figure*, 12", mark is a incised "Hamilton" in a circle (see *Godey Lady* on page 37 for a picture of mark), $900.00; *Sari* from a backview, 14½", $1,500.00; *Head with Hair*, 11", $2,500.00+. Note: In the Hamilton estate photo, which shows two Saris flanking a bowl, the bowl is 13" Cosmic (see page 47 for example).

Sari, 14½", front and back views, facing Spheres (sometimes named Rose Bowl) No. 3 (6"). One of the two *Sari*s in this picture was once owned by 20th Century Fox. Besides white, *Sari* has been found in pink and blue. Sari, $1,500.00. Spheres, $250.00.

Photo showing the 20th Century Fox prop room mark on the base of one *Sari* pictured.

The bowl is Cosmic, 13" diameter, 6¼" tall, with sloped sides to ringed 1" deep footed base. $700.00.
Daniel J. Trueblood photo.

More fine examples of the 1930 period work by the Hamilton sisters are seen in the following pictures.

Backview of *Head with Hand.*

Backstamp.

Head with Hand, 12" tall, sculpted by Diane May Hamilton deCausee. May or may not be inscribed with her signature across the base. One of these figures was found mismarked and was mistakenly attributed to Jane Bennison. The figure was in RKO's 1945 *Zombies on Broadway.* Rare. $2,500.00.

Prices in 1937 and 1938 were as follows: *Head with Hair,* $8.00; Pierced Plate, $12.50; Carved Ovoid, $10.00; Hors d'oeuvre, $10.00.

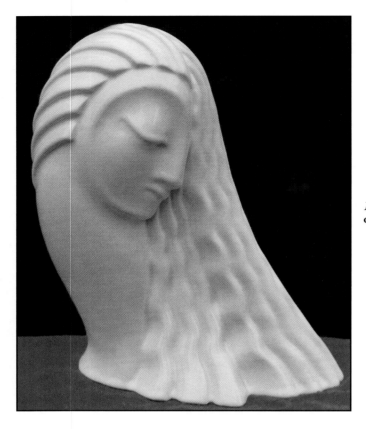

Head with Hair, 11". This has been seen in a background scene of the movie *Star Dust.* Few known, very rare. $2,500.00+.

Head with Hair backview. *Daniel J. Trueblood photo.*

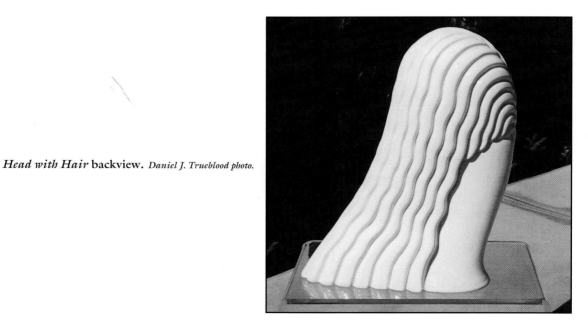

Detailed view of sculptured monkey design.
Daniel J. Trueblood photo.

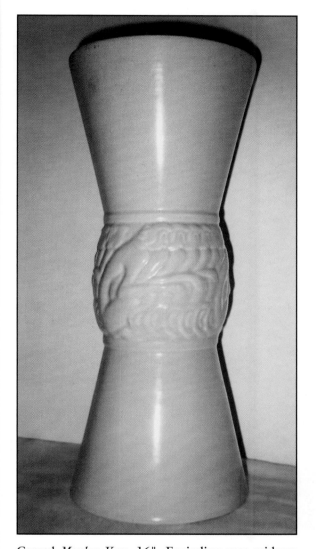

Carved *Monkey Vase*, 16". Encircling vase midway is a wide embossed band picturing a monkey profile. The monkey is in a seated position, with an elongated arm that is extended forward and a long curled tail. Colors known are dark blue, white and Pistachio (Sea Foam Green), and Turquoise. Difficult to find today. Diane May Hamilton was the designer. 1936 National Prize winning design – Robineau Memorial Ceramic Exhibit. Selected for 1937 European Circuit Tour by American Ceramic Society. Whitney Museum Exhibit, 1937. $1,500.00+. *John and Joanne Barrett photo.*

Backstamp.

Hollywood Figure in yellow, 12" tall.
Rare. $900.00. *Dennis Donnal photo.*

Back view.

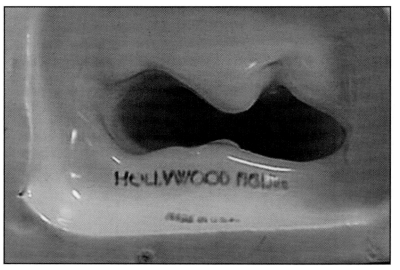

Backstamp.

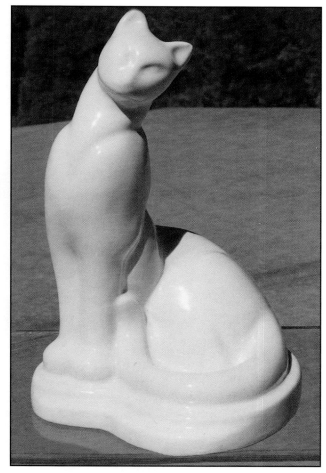

Cat Figure, 7¼". Appeared in *House Beautiful* magazine, November 1934. Two *Cats* were found, each with a different mark: one had "Made in USA," and the other had the early Hamilton mark. $1,000.00. *Daniel J. Trueblood photo.*

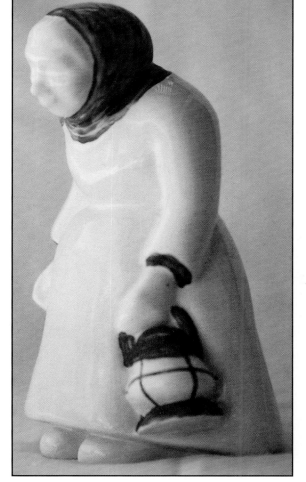

Mrs. O'Leary Figure. Size not known. PND.

Other Hamilton pottery pieces that are known (initials after figure indicate May Hamilton or Vieve Hamilton attribution): *Mrs. O'Leary's Cow* (VH), *Baboon* (*Monkey*, crouching on base) 8⅝"; *The Way-Shower* (sculptured head of Christ, VH), *Neckers* (Pair of Giraffes, MH, 11½"), *Giraffes* (trio figure), *Indian Woman with Baby*, *Man Figure*, *Woman Figure*, *Torso* (female nude, VH), and *Polar Bears* (pair). Some copies of original studio photos were made available for this book. Although lacking in clarity, the author elected to picture them due to the rarity of these Hamilton pieces. The original photos are from the Hamilton estate collection of Al Alberts.

For the most part, the studio prints were dated 1934.

Man and Woman. **PND.**

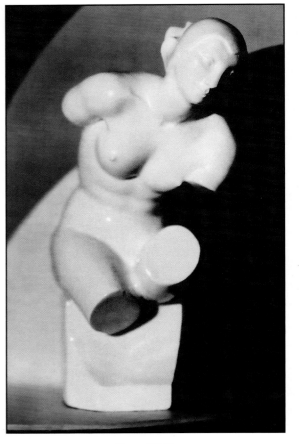

Torso. **PND.**

Indian Woman with Baby. **PND.**

Mrs. O'Leary and her *Cow.* PND.

Neckers, 11½" high. PND.

Arriving the last hour before the book went to print, a picture of the *Baboon* is replacing the Hamilton estate reprint. The pictured figure formerly belonged to Jane Bennison. *Baboon* (or *Monkey*), unmarked, 8½" tall, base 5½". PND.
Photo courtesy of Laguna Vintage Pottery, Seattle, Washington.

53

Polar Bears. PND.

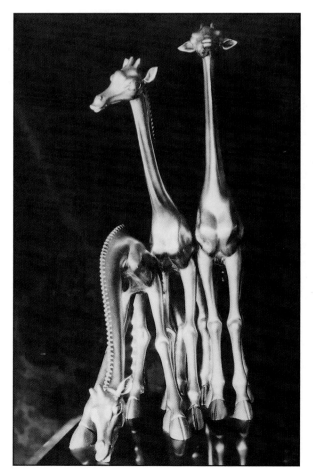

Giraffes. PND.

Rythmic and Rippled dinnerware by the Hamiltons is seen in the next set of pictures. The Rippled pattern has graduated narrow rings on the rims. Known colors are pink, green, yellow, ivory, orchid, beige, orange, and bright blue. The Rythmic design has three wide, exactly-spaced stepped rings. Saucers have three rings. Known colors are orange, yellow, pink, blue, green, and white. The lines of the hollow ware pieces in Rythmic are rounded compared to the more severe lines of Rippled. Dinnerware may be found unmarked. If marked, it may have pattern name only, the Hamilton mark (32) only, or with mark 32 and the pattern name.

In February 1981, *The Glaze*, no longer in publication, featured several Rythmic pieces on the cover — a teapot, a creamer and sugar, two sizes of plates, and a cup and saucer. In that same issue, an article by Allen Kleinbeck stated that the cover grouping was from a larger set that included "chop plate, salad plate, and a large salad bowl" and that "the set was originally owned by Mrs. Arthur Eisenhower, sister-in-law of former President Dwight D. Eisenhower."

Below is a picture showing a partial table setting and serving pieces of this same Rythmic dinnerware from the Eisenhower estate.

Rythmic dinnerware.
LEFT: 14½" chop plate, $400.00; 10½" dinner plate, $100.00; 9½" luncheon plate, $100.00; 7¾" salad plate, $75.00. There is also a 22" Rythmic chop plate, $600.00.
CENTER: Very rare 15½" salad bowl, $750.00; teacup and saucer, $100.00.
RIGHT: Scarce tea pot, $500.00; covered sugar, $150.00; creamer, $150.00; teacup and saucer, $100.00.
Daniel J. Trueblood photo.

Close up view of very rare 15½" Rythmic orange salad bowl, $800.00.
John and Joanne Barrett photo.

Picture of Rythmic mark.
Daniel J. Trueblood photo.

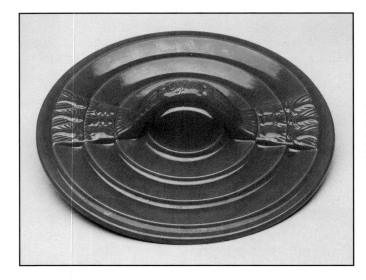

Hors d'oeuvre handled serving plate, 16", sculpted fish form design on large handle. Plate has the stepped rings of Rythmic. Some collectors suggest this is part of the Rythmic line. Has been seen mismarked "Carved Handle." $700.00.+.

A cocktail mixer and its accompaning cocktail goblets are pictured here. This mixer is one of only two known at this time. Prior to knowledge of the existence of the mixer, the goblets were identified as Rippled egg cups, but they are now believed to have been made for use as cocktails. Some collectors suggest that the cocktail mixer and goblets may have been part of the Rippled dinnerware line.

Cocktail mixer, 10". Few survive today. $650.00 +.
Cocktail goblets, 3" tall. $200.00+ each.
Daniel J. Trueblood photo.

LEFT TO RIGHT: Rippled 7" tab-handled chowder or fruit, $50.00; teacup and saucer, $75.00; 10½" plate, $75.00; Rythmic plates, 6½", $50.00; 7¾", $75.00; 9½", has greenish undertones and is the only unmarked piece, $100.00; Rippled 4-cup teapot, $400.00. Note the down turn to handles of Rippled hollow ware.

Close up view of Rippled tea pot, 5½" tall, $400.00.

Daniel J. Trueblood photo.

Close-up view of Rippled salad bowl. 14½" diameter, 7½" tall. Awarded the 1936 National Prize for winning design at the Robineau Memorial Ceramic Exhibit. Difficult to find. $500.00+.

Dennis Donnal photo.

Close up view of different sizes of superimposed Rippled plates. 16½" tab handled chop plate, $400.00; 10½" dinner plate, $75.00; 9½" luncheon plate, $75.00; 7½" salad plate, $50.00. Not pictured is a 6" bread an butter plate, $40.00.
Daniel J. Trueblood photo.

A set of Rippled purchased from the original owner was said to have been bought at a San Francisco store in the 1930s. Included in the set was an orchid butter dish (missing cover) with the Montecito Rippled-style handles. The tray had mark 10.

Close up view of Rippled tab-handled chowders. 6" diameter excluding handles. $50.00.
Daniel J. Trueblood photo.

Closeup view of Rippled sherbets in orchid, blue, and yellow, $75.00. Sherbets 2¾" tall, 3¾" diameter. *Daniel J. Trueblood photo.*

View of bottom markings on two of the sherbet cups shown above. *Daniel J. Trueblood photo.*

Pair of Rippled cocktail goblets, $200.00+ each, and Rythmic teacup and saucer, $100.00. *Daniel J. Trueblood photo.*

∽ Famous Artists — Designers ∽

Harry Bird ∽

During the art ware period, Harry Bird was associated with Vernon Kilns. Little is known about the man. Before joining Vernon, Bird is believed to have had his own pottery studio in Pasadena, California, where he often used Vernon Kilns wares. According to Jane Bennison, he later made an arrangement with Vernon Kilns to use its facilities and decorate its dinnerware with his own patented designs. This may explain why some Bird decorated pottery is found without the Vernon Kilns name. His personal trademark depicted either his name in script signature (mark 30) or a bird over the name Vernon Kilns (mark 31). Sometimes the only mark found will be "Bird Pottery," in block letters.

Innovative and captivating, his designs were executed on the Montecito shapes, both angular and round, with few exceptions. Though his was not the sculptured ware of Bennison and the Hamiltons, his patented "inlaid glaze" process helped to produce dinnerware designs that were unique in artistic style. His florals, animal, and bird themes suggest that he was a man with a love of nature. Harry Bird pottery is not plentiful and is avidly sought. For more about Bird's pottery and examples of patterns, see the Montecito section in Dinnerware. (pages 150 – 165).

Gale Turnbull ∽

There was an overlap of the art ware pottery period and the hiring of Gale Turnbull as art director in 1935.* Turnbull, a painter and engraver, had already achieved recognition for his designs in 1930 at Leigh Potteries of Alliance, Ohio, and his later designs at Sebring Pottery.

His credits include a listing in Who's Who in American Art, membership in the American Art Association of Paris, France, and exhibitions in the Museum of Modern Art in Paris and the Brooklyn Museum in New York.

The renowned and highly respected Frederick Rhead in his "Art and Design Committee Report" to the 55th Annual Convention of the U. S. Potters Association in 1933 said, "The acquisition by the tableware manufacturers....of men such as Gale Turnbull, Joseph Thorley, and Viktor Schreckengost has already resulted in development activities which have raised the standards of tableware design and by examples exercised favorable influence over those concerns who do not yet employ art specialists." In his report at the 56th Annual Convention in December 1934 he said, "Gale Turnbull is the first ceramic artist in the American tableware game to emphasize the beauty of color in tableware decoration." And again, at the 58th Annual Convention in December 1936, he reported, "The Vernon Potteries of California, who within the past year [1935] acquired Gale Turnbull, have produced some interesting printed and filled-in [hand-tinted] ware, and also some hand-painted underglaze craft types, of a Continental flavor. Both shapes and decorations are fundamentally sound, and the potting is among the best we have seen in semi-vitreous practice."

Vernon Kilns was a pacesetter with Gale Turnbull as art director. Celebrated artists personally hired by Faye Bennison were given the freedom to create their best, in their own studios and in various parts of the country, with Mr. Turnbull traveling to supervise. Again Frederick Rhead, in his 60th Annual Convention report of January 1939, stated, "One of our group, Vernon Potteries of Los Angeles, has made a most interesting experiment in this direction (underglaze printing). With Gale Turnbull as art director they turn up at this year's Pittsburgh Show with two tableware decorations by Rockwell Kent and two more by Don Blanding. Three of the patterns are underglaze prints in one color; the fourth, also underglaze, is in outline and beautifully hand tinted by well-trained art students." He went on to report, "It is enough to state without any reservation that it is the greatest and most inspiring development since the production of Wedgwood's Queensware and the old Staffordshire underglaze prints. It is so far above anything that has been done in any country, by any potter since that time, that comparison would be idiotic. Anyone at present in the tableware business who fails to appreciate or to recognize the significance of this development is in that class of potters whose organizations have ceased to exist for no other reason than that they starved themselves to death for lack of creative vision."

*Announced in *Crockery & Glass Journal,* October 1935.

And finally, in his committee report at the 61st Annual Convention of the U.S. Potters Association in January 1940, he commented, "The Rockwell Kent American series cannot be ignored; it is another advance in this history of American ceramic creative development. With proper care and attention to marketing, The Rockwell Kent and Don Blanding decorations will last for generations." In essence, these few words of Frederick Rhead echo the thought expressed by Faye Bennison in his *Our Family*, and are evidenced in the pottery of Vernon Kilns. Rhead's recognition of Turnbull's talent, and the importance of hiring him as head of the art department, are evidence too of Fay Bennison's far-sightedness and outstanding leadership.

During his years with Vernon, Turnbull's output of designs was abundant. He is credited with the Ultra shape and with many hand-painted, printed, and hand-tinted designs pictured in the Dinnerware section of this book. Marks 33 or 34 were used on Turnbull designs, sometimes with only his initials as part of the mark. It is not known for certain when Turnbull left Vernon, but it was probably in the early 1940s. Nevertheless, his creative influence remained for the duration of the company.

Gale Turnbull's extraordinary talent is illustrated in the sculpture in the photo on the right, named by its owners *Jazz Band*. Signed by Gale Turnbull, there is no other identifying mark on this piece. The band is comprised of seven figures all dressed in tuxedos. The tallest figure is playing a saxophone; to the right is a bass player. To the left, a figure appears to be playing a harmonica. The figure on the lower right looks to be playing a piano, and the figure to the left of the drummer, who is front and center, is playing a clarinet. The figure on the lower left is holding a string instrument with a long neck. The piece is 8 inches high and 6 inches wide; PND.

Another known Turnbull sculpture is *Tropical Fish*, a figure of a fish riding the waves.

John and Joanne Barrett photo.

Hand-painted plate by artist Gale Turnbull presented as a wedding gift to Jane Bennison and her husband, B.N. "Bud" Howell. *Bill Stern photo.*

Don Blanding ∞

Under Gale Turnbull's supervision, Don Blanding (1894 – 1957) was the first of the famous artists to design and add his signature to pieces of Vernon Kilns dinnerware. Known as the "Hawaiian poet," he was a globe-trotter, author, and lecturer as well as an artist and illustrator. His travels took him to the tropics, where he worked and lived among the Hawaiians, writing and illustrating many delightful books of poetry, such as *Hula Moons, Leaves From a Grass House,* and *Vagabond House* — all collector's items today.

While associated with Vernon, Don Blanding worked from his studio in Carmel-by-the-Sea, California, and lived at Vagabond House, an old rambling redwood inn (which last the author heard was still standing). It has been said that the proprietor will eagerly point out the room where Blanding lived.

Blanding created four basic tropical designs; two were floral and two were fish. Identical designs in different colors were often given different pattern names; this resulted in a total of ten known patterns on the Ultra shape. His Lei Lani, one of the most popular Vernon Kilns patterns of all time, appeared in 1939 magazine ads and was still available by special order as late as June 1955. In 1942, Lei Lani was executed on the Melinda shape for a short time and called Hawaii. By 1947, the San Marino shape had been designed and production of Lei Lani was continued on it. Blanding's patterns were almost always marked with his signature, "Aloha, Don Blanding," and the Vernon Kilns name, though sometimes the pattern name was not included. (See mark 35.)

Mr. Bennison mentioned that he had a special attachment for Don Blanding as the son he never had. It was with great sorrow that he learned too late that Don Blanding had become ill and had passed away at the Sawtelle Hospital in Los Angeles — a few miles from Mr. Bennison's home.

Rockwell Kent ∞

In the late 1930s, Mr. Bennison went to New York to contact Rockwell Kent (1882 – 1971), a celebrated painter, author, lecturer, and illustrator. He hired him to design dinnerware patterns which are now museum pieces. An artist of the social realist school, Kent illustrated everything from large-scale public works murals, greeting cards, magazine ads, book plates, and record album covers to dinnerware. The Kent dinnerware is considered by Kentiana collectors to be the scarcest of all Kent. Kent, who became a controversial figure during the McCarthy investigations of the 1950s, is today honored as one of America's outstanding artists of the twentieth century.

Between 1938 and 1940, Kent designed pictorials which were to decorate three dinnerware patterns: Salamina, Moby Dick, and Our America. Each piece would have Rockwell Kent's signature over the Vernon Kilns name, mark 36. All the Kent patterns were transfer-print designs, and Salamina required some tinting. The Kent dinnerware, unfortunately, was way ahead of its time, and although major stores throughout the country placed large orders, about half of the dinnerware was returned because it did not sell — this according to Mr. Bennison. Production was soon discontinued; consequently, not too much of Kent's dinnerware is found today. Kent was unhappy, and blamed the "upside-down" handles of the Ultra shape. However, contrary to his criticisms, the handles were functional and comfortable, and the pitchers did pour.

In 1929, Kent visited Greenland, and returned again in 1931 for a year's stay. He later wrote and illustrated the book *Salamina*, named for his faithful housekeeper in Greenland. The colorful Salamina dinnerware pictures her among the icebergs of the Arctic Circle and the flaming rainbows of the Northern landscape. The company brochure described this dinnerware as "beautiful enough for the wall of an art museum," and it truly is!

For Our America, Kent drew over 30 different designs illustrating scenes and activities typical of the various regions of the United States. Moby Dick features whaling scenes from Kent's illustrations for the Herman Melville classic. Mr Bennison said that it was the most popular of the Kent dinnerware. A Vernon Kilns 12-piece place setting of Moby Dick in walnut brown, a gift from Kent's widow, Sally Kent Gorton, is housed at Columbia University in Special Collections. Further details about the Kent ware are outlined in the Dinnerware section.

Both Kent and Blanding plates and bowls are sometimes found encased in Farber Brothers metal display rims. Farber Brothers of New York City — not Farberware — bought the ware, specifying hand tinting on the Moby Dick plates and their own backstamp, and sold the finished product. Mr. Bennison said that during World War II, the metal transfer plates of all the Rockwell Kent designs were melted down for the zinc and copper necessary for defense production.

Today, there is an international group of Rockwell Kent collectors, and the Vernon Kilns Kent-designed dishware is some of the most sought Kentiana. A source of information for collectors is *The Kent Collector,* a triannual journal that contains articles, acquisitions, exhibitions, auctions, sale items, etc., regarding Kentiana. *The Kent Col-*

lector was first published by the late George Spector in 1974 and, after his death in July 1987, was continued for a short time by his widow, Gladys. During this time, the Docent Program of the SUNY Plattsburgh Art Museum in Plattsburgh, New York, offered to continue the journal publication. It seemed fitting, since the museum's Rockwell Kent Gallery is a center for scholarly work about Kent. The editor, Evelyn Heins, is happy to communicate with people interested in Kent's life and work. Subscription cost in 1992 was $15 annually, payable to *The Kent Collector* and sent to Evelyn Heins at the Rockwell Kent Gallery.

Walt Disney ∞

Vernon Kilns signed a contract on October 10, 1940, with the famous Walt Disney Productions to make figures of the characters from the animated film classics *Fantasia, Dumbo,* and *The Reluctant Dragon.* During the contract years (1940 – 1941), vases and tableware were also produced using various *Fantasia* designs.

Fantasia is an animated film that gains in popularity and prestige the older it becomes. During production — over four years at Disney Studios in Burbank — many of the thousand or so people involved in the various aspects of *Fantasia's* production felt that the film was too daring and experimental for Disney. Unfortunately, the 1940 public was not ready for such a concept and stayed away from the film, even though the critics agreed that it was well worth viewing. Walt Disney was disappointed and felt the film was a commercial failure — and his judgment remained unchanged for the rest of his life. Today, the movie is considered one of the great film classics and attracts large audiences at frequent revivals.

The Disney artists attempted to portray, through eight sequences in *Fantasia,* the mental images that occur when listening to classical music. The eight sequences were brought to life in cartoon form against the musical backgrounds of "Toccata and Fugue in D Minor," "The Nutcracker Suite," "The Sorcerer's Apprentice," "Rite of Spring," "The Pastoral Symphony," "Dance of the Hours," "Night on Bald Mountain," and "Ave Maria." The figurines made by Vernon Kilns were produced from the actual models used in the production of the film and are extremely rare. All Vernon figures are believed to be numbered and bear the trademarks "Vernon Kilns, U.S.A." and "Disney, Copyright 1940" or "1941." This mark is a black ink-stamped block letter mark on the bottom rim (mark 38), and the number of each figurine is impressed in the unglazed underside of the body. Each high-glaze figure took a minimum of 30 minutes to hand paint, and the figures sold for $1.00 to $2.50. Due to high production costs, the figures were discontinued after a short run.

Listed and numbered Fantasia figures are:

1	4½" Satyr	19	4½" Baby Pegasus, black
2	4½" Satyr	20	5" Pegasus, white, head turned
3	4½" Satyr	21	5½" Pegasus, white
4	4½" Satyr	22	8½" Centaurette
5	4½" Satyr	23	8" Nubian Centaurette
6	4½" Satyr	24	7½" Nubian Centaurette
7	4½" Sprite	25	5" Elephant
8	3" Reclining Sprite	26	6" Elephant with trunk raised
9	4½" Sprite	27	5½" Elephant
10	4½" Sprite	28	6" Ostrich
11	4½" Sprite	29	8" Ostrich
12	4½" Sprite	30	9" Ostrich
13	5" Unicorn, black with yellow horn	31	10" Centaur
14	5" Unicorn, white, sitting	32	5½" Hippo
15	6" Unicorn, white, rearing	33	5" Hippo
16	5½" Donkey Unicorn, white	34	5" Hippo
17	5½" Reclining Centaurette	35	3½" Mushroom pepper shaker
18	7½" Centaurette	36	3½" Mushroom salt shaker

The pair of 3½" mushroom salt and pepper shakers, numbered 35 and 36 and known as Hop Low, were added to the line in June 1941 and were sold to benefit the United China Relief. These were also made by American Pottery.

Vases and bowls also were designed with different motifs from *Fantasia*. The designs are in high relief and are found in different color combinations, sometimes hand decorated. These are marked "Designed by Walt Disney, Copyright 1940" and "Vernon Kilns, Made in U. S. A." (mark 39). The mark was stamped in block letters and numbered under the glaze. Sometimes there is also an embossed number.

Known Fantasia vases are:

120	Mushroom bowl, rectangular, 2" high, 12" x 7"		124	Satyr bowl, 3" high, 6½" diameter
121	Goldfish bowl, 6" high, 6" diameter		125	Sprite bowl, 3" high, 10½" diameter,
122	Winged Nymph bowl, 2½" high,		126	Goddess vase, 10" high, 6½" wide, 4½" across
	12" base diameter		127	Pegasus vase, 8" high, 12" wide, 5" across
123	Winged Nymph vase, 7" high, 4" diameter			

The Fantasia dinnerware patterns were made to complement the figures and vases. There were 51 pieces in the open stock sets, according to a reported article of January 1941. Patterns were Milkweed Dance, Autumn Ballet, Fairyland, and Fantasia (all identical patterns but in different color combinations), and Flower Ballet, Enchantment, Dewdrop Fairies, and Nutcracker (identical, different color combinations). One other reported pattern, called Firefly, has not been identified. According to the Walt Disney Archivist, another company had a previous right to use the word *Fantasia* on a set of chinaware. Vernon Kilns apparently made a few sets before they were informed of this.

Each piece of dinnerware has the pattern name backstamped in block letters under the glaze, along with "designed by Walt Disney" (script signature), the copyright date, and "Vernon Kilns, Made in U.S.A." (mark 37). Dinnerware patterns are described and pictured in the Dinnerware section (pages 246 and 247).

Dumbo figurines recreated by Vernon are:

38	6" Timothy Mouse		41	5" Dumbo
39	5¾" Crow		42	8¾" Stork
40	4" Dumbo			

Dumbo was typical of Disney's successful animated films and won immediate acclaim. Vernon's Dumbo figurines are dated 1941 and have the Disney copyright and "Vernon Kilns, U. S. A." (mark 38). Unmarked Dumbo figures identical to Vernon Kilns are probably Evan K. Shaw's American Pottery figures, although many companies have made these figures. A Dumbo figural planter vase has also been reported, but its number is unknown.

Baby Weems, from the full-length feature film with animated sequences *The Reluctant Dragon*, was another Disney figure designed by Vernon Kilns. The 6" Baby Weems, No. 37, dated 1941, has both the Disney and Vernon Kilns trademarks (mark 38).

Extremely rare are personalized Baby Weemses made expressly for Mr. Edward J. Fischer, last president of Vernon Kilns, and given to friends in 1942 to announce the birth of the Fischer daughter. Personalized words appear on the base of each of these.

American Pottery Fantasia and Dumbo Figures

Vernon Kilns manufactured and sold Disney designs for only a year and a half. On July 22, 1942, Disney agreed to let Vernon Kilns assign its contract to Evan K. Shaw's American Pottery Company.* Shaw purchased Vernon's stock of figures on hand at that time, along with all the molds, blocks, and cases. It was learned from the Disney archivist that Shaw continued to manufacture the two Dumbo designs. An unmarked Timothy Mouse has also been found. Two Fantasia figures with American Pottery paper labels have been reported — a hippo and an elephant — as well as the mushroom shakers. For this reason, one can conjecture with some certainty that unmarked Fantasia or Dumbo figures are American Pottery pieces missing paper labels. The writer has discovered certain distinctions between unmarked and marked figures. Vernon Kilns figures are usually marked with an incised number in the unglazed underside body. American Pottery figures that have been examined do not have any numbers and are glazed inside the body cavity. Further, they tend to be slightly larger than Vernon's and their glaze and handwork sometimes seem to lack some of the quality and detail of Vernon's. However, all of these figures are rare, and this is not an attempt to discount any, only to point out differences between those made by Vernon Kilns and those made by American Pottery.

Disney figures by Vernon Kilns are adorable and saucy creatures that capture the imagination. It is believed the Vernon Kilns figures were always numbered and marked (38). Pictured are Vernon Kilns figures from *Fantasia*.

* Evan K. Shaw acquired Metlox Pottery of Manhattan Beach, California, in 1946. He passed away in February 1980.

Sprites and Satyrs.
LEFT TO RIGHT: Sprites 12, 10, 9, 7, 8, 11; Satyrs 3, 2, 5, 1, 6, 4. © *Disney Enterprises, Inc.*
Sprites are $250.00 – 300.00 each, with the exception of No. 8, which is hard to fine and sells for $300.00 – 400.00.
Satyrs are $200.00 – 250.00 each.

Unicorns and Pegasus.
LEFT TO RIGHT: Pegasus 21, $200.00 – 300.00; Donkey Unicorn 16, $600.00 – 700.00; Rearing Unicorn 15, $400.00 – 500.00; Sitting Unicorn 14, $400.00 – 500.00; Pegasus 20, $700.00 – 800.00 (hard to find). © *Disney Enterprises, Inc.*

Variations in color.
LEFT TO RIGHT: Black Baby Pegasus 19, gray or black, $250.00 – 300.00; Black Unicorn 13, gray or black, $300.00 – 350.00.
© *Disney Enterprises, Inc.*

Elephants, Hippos, and Hop Low shakers.
TOP: Hippo 33, Elephant 26, Hippo 32, Hippo 34, Elephant 27, Elephant 25. Hippos, $350.00 – 400.00. Elephants, $300.00 – 400.00.
BOTTOM: Hop Low 35 and 36, $50.00 –75.00.
© *Disney Enterprises, Inc.*

Centaur and Centaurettes.
TOP: Centaurette 18, $700.00 – 1,000.00; Nubian Centaurette 24, $800.00 – 900.00; Centaur 31, $1,100.00 – 1,200.00; Nubian Centaurette 23, $1,000.00 – 1,100.00; Centaurette 22, $1,000.00 – 1,100.00.
BOTTOM: Centaurette 17, $600.00 – 800.00.
© *Disney Enterprises, Inc.*

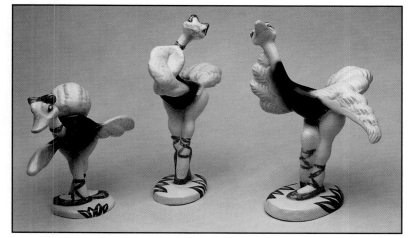

Ostrich 29, $1,000.00 –
1,200.00. Ostriches 28, 30,
$1,200.00 – 1,500.00.
© *Disney Enterprises, Inc.*

Pictured are all known Fantasia vases and bowls designed by Walt Disney and made by Vernon Kilns. Various solid colors have been reported for most of these, as well as hand-decorated versions. A backstamp which includes the vase number, mark 39, and usually an embossed number appears under the glaze of each.

Note: Hand-painted or decorated vases and bowls are generally worth double the standard solid colors.

TOP: 127 Winged Pegasus vase, 7½" x 12" (widest point), $500.00 – 700.00; 126 Goddess vase, 10½", $800.00 – 1,200.00; 121 Goldfish bowl, 6", $300.00 – 400.00; 124 Satyr bowl, 3½" high, 7" diameter, $200.00 – 300.00.
BOTTOM: 120 Mushroom bowl, 2" x 7" x 12", $150.00 – 200.00; 122 Winged Nymph bowl, 2½" x 12" base diameter, $200.00 – 300.00; 123 Winged Nymph vase, 7", $300.00 – 500.00; 125 Sprite bowl, 3" x 10½" diameter, $300.00 – 500.00.
© *Disney Enterprises, Inc.*

Close-up view of hand-decorated 121 Goldfish bowl, $500.00 – 600.00. © *Disney Enterprises, Inc.*

Two decorated bowls.
LEFT TO RIGHT: 122 Winged Nymph bowl, $400.00 – 600.00; 124 Satyr bowl, $400.00 – 600.00.
© *Disney Enterprises, Inc.*

Cameo Goddess vase. 126 Goddess vase has two colors, giving it a cameo effect, $1,500.00 – 2,000.00. © *Disney Enterprises, Inc.*

127 Winged Pegasus vase, decorated, rare, $1,200.00 – 1,400.00.
© *Disney Enterprises, Inc.*

Figures from Dumbo.
LEFT TO RIGHT: Dumbo 40, $75.00 – 150.00; Dumbo 41, $75.00 – 150.00; Stork 42, $1,500.00 – 2,000.00; Crow 39, $1,200.00 – 1,500.00; Timothy Mouse 38, $300.00 – 500.00. © *Disney Enterprises, Inc.*

Baby Weems 37 from *The Reluctant Dragon,*
$250.00 – 350.00. © *Disney Enterprises, Inc.*

Royal Hickman ∞

Royal Hickman, a familiar name in the field of design, was also associated with Vernon Kilns. In January 1942 at the Pittsburgh, Pennsylvania, show held in the William Penn Hotel, Vernon Kilns introduced Melinda, an elaborate dinnerware shape designed by Hickman. At the time, he was world famous for his creations in Swedish glass and artware, and noted for his animal designs for Heisey of Newark, Ohio. According to the late Clarence Vogel, who was editor of the *Heisey Glass Newscaster* out of Plymouth, Ohio, Hickman was an artist who did contract work for many companies in the metal, paper, glass, and pottery fields. He was known to have moved about the country, and he lived his final days in Guadalajara, Mexico, where he passed away in September 1969*. Vogel also stated that Hickman was an artist of exceptional ability who had a very characteristic style.

* Social Security death index.

Janice Pettee ∞

Janice Pettee sculpted the rare and almost legendary movie star figurines, believed to be the only such pottery figurines ever made. The figures known to date are Gary Cooper, Preston Foster, Walter Hampden, Dorothy Lamour, Bette Davis (two different poses, one of the poses done both with and without base, pictured on page 72), Paulette Goddard, Madeleine Carroll (two different figures), Anne Shirley, Wallace Beery (three different sizes and poses), Robert Preston, Lynne Overman, Victor McLaglen, Sally Rand (two different poses, the Balloon Dance and the Fan Dance), and Evelyn Venable. It is not known how many of these were produced, and only a few have been found. A number of the figures portray characters from the Paramount Studios movie, *North West Mounted Police*. Some are dated and marked Vernon Potteries, Ltd.; others have the company name Vernon Kilns. In addition, all have been marked "Approved by (signature facsimile of the respective movie star)" on the bottom and have the signature facsimile "Sculptured by Janice Pettee."

In my telephone conversation a few years ago with Evelyn Venable, a leading lady of the 1930s who was frequently cast in demure roles, she revealed that the 11" figure of her portrayed her as Shirley Temple's mother in *The Little Colonel*. Neither date nor movie was indicated in the mark on the base of her figure. Miss Venable believed that the figure may have been merchandised in shops where mementos of this nature were sold. She remarked that one had been given to her at the time it was made. Several of her figures have been found. All figures are considered extremely rare.

A figure of Will Rogers is known. It is unmarked, all white, and is almost certain to have been a Vernon Kilns figure.

It has been reported that in a 1940s trade journal, there was a list of Trade Names stating "Hollywood — dinnerware and art pottery, Vernon Potteries, Ltd." Could the movie star figures be what were referred to as the Hollywood line?

Other Artists — Designers ∞

Paul L. Davidson ∞ Of all the Vernon Kilns artists, he must have had the longest tenure. The earliest known dated picture plate, *The Arkansaw Traveler* (copyright 1936) and its companion plate, *Turn of the Tune*, are signed by Paul Davidson. Through the years, multitudes of picture plates have had his signature. His work also included the Winchester '73 designs for dinnerware introduced in 1950 (made to coordinate with Heisey's etched glass design of the same name), R.F.D. in 1951, and Countryside and Spice Islands, two patterns made for dā Bron (see page 310).

Allen F. Brewer, Jr. ∞ Brewer, of Lexington, Kentucky, was internationally known for his equestrian art and designed two race horse series for hostess tableware sets: Coaltown and Greyhound, picturing famous horses. His signature appears on the face of every plate. According to a 1950 company catalog, this series included two sizes of plates, 10½" at $3.00 and 8½" at $2.00, and cups and saucers at $3.00 per set. It is relatively scarce. (See pages 115 and 117.)

LEFT TO RIGHT: Evelyn Venable, 11"; 16½" statue of Gary Cooper, "Dusty Rivers, *North West Mounted Police*, A Paramount Picture"; Dorothy Lamour, 10", almost certain to be from the 1947 film *Road to Rio*, although not indicated in mark, co-stars were Bob Hope and Bing Crosby; "Sergeant Bret," 11½", as played by Preston Foster in *North West Mounted Police*; "Chief Big Bear," played by Walter Hampden in *North West Mounted Police*. (Incidentally, there is a Royal Doulton Indian figure of similar quality, size, position, and detail.) All the *North West Mounted Police* figures were dated 1940. Figures are all marked "Sculptured by Janice Pettee" (signature) and "Vernon Potteries, Ltd.," except for Evelyn Venable figure, marked "Vernon Kilns." All say "Approved by," followed with the respective star's signature facsimile. In the film *The Little Colonel*, in an opening scene the character portrayed by Evelyn Venable is dressed in the same costume seen on the Vernon Kilns figure. All PND.

LEFT TO RIGHT: Lynne Overman, 8½", "Tod McDuff," and Paulette Goddard, 10", "Louvette," both were characters in the 1940 Cecile B. DeMille Paramount film and are marked *"North West Mounted Police*, Vernon Potteries, Ltd."; Evelyn Venable, 11" (see picture above for description of figure). This figure had a "Mottman's Giftwares" sticker label, apparently from a gift shop where the figure was sold. Lionel Barrymore and Bill Robinson also starred in *The Little Colonel*, the 1935 Shirley Temple movie that inspired this piece. Dorothy Lamour, 10" (same as in above picture); Wallace Beery, 7½", figure is possibly from *20 Mule Team*, a 1940 MGM film where Beery portrayed a character who trekked through Death Valley dressed in boots and a gunbelt. All PND.

Rear view showing details of figures.
LEFT TO RIGHT: Lynne Overman, Evelyn Venable, and Dorothy Lamour. Dorothy Lamour passed away Sept. 22, 1996, at age 81. She had appeared in seven *Road* movies, beginning with *Road to Singapore* in 1940, and appeared in about 60 other movies as well. All PND.

Bette Davis, 16½", from movie and marked "*All This and Heaven Too*, Warner Brothers, Vernon Kilns." She played a governess in this film. PND.

Bette Davis figure without a base, 14½" tall, is identical to the figure with the base. The mark is the same, except it reads "Vernon Potteries, Ltd.," and is backstamped within the body. PND.

This is a 10½" Bette Davis figure in a different costume from the same movie, with the same bottom markings. Other stars who appeared in the 1940 film were Charles Boyer and June Lockhart. Is it possible there are other figures from this film? PND. *Judi Thompson photo.*

Group of figures.
TOP: Wallace Beery, 17", marked "Copyright 1940, by Vernon Potteries, Ltd., Made in U.S.A."; Victor McLaglen, 17", not dated, marked "Vernon Kilns."
BOTTOM: Anne Shirley, 11", not dated, "Vernon Kilns"; Robert Preston, 10", marked "*North West Mounted Police*, A Paramount Picture," portrays Ronnie Logan, "Copyright 1940, by Vernon Potteries, Ltd., Made in U.S.A."; and Madeleine Carroll, 10½", "Copyright 1940, by Vernon Potteries, Ltd., Made in U.S.A." All are marked "Approved by (signature facsimile)" and "Sculptured by Janice Pettee." All PND.
Frank Tosto photo.

LEFT: Another Madeleine Carroll. 17" figure of Madeleine Carroll as she portrayed April Logan in *North West Mounted Police*, with the same markings as other figures from the film. PND. *Judi Thompson photo.*
RIGHT: Mark within the hollow base of the Madeleine Carroll figure. *Judi Thompson photo.*

Wallace Beery, 10", same figure except for size and paint job sa found in the group picture on page 71. Believed to be the character from *20 Mule Team*, a 1940 MGM film. PND. *John and Joanne Barrett photo.*

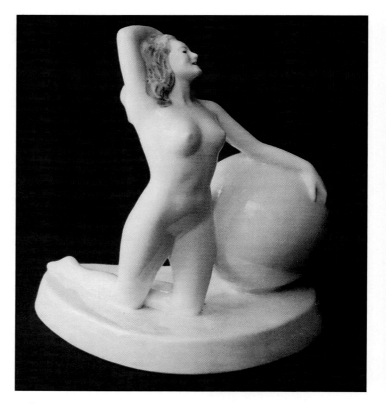

Sally Rand Balloon Dance figure, 7¼", 6½" wide, 4⅛" deep. Sally Rand was an exotic dancer in the 1930s. Though artistic, her dances were considered quite risque at the time. This figure and the Fan Dance figure are stamped "Approved by Sally Rand (signature facsimile), sculptured by Janice Pettee (signature facsimile), Vernon Kilns, Made in U.S.A." PND.

This 16" figure is of Sally Rand performing her famous Fan Dance as an entertainer on the Midway at the Century of Progress Exposition in Chicago 1933-1934. In the late 1930s, the author saw her perform the Fan Dance in Seattle, Washington. PND. *John and Joanne Barrett photo.*

Orpha Klinker ∽ Klinker (1891 – 1964) was Iowa born, raised in California, and best known for her painted historical and desert subjects and portraits. Her artwork and signature appear on many Vernon Kilns picture plates. She had studied in America and Europe, and was an academician from the American International Academy, Washington, D.C. She was listed in *Who's Who in American Art*, 1962, and received honors in France, Belgium, Mexico, and India. Her paintings were in the collections of Winston Churchill, Franklin Delano Roosevelt, and Edgar Bergen, to whom she also gave art lessons. There is a family story about the naming of Bergen's old maid. Orpha was nicknamed "Effie" by her brother, Zeno, who was a writer for Edgar Bergen. It was Zeno who suggested the name Effie for the character dummy.

Cavett ∽ Early in the 1940s, a young Mr. Cavett (no one rememered his first name) had his art career cut short when he took a leave of absence from his job at Vernon Kilns to join the military. He was killed while in training for the paratroopers. He is best known for the very popular Bits plate series; most plates in it carry his name in the lower right-hand corner of the picture. An exception is the Bits of the Old Northwest series by E. Fortier. (See pages 115 and 116 for examples of the Bits plates.)

Till Goodan ∽ Goodan was an artist famous for his western themed china ware ,and it is reported that he worked at Vernon Kilns sometime in the 1940s. While there, he probably did the original art work for the western ware that was ultimately produced by Wallace. Pictured on page 202 is a 9½" Rodeo plate; the design was hand painted and signed by Goodan on an unmarked Montecito plate.

Elliott House ∽ Elliott House was art director in 1952 and is believed to have remained with the company until it went out of business. Under his direction, many artists continued to be hired.

Sharon Merrill ∽ In the 1950s, Miss Merrill designed Chatelaine, a highly stylized dinnerware pattern. Her signature appears on almost every piece. (See mark 47 on page 8 of Evolution of Marks and pages 289 and 290 for pictures of the pattern.) In an article in the Winter 1996 issue of *Vernon Views*, editor Pat Faux wrote that "Merrill did more than just design dinnerware." A booklet, *California Originality: A Sharon Merrill Presentation*, stated that "the fashion conscious buyer is scanning the horizon for the new in decorative accessories to meet the taste of this new America that has dawned upon us. The upswing is modern." The *Views* article goes on to say that Merrill, who was a multi-faceted individual, also promoted the designs of many California artists at gift shows, including those in New York City. Artists such as Harriet Guppy, Velma Allen, and George Goldammer were among these fortunate artists. She also promoted a pattern she developed on her own — Our Homeland, a complete departure from the modern Chatelaine. The dinnerware pattern pieces pictured in the *Views* article were a red barn cookie jar and jam jar with cover, a silo salt and pepper, a hub mug, a wagon wheel condiment plate, a pitchfork relish, a shovel serving plate, etc. During this period of her career, Miss Merrill was living on Venture Boulevard, in Studio City, California.

Jean Goodwin Ames ∽ Ames was the designer of the 1950s pattern Sun Garden (see page 276). Under Evolution of Marks on page 8, her mark (46) may be seen. A noted muralist and botanist, she was a professor of art at Claremont Graduate School and Scripps College in California, and taught at Scripps from 1940 until her retirement in 1962. Murals painted by Mrs. Ames were placed at the University of Southern California, Newport Harbor Union High School, and Santa Ana College in Orange, California. Her enamels and ceramics were displayed at the Brussels Worlds Fair in 1958 and at national ceramics exhibitions. Much of her work was done in association with her husband, who died in 1975. She passed away in 1986, at age 82.

Robert Mayokok ∽ A full-blooded Eskimo, he was the artist of the Alaska scrimshaw plate. He was born June 1, 1903, in Wales, Alaska, a tiny Eskimo village about 50 miles across the Bering Strait from Siberia. A lifelong resident, he was well known for his ivory carvings and his drawings with pen and ink, and as an author of several books on Eskimo culture. At age 15, he lost both parents and began exploring the Arctic with excursions into eastern Siberia. Twice he traveled to the lower 48 to transport live reindeer; on the second trip, he took reindeer to the 1939 World's Fair in New York. He died February 7, 1983. This information was obtained from the obituary of Mayokok as it appeared in the February 17, 1983, issue of the *Tundra Drums* newspaper of Bethel, Alaska, sent by a collector who lives in Alaska. (Examples of Mayokok's work can bee seen on pages 112 and 114.)

Some of the many other artists whose names appear on the picture plates are Lloyd Hicks (who designed the Cocktail Hour series), Nick Goode, Annette Honeywell,* Frank Bowers (reported to have designed sets for *Gone*

With The Wind), Eugene Derdeyn, H. Fennell, Erik Sederling, Margaret Pearson Joyner, D. Klein, Joe C. Sewell, Mary Van Gelder, Robert Schepe, T. R. and N. W. Kingston, Mary Petty, Helen Chandler, E. Fortier, Eric Houghton, Lucille Mollacher, H. Monroe, Emax (designed the Farmers Market plate and was also an illustrator for the *New Yorker, Esquire,* and *Yank* magazines), David Rogers, Willie Rowe, Vandruff, Bert Williams, and others who are not named here. These were mostly artists who were involved in the artwork of the picture plates and worked out of their own local studios. Often the artists' signatures or initials are hard to find; sometimes they are in the border design or obscured somewhere in the picture.

In February 1990, it was my pleasure to meet and interview artist Robert Schepe in his studio/home in Borrego Springs in the Anza-Borrego desert, the southernmost desert in California. Here is where he and Mrs. Schepe spend their winters. The studio was filled with his paintings of desert landscapes as well as with mountain scenes of Montana, where they reside in the summers. His recollection of association with Vernon Kilns was dim, but he did say that he worked with Lloyd Hicks out of Hick's studio in Long Beach, California, during that period of his career. The only contact with Vernon Kilns was through an art department representative who would call upon them at the studio.

There were many unnamed employees with artistic flair who worked on the production line hand painting popular patterns such as Brown Eyed Susan and the Plaids.

*Annette Honeywell also created the concept for Franciscan's Desert Rose.

Vases and Bowls

There is a series of vases and bowls that is believed to have been produced for a short time during the same period as the Disney bowls and vases. Though they are similar, these are not Disney-designed pottery, a fact confirmed by the Disney Archives. Found in solid colors or hand decorated, none are artist signed. The series numbers start upwards from the Disney Fantasia numbers (120 through 127). Bowls 128, 129, 130, 134, 135, 137, 138, 139, 140, 141, and 142 are pictured. There are probably vases or bowls for the missing numbers 131, 132, 133, and 136, and the series may not end at 142. The series will have mark 12 if undecorated; if hand decorated, the words *hand painted* will be added to the mark 19. Bowl numbers are embossed or stamped on the bottom. Both 129 and 139 have been adapted for use as serving bowls for some Melinda patterns (See Dinnerware section, page 255), e.g., Cosmos and Blossom Time.

Vases and bowls, not artist signed.
TOP: 135 Flower bowl, 10½", $50.00; 134 decorated figural bird bowl, 8", $65.00.
CENTER: 130 embossed rim bowl, 6½", $40.00.
BOTTOM: 142 decorated duck bowl, 13", $115.00; 141 ash tray, 8½", $35.00; 138 decorated wave bowl, 11½", $60.00.

TOP: 135 decorated Flower bowl, 10½" (note: the number *135* may have been embossed backwards, appearing to read *132*), $65.00; 128 Vintage two-handled bowl, 13½", $95.00; 129 bowl, plain rim, 10", $35.00. BOTTOM: 140 Leaves and Flower handled bowl, 9½", $45.00; 139 Petal bowl, 9½", $45.00. The 129 bowl has been reported as seen decorated with hand-painted cherries, marked with Vernon Kilns mark 12 and "Tyrene Studios." The Vernon Kilns series will have mark 12, and if hand painted, the words *hand painted* will have been added to the mark (19). (See page 255 for 139 bowl decorated with Blossom Time pattern).

Ribbon bowl No. 137, approximately 11" long x 6" at its widest point and 1½" deep. Sides have an embossed ribbon look. $55.00. *John and Joanne Barrett photo.*

Bowl No. 140, hand-painted touches, bowl diameter 6"; including handles, 9". The plain version is shown in the photo at the top of the page, second grouping, lower row on the left. $65.00. *John and Joanne Barrett photo.*

By 1940, Vernon Kilns was well established in two lines of production, specialty ware and dinnerware. Yet during the early years of World War II, the future of the pottery business looked bleak, since so many employees were going into the armed forces or the vital defense industry. High school boys were hired to supplement the work force and were willing workers. English, German, and Japanese pottery imports were not available during those years, and there was increased demand for American dinnerware. Vernon Kilns was quick to take advantage of this situation and designed new molds and patterns, nearly duplicating English patterns, to meet the demand from American housewives who wanted to match their English dishes. Specialty wares with patriotic themes were also in big demand. Thus, the company was able to maintain peak production.

After the war, a fire occurred in 1946 and burned half of the main building, but it was soon rebuilt. In 1947, two days after Christmas, a second devastating fire hit the 30-year-old wood and sheet metal structures and burned everything to the ground. This fire was caused by a rupture of the main gas line that went through the center of the building. The plant had been closed down for the Christmas holidays, which was traditional, in order to repair equipment and take inventory. The factory building was fully insured for over a million dollars. Mr. Bennison considered retiring at this time and dissolving the company but, according to him, Eddie Fischer and key employees urged him to rebuild the plant. The employees were willing to take a cut in pay to keep things going rather than work elsewhere. The decision was made to rebuild the factory and carry on with the business.

With the rebuilding of the 130,000 square foot factory, all the old beehive kilns were replaced by tunnel kilns, and tracks and the cars that rolled along them were added. A car loaded with ware took 54 hours to go through the 1800-plus degrees kilns. The system greatly increased the overall production capacity of the factory.

The new building was a modern plant of steel-reinforced concrete and had an automatic sprinkler system. Suppliers of the equipment sent representatives from all over the country to view the model plant and equipment, as the very latest innovations devised by Vernon Kilns. For a short period, Memento plates and ash trays were given free to visitors of the new factory, which now showed the address 2300 East 52nd Street, Los Angeles.

Company photo of rebuilt factory as it looked in 1950.

Manufacturing Process

As was the case in the old plant, only top grade materials were used at the rebuilt Vernon Kilns. An adhesive-type ball clay from Tennessee was one of the favorite clays, as well as English, Kentucky, and North Carolina varieties. The clays were stored in clay bins adjacent to the railroad spur in back of the plant. From the storage bins, the clay was conveyed to the vats immediately inside. Water was added for the mixing process, and the clay was then formed into slip; this slip was pumped into a filter press, the function of which was to squeeze out the water. From there, the clay went into a pug machine to be de-aired. It then had a consistency that allowed it to be worked into 10" or 12" rolls. The rolls were transferred to the jigger. The jiggerman would take a handful of batter and would flatten it onto the plaster of Paris mold with a bat, in the same method as had been used at the old Poxon factory. This would form the plate, and while it was on the revolving mold, the edges of the piece would be trimmed. After the bisque was decorated, it was fired in the bisque kiln at high temperatures. Finally, the glaze was applied, and a second high firing, in the glost kiln, completed the process.

The glazes were made from silica mined in central California and were, like the clays, of very good quality. The glazes were guaranteed against crazing for 25 years. They have stood the test of time.

The decorating was done by hand on patterns such as Brown Eyed Susan, the Plaids, and Barkwood. No two pieces will be found that are identical. The method for the patterns, such as the earlier Blanding, Kent, and Disney dinnerware, and the specialty ware, was much the same as that invented in the 1750s in Liverpool, England, to produce historic Staffordshire transfer-printed pottery. The designs were printed on special paper, from designs that had been etched onto a copper cylinder. The copper roll revolved, printing an outline on tissue-like paper transfer sheets that picked up ink as it revolved and transferred the drawing to the bisque pottery, much like a printing press. The plain print was hand tinted on some patterns and specialty ware, a method that the industry termed "print and fill-in." The plain print (plain indicating not hand tinted) was mostly produced in colors of blue, brown, or maroon on a cream ground. Some was produced in green, black, purple, or orangy-yellow on cream ground. Vernon Kilns used the same hand-painted backstamps for the print and fill-in designs as for the hand-painted patterns.

Vernon Kilns was a pioneer in the transfer print process. Frederick Rhead, in his *Report of the Art and Design Committee* at the U.S. Potters Association 61st Annual Convention in January 1940, remarked that Vernon Kilns underglaze printing was "another advance in the history of American Ceramic development ... We may find increased interest in underglaze printing either from etched or engraved rolls." (In the Our America dinnerware pattern, which had over 30 designs, transfer printing became very costly.)

The manufacturing process is described in *Entertaining Table Ideas*, published in 1954 by Vernon Kilns.

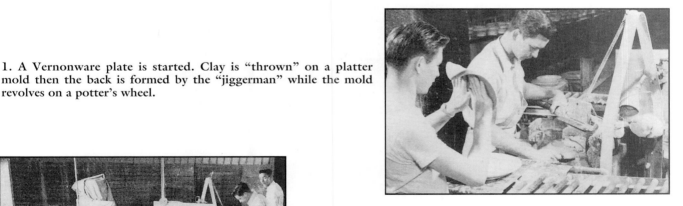

1. A Vernonware plate is started. Clay is "thrown" on a platter mold then the back is formed by the "jiggerman" while the mold revolves on a potter's wheel.

2. Every hour hundreds of Vernonware plates travel slowly through a forced-air dryer on a moving steel belt.

3. The dry, formed clay now known as "greenware" is edged and sponged by a finisher who inspects each dish for flaws.

4. Holloware is formed by pouring liquid clay or "slip" into a mold. Excess is poured out when the slip has jelled to the desired thickness and edges are smooth. The mold is then removed and the holloware is ready for drying and firing.

5. A car of greenware starts its 54-hour trip through Vernon's giant bisque kiln. As it travels the firing heat builds up to 2300 F°, forming a strong, durable bisque body.

6. Inspected again, perfect bisque is hand-decorated with ceramic colors by skilled artists.

7. Mounted on whirling tripods, the Vernonware receives a complete and thorough coating of raw glaze. Fired a second time in the "glost" kiln at about 1800 F°, the bisque and glaze are almost completely fused and Vernonware is now semi-vitreous, fine earthenware with its pattern completely under the hard, glass-like finish.

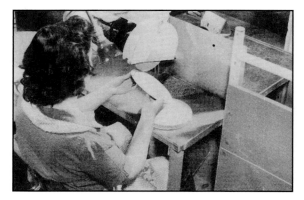

8. The tiny pin marks left from the glost kiln firing are burnished smooth on an emery wheel and every piece is inspected and graded.

Specialty Ware

Today, many people identify Vernon Kilns with its transfer-print specialty ware, the picture plates. Beginning in the 1930s, vast amounts, either stock or special order, were produced. Information for stock items is limited, as the only company catalogs available were for the period between 1950 and 1956. Two of the earliest known dated picture plates were *The Arkansaw Traveler* (Arkan*sas* is spelled Arkan*saw* here) and its companion, *The Turn of the Tune*, in 1936. A span of 14 years exists between the 1936 and the 1950 company catalogs, during which time the company continued to produce specialty ware. For special order items, there was no company documentation. Literally hundreds of souvenir and commemorative-type wares have been found. Only through the help of collectors and dealers who have provided listings and examples has it been possible to record and, within limits, picture some typical and some scarce stock and special order items.

Of invaluable help as a reference is a company list of available plates and where they could be purchased. It was sent to a collector in 1943 and was loaned to the author for the creation of this book.

The *Vernon Views* newsletter was an invaluable source of information for collectors for 22 years; its editor, Pat Faux, decided to cease publication with the 2003 winter issue.

An excellent source of information today is the website for Vernon Kilns Pottery by Tim and Linda Colling, http://www.vernonware.com. The website covers pottery identification and has a question and answer page, an e-mail newsletter, and more.

Stock Items

Ashtrays Ashtrays appeared as stock items in the 1950 catalog only. Described as 5½" wide and as offering a "choice of any State picture except Alabama," the ashtrays had the same pictures used on the 10½" plates. The ashtrays were done on the San Marino shape. Deep pink (or maroon) on ivory ground is the common color, and no colors have been reported in stock ashtrays. There is an *Alabama* picture ashtray, even though in the 1950 catalog there was none listed. In the same catalog, two were listed for Alaska: the Husky and the Bear. Some state map ashtrays have been reported: Florida, Georgia, South Carolina, Kansas, and South Dakota. The ashtrays sold for 85 cents. They were also designed by special order (SO and will be found in other colors as well as deep pink). Besides states, other subjects that may be found are universities, cities (both domestic and foreign), and famous people (some of these may have been special order items). An ashtray of the same design as the Memento plate was also made and given to visitors of the factory. (See pages 92, 93, 94, 123, and 126 for examples of these ashtrays.)

Picture Plates Picture plates were readily accessible to shop owners, generally in minimum orders of 100, mixed or matched, available on different shapes (the same as the dinnerware shapes), and usually 10½" in size. Of the shapes, Ultra was most common, Melinda next; less common were the San Fernando and Montecito, and even more rare the San Marino. (See Dinnerware section for a description of these shapes.) The earliest Ultra had the typical dipped rim; later, the shape was modified so that the dipped rim became flattened or turned up. Many collectors now refer to the rims as follows: turned up is "standard," flat is "flattened," and dipped is "Ultra." Backstamps were varied; a descriptive paragraph, a state seal, or simply "by Vernon Kilns, U.S.A."; occasionally, if requested by a "jobber," plates were made without the Vernon Kilns mark — but more on that later.

Until 1953, stock plates were plain print (PP), and hand-painted plates were available by special order. Colors were chiefly maroon, blue, or brown on a cream ground. Other colors, used infrequently, were green, black, and purple. In 1953, hand-painted (HP) plates were added as stock items. According to company price lists, hand painted meant hand tinted (print and fill-in). Today, collectors refer to these as multicolor. By 1954, only hand-painted plates were stock. Plain print was available only by special order, and by 1955, only in minimum lots of 1,000 of each subject (SO-M).

The following chart with codes indicates availability and prices of stock items for the period 1950 – 1956, with years 1951 and 1952 not known. Information is from company price lists.

Item	1950	1953	1954	1955	1956
State Picture	PP $1.75	PP $1.85	HP $2.75*	HP $2.75*	HP $2.95*
		HP $2.50	PP SO	PP SO-M	PP SO-M

In the 1950 through 1956 catalogs, all states were listed, including District of Columbia and two for Alaska (the Bear and Husky), except that Alabama was not on the list for years 1950 and 1953. Though the list shows only Alaska having two different pictures, there are two or more plates for many (if not most) states. Also contrary to catalog information, there is a hand-painted version of the Alaska Husky plate.

State Map	PP $1.75	PP $1.85	PP SO	—	—
		HP $2.50			

All states except Hawaii and Alabama. Also a state map of the entire U.S. As yet, no hand-painted map plates are known.

Cities	PP $1.75	PP $1.85	—	—	—
		HP $2.50			

Los Angeles, San Francisco, Phoenix, Hollywood, and Washington, D.C. Many more city plates are known, some of which may have been stock items before 1950.

Famous People	PP $1.75	PP $1.85	—	—	—
		HP $2.50			

*F.D. Roosevelt, Teddy Roosevelt, Woodrow Wilson, George Washington, Abraham Lincoln,** Andrew Jackson, The Atlantic Charter with Roosevelt and Churchill, Robert E. Lee, Stonewall Jackson, Will Rogers, and the Presidential Gallery (all presidents on one plate; at least two 10½" and one 12½" edition are known).*

Special	PP $1.75	PP $1.85	—	—	—
		HP $2.50			

*The Missions (California missions also pictured on 12½" and 14" plates), Cable Car San Francisco, Our West, Yellowstone Park,** Mount Rushmore,** Mother Lode, and Deep in the Heart of Texas.*

California Centennial, 1849 – 1949	PP $1.75	—	—	—	—
	Brown or blue				

Transportation, El Camino Real, State Capitol, Discovery of Gold, Campo de Cahuenga, and Historical Trees.

California Commemoratives	PP $1.75	—	—	—	—

There are twelve in this series: Marshall Discovers Gold at Coloma, 1848; University of California, Berkeley, 1873; Bear Flag Raised at Sonoma; Santa Barbara Mission, 1786; Golden Gate, 1855; Pico Capitulates to Fremont, 1848; Monterey (first capitol of California), 1850; Cabrillo Discovers California, 1542; Cradle Rocking During Gold Rush, 1849; San Francisco Bay, 1849; California-Oregon Stagecoach Passes Mount Shasta, 1860; and Mammoth Tree of Calaveras County, 3,000 years old. Known colors are blue and maroon.

Commemoratives	—	PP $1.85	—	—	—
		HP $2.50			

Only one listed in 1953 company price list: St. Mary's in the Mountains in Virginia City, Nevada.

Universities	—	PP $1.85	—	—	—

University of Notre Dame, University of Ohio, University of Michigan (all that were listed in 1953).

*Alaska was the only state not included in hand-painted stock.
**Subject available in another version in an 8½" plate, by special order.

Spoon Holders ∞ Spoon holders were available for awhile in the 1950s. Special designs were made upon request. Though prices are not known, the dinnerware spoon holders during the same period sold for approximately $1.35. Scarce. Examples are pictured on page 127. Of particular interest is one that was used as an invitation to a gift show to "meet Mr. and Mrs. Faye Bennison of Vernon Kilns, July 9, 1952, at the Gotham Hotel, 5th Avenue, New York City..." (page 103).

Miniature Plates ∞ Miniature plates had the same subjects as 10½" picture plates but were reduced in size. The Montecito 4½" plate was used for this purpose. It is not known whether these were stock items or special orders. Not plentiful. Examples are pictured on pages 93 and 127.

Bits Series ∞ Bits was a name given to seven groups of plates, six that divided the United States into regions, and one that represented Old England. For each group, there were eight 8½" plates and a 14" chop plate (there was not one of these for the Northwest) that pictured typical scenes of the region. Executed on the Ultra shape, the bit plates had dipped rims when first produced; later, the rims became flattened or turned up. Scenes were hand tinted and, except for Bits of Old Northwest, which bears E. Fortier's signature, bear artist Cavett's signature. The Bits were probably first introduced around 1940, since Cavett was an artist for Vernon Kilns at that time. Since they were not listed in the company catalogs from 1953 on, it may be assumed they had been discontinued by then. In 1950, the 8½" plates were priced at $1.75 each and the 14" chop plate was priced at $6.50. Variations have been reported, e.g., the *Tapping for Sugar* chop plate in the Melinda shape, and a blue 8½" *Tapping for Sugar* plate. Examples of the Bits plates can be found on pages 115 and 116.

In the Bits of Old England, the plates were not titled, but were numbered one through eight. An exception was for the No. 8 14" chop plate, which was titled *Golden Spur*.

Bits of Old New England

The Old Covered Bridge
Haying
Sunday Morning
The Cove
Old Dobbin
The Whaler
*Tapping for Sugar
Lighthouse

Bits of the Middle West

End of the Drought
Saturday Night
The Mail Train
The County Fair Blue Ribbon
The Corn Huskers
River Commerce
*R. F. D.
Fourth of July

Bits of the Old South

*Down on the Levee
Off to the Hunt
A Southern Mansion
Cypress Swamp
The Old Mill
Tobacco Field
Houseboat on the River
Cotton Patch

Bits of the Southwest

*Pueblo
Grinding Meal
Blanket Weavers
Hogan Dwellers
Baking Bread
Medicine Man
Basket Weaver
The Potters

Bits of the Old West

The Fleecing
*The Horse Thieves
The Train Robbers
The Stage Arrival
The Stage Robbers
The Bar Fly
Thirst
The Posse

Bits of the Old Northwest

Branding Time
Come and Get It
Fur Trapping
Logging
Logging Train
Log Jam
Sheep Herder
Unloading the Nets
(No chop plate for this series)

*Chop plate has this scene.

Mormon Series ∽ Temples of the Church of Jesus Christ of Latter-Day Saints. Though not documented, a Mormon Temple series of plates was done in the same style as the Bits series. The 8½" plates picture temples in Mesa, Arizona; Idaho Falls, Idaho; Cardston, Alberta, Canada; St. George, Logan, Manti, and Salt Lake City in Utah; and Honolulu, Hawaii. In addition, there is also a ninth 8½" plate which pictures a model of the future Los Angeles Temple. See page 120 for Mormon series examples.

Several other individual plates were done in the Bits style, such as the Virginia & Truckee Railroad; Avalon Bay, Santa Catalina Island; and The Alamo, San Antonio. See page 118.

California Missions Series ∽ California Missions was another series done in the Bits style. The group has 16 8½" plates picturing 16 different missions, plus 14" chop plate. According to collectors, the northern California mission plates listed in the right column are harder to find.

Distinctions between the northern mission plates and the southern mission plates are noted as follows: The northern mission plates are all signed by Orpha Klinker; the southern are unsigned but are clearly not Klinker's art style of bold lines.

The fronts of either northern or southern plates included the name of the mission, the date of its founding, and its location. The southern plates also include the names of the founders of each mission. See pages 118 for examples of the California Missions series.

California Missions

San Fernando Rey	San Francisco Solano
San Juan Capistrano	Carmel, San Carlos Borromeo
San Gabriel Archangel	Santa Clara
Santa Barbara	San Rafael Archangel
San Diego de Alcala*	Santa Cruz
La Purisima Conception	San Jose de Guadalupe
San Buenaventura	Dolores
San Luis Obispo de Tolosa	San Juan Bautista

*Chop plate has this scene.

Besides the series, other mission plates are the 14" El Camino Real, first edition, by Annette Honeywell and showing 21 missions and their founding dates, a 12½" chop plate on the Melinda shape, and a 10½" plate by Orpha Klinker.

The next groups, though they did not resemble the Bits series, were also stock items done in series of eight 8½" plates:

French Opera Reproductions ∽ These plates were copies of 19th century French plates and depicted scenes from eight operas. In the original French series, there were 12 scenes. In the Vernon Kilns series of eight, operas 2, 4, 8, and 11 were not reproduced. The Vernon Kilns operas are: 1. *Le Pre Aux Clercs*, 3. *Le Barbier de Seville*, 5. *Guillaume Tell*, 6. *Les Dragons de Villars*, 7. *La Dame Blanche*, 9. *Lucie de Lammermoor*, 10. *La Musette de Portici*, and 12. *Faust*. (See page 119). A 14" chop plate with the No. 3 opera, *Le Barbier de Seville*, was made for this series.

The artist's signature on the face of the plates is also reproduced from the original and is not that of a Vernon Kilns artist. Another company in the United States, with the trademark *PV* (Peasant Village), also reproduced the plates for an importer, Mitteldorfer Straus, Inc. of New York City. This has caused some confusion to collectors. Though it is sometimes difficult to distinguish the *PV* plates from Vernon Kilns on the surface, Vernon's are backstamped "French Reproductions by Vernon Kilns, U.S.A." The series is executed on the Ultra shape and is hand tinted.

No. 1, *Le Pre Aux Clercs*, has also been reported in plain brown print and with the opera number omitted.

Music Masters Series ⨯ Music Masters featured portraits of great composers, with a facsimile of the composer's signature on each plate. An actual score of music composed by each forms the border. A short biography is on the reverse side. Found in sepia brown tones, sometimes in blue, on cream background and executed on the Ultra shape, they sold for $1.25 in 1950. The eight composers in the series: Peter Tschaikovsky, Ludwig van Beethoven, Felix Mendelssohn, Edward Grieg, Ignace Jan Paderewski, Frans Schubert, Fredric Chopin, and Franz Liszt. Examples are shown on page 119.

The Cocktail Hour Series ⨯ The Cocktail Hour plates are very popular. These were done in sepia brown on cream background on the Ultra shape, and in 1950 were listed at $1.25 each. Each pictures a young lady, with the border design featuring the name of a various cocktail (L. Hicks, artist). The eight cocktails are Bacardi, The Bronx, Hot Toddy, Manhattan, Old Fashioned, Pink Lady, Singapore Sling, and Whiskey Sour. Some of these can be seen on page 119.

Mother Goose ⨯ Mother Goose, a single plate, was described in the company price list as in "deep pink only." Nevertheless, the one pictured on page 109 is brown. The Mother Goose plate depicts nursery rhyme figures. It originally sold for $1.25 and is scarce.

Children's Dishes ⨯ Children's dishes are included in this section, since it is not known whether these were stock or special order items. The Ultra and Montecito ware, the backstamp, and the dress style would indicate production during the 1930s.

One line features children; the 7½" Montecito plate portrays and is entitled *Little Miss Muffet*; the matching Playmates mug portrays two little children and Little Miss Muffet on the reverse side. Both are marked "designed by Amanda Owens" with the Vernon Kilns mark 9. Interestingly, the 6" bowl in this set is on the Ultra shape and the backstamp identifies it as *Bubbles*; it pictures the same two children on the mug, is signed by the same artist, and has the same mark as the mug.

The other children's dishes are all on the Ultra shape; they picture a 7⅜" frog plate, No. 792; a 6½" bunny bowl, #790; and a Scottie mug (neither numbered nor marked). The design is done in airbrushed stencil. Pictures of these items are on page 129.

Four 6½" plates on the Montecito shape are pictured on page 130: a cat peering at a goldfish bowl, a black and white spotted cow looking at a little dog, children looking in a kitchen window, and a lady looking out a door. All that is known of these plates is that they are signed "BLO," the artist's initials, and have Vernon Kilns mark 13.

Another piece reported is a sugar bowl with the Melinda shape, with the airbrushed stencil design scene of the cat eyeing the fish in fishbowl.

Race Horse Series ⨯ Race Horse series hostess sets were available in 1950 and listed two subjects, Coaltown and Greyhound. Each was signed on the face by internationally famed equestrian artist Allen F. Brewer, Jr. The sets consisted of hand-tinted 10½" and 8½" plates, and cups and saucers. Plates were $3.00 and $2.00; cups and saucers were $3.00. These pieces are considered scarce and are pictured on pages 115 and 117.

Christmas Series ⨯ The Christmas series had three themes: Christmas Tree (on both Montecito and standard shapes), and Santa Claus and Ye Olde Tymes (both produced on the standard shape) scenes, which decorated 10½" plates and two-tier tidbit servers. The signature of L. Hicks is found on both Ye Olde Tymes (on the mailbox) and Santa Claus (to the left of Santa's ear) plates as well as saucers. Plates seem to be more plentiful than cups and saucers in the Christmas series. The information for the detailed descriptions of the Christmas series that follow was contributed by Bob Hutchins.

The shapes used to describe the Christmas series by collectors are "standard," meaning the outer rims turn upwards from the inner rims, rather than downwards, and "flattened," meaning the rims are relatively flat. Both are variations of the Ultra shape.

The Christmas Tree plate is the only one of the series that was included on the 1943 list of specialty plates (page 137). It is believed that it was executed on the Montecito plate, and that the Christmas Tree on the more familiar standard-shape plate was introduced later, along with the Santa Claus and Ye Olde Tymes patterns. There are at least four different styles of the Christmas Tree plates: an undecorated solid brown transfer on a Montecito blank (see page 111), two hand-tinted transfers on a Montecito blank, with either solid brown or solid red bands on the rims (like the Christmas Tree cup and saucer with red bands on page 109), and a design of holly leaves decorating the rim of a standard-shape blank (as seen in the tidbit server on page 112).

Christmas tree cups and saucers were decorated with parts of the same transfer. Rims were varied; some pieces had red rims, as mentioned above, and other pieces were holly decorated.

Backstamps varied. Until the mid-1940s, mark 19 without the pattern name appeared on the decorated plates that had brown rims or red rims. Both the undecorated Montecito-shape transfers and those with the red rims have backstamps that read "Vernon's Xmas Tree By Vernon Kilns U.S.A." The "Xmas" designation was likely discontinued by 1950. The backstamps on the later, standard-shape Christmas Tree plates and cups and saucers read "Vernon's Christmas Tree By Vernon Kilns U.S.A."

It is believed that Vernon Kilns wished to distinguish its Santa Claus and Ye Olde Tymes plates from the special orders and did so in several ways.

The Ye Olde Tymes stock plate, standard shape, pictures a side view of a woman with a little girl in the scene, and is not titled on the front (see close-up on page 111). The backstamp on stock plates and cups and saucers is "Ye Olde Tymes By Vernon Kilns, U.S.A."

On special order Ye Olde Tymes plates, the transfer is on a flattened blank and pictures the back view of a lone woman in the scene. It is titled *Christmas* on the front, as seen in the picture on page 109, 3rd row, far right. The backstamp for this version reads "Merry Christmas and Best Wishes for a Happy New Year by Vernon Kilns, U.S.A."

The image on the cup features a view of a house that differs from that on the plate. The saucer pictures a stagecoach.

Santa Claus stock plates were on the standard shape and have a holly border (page 109). The special order version used a flattened plate and has a more elaborated rim design. The holly is interspersed with a scene of Santa in his sleigh. The special order will be found with the *Christmas* on the front.

Santa Claus cups and saucers include images of Santa's face (page 109). The backstamp for stock plates and cups and saucers reads "Vernon's Santa Claus By Vernon Kilns U.S.A." The backstamp for special orders reads the same as it does on Ye Olde Tymes, "Merry Christmas and Best Wishes for a Happy New Year by Vernon Kilns, U.S.A."

Both Ye Olde Tymes and Santa Claus plates were special ordered for the Austin Company (still in business in Irvine, California) and have the words "The Austin Children's Christmas Party" at the base of the pictures. The backstamp reads "Merry Christmas and Best Wishes for a Happy New Year from the Austin Company (signature facsimile) by Vernon Kilns U.S.A."

Other variations have been noted in this series of plates. Two versions of a 12" Montecito-shape Christmas Tree chop plate, one with a red rim and the other with a green rim, have been reported. A picture of the chop plate with the green rim is on page 111. No other Christmas Tree pieces with a green rim are known. Both chop plates are backstamped with the name and address of the store, "Plummer Ltd. in New York City with locations at 7 East 35 Street and 695 Fifth Avenue," and were specially ordered.

One other Christmas-related item by Vernon Kilns is a 9½" Montecito-shape plate by Harry Bird showing two Christmas trees in pots and a holly border. The backstamp is a variation of mark 31 but does not include "Made in U.S.A." This may have been Vernon's earliest Christmas ware. See page 111 for close-up view.

Scenic America Series of After Dinner Cups and Saucers ∽ These items were an assortment of 24 views of Scenic America subjects, in colors of brown, pink, or purple print with hand-tinted scenic panel borders. One has also been seen in plain green print. These came packaged in a special carton and sold for $0.85 each. A six-color counter card displayed three different shapes: Melinda, Montecito, and San Fernando. Examples are on pages 109 and 122.

Subjects for Scenic America After Dinner Cups and Saucers:

First Confederate White House, Alabama

Grand Canyon, Arizona

Apache Trail, Arizona

Monument Valley, Arizona

Monterey Cypress, Carmel, California

Lone Cypress, Carmel, California

Singing Tower, Lake Wales, Florida

Cypress Gardens, Florida

Little White House, Georgia

My Old Kentucky Home

Mississippi River Steamboat

Statue of Liberty, New York

Niagara Falls, New York

Plantation Home, South Carolina

Lookout Mountain, Tennessee

Andrew Jackson Home, Tennessee

Christ Church, Virginia

Jefferson Davis' Home, Virginia

Monticello, Thomas Jefferson's Home, Virginia

Natural Bridge, Virginia

University of Virginia

Mt. Vernon, Washington's Home, Virginia

Jefferson Memorial, Washington, D. C.

Washington Monument, Washington, D. C.

Other scenic demitasse cups and saucers were made, such as Old Church Tower, Jamestown, Virginia; Golden Nugget, Las Vegas; and Carlsbad Caverns, which may have been special order.

Special Order Items ⤬

Besides stock items, myriad wares were designed for special orders from organizations such as department stores, national parks concessions, businesses, organizations, etc. Plates (4½" to 14"), ashtrays, spoon holders, dinnerware sets, hollowware (cups and saucers, pitchers, vases), and even some specially-designed shapes (such as the Lake Tahoe tray on pages 127 and 128) were available. Most were marked "Made expressly for (sponsor)" or "Especially for (sponsor)" and "by Vernon Kilns"; sometimes the name Vernon Kilns was omitted. Two examples are the Washington, D.C., plate backstamped "Capsco Product" (Capitol Souvenir Company, Washington, D.C.) and the Alaska State Bear plate backstamped "Wesco Kilns" (West Coast Kilns). Capsco also ordered souvenir plates from Adams of England. Probably more wares were ordered from Texas than any other area except California.

Ashtrays ⤬ Ashtrays were available for special designs, often the same ones that could be found on the 10½" plates. Ashtrays picturing the State seal of Florida and the Territorial Seal of Alaska have been reported. Pictured on page 94 is the Memento astray given to visitors to the pottery company. A Rotary ashtray with a Rotary dark blue transfer on Modern California light blue ashtray stock was a rare find and a departure from the usual San Marino stock used for ashtrays (see page 101). Yosemite Half Dome is shown on page 128.

Picture Plates ⤬ Picture plates, 10½", were the speciality pieces ordered most often and were therefore the most numerous. Subjects were cities, states, state maps, famous people, counties, universities and schools, World War II, religious groups, organizations, transportation, advertising, foreign countries, souvenirs, and children's themes. Many plates were produced as souviners. A few examples of picture plates are given:

Cities: Flint, Michigan, Home of General Motors, made expressly for McLogan & Austin, The China Closet; Memphis, Tennessee, designed for The John Gerber Company; Chicago, made exclusively for Marshall Field & Co. All are pictured on page 93. Flint plate, with its automobile motif, has double collectibility. There was a Tri-Cities picture plate — Davenport, Iowa; Rock Island, Illinois; and Moline, Illinois — made for Peterson-Harned-von Maur, Davenport, Iowa. City map plates, too, were ordered: St. Louis, Missouri, for Scrugg-Tandervort-Barney is one example.

Counties: Historic Anson County, North Carolina, 1749 – 1949, for Thomas Wade Chapter, D. A. R., Wadesboro, Calhoun County, Texas, for Port Lavaca Cemetery Association; Liberty County, Georgia, for Mary Eliza Shop, Hinesville; Surry County, Virginia, for Thomas Rolfe Branch Association for Preservation of Virginia Antiquities.

State Picture: Florida, made for Yowell Drew Ivey Co., Orlando; Illinois, made for A. C. McClurg Co.; Kentucky, made for Belknap Hardware & Manufacturing Co.; Minnesota, made for A. C. McClurg & Co.; Vermont, for C. T. Bodwell, The Picture Plate Man; Wyoming, made for Dan S. Park & Co., Jewelers; and the Alaska Bear for Wesco Kilns (unmarked Vernon Kilns found on page 93).

State Map: Georgia, made for Georgia's Leading Jewelers, Thomas Freeman & Bros., and Michigan, for the Automobile Club of Michigan (unmarked Vernon Kilns), are two examples.

Famous People: Two editions of General Douglas MacArthur (also a stock item), the first edition for Barker Bros. (a Los Angeles furniture store no longer in business). This subject also is a double collectible appealing to World War II collectors, and is quite plentiful. James Stephen Hogg, for Daughters of the Republic of Texas; Franklin D. Roosevelt, for the Little White House Souvenir Shop, Warm Springs, Georgia (page 102); William Pryor Letchworth, for A. B. Davis, Glen Iris Inn; and Generalissimo and Madame Chiang Kai-shek (backstamped "A CDGC Creation, Made in U.S.A." — unmarked Vernon Kilns).

Universities and Schools: Three 10½" plates were listed as stock items in 1953 (see chart on page 82). However, University of Notre Dame and University of Michigan have also been found as special orders. Listed are some of the many that were produced, whether special order or not: John Brown University, Arkansas; Christian College, Columbia, Missouri; Brigham Young University, Utah; Culver School for Boys; Duke University; Fresno State College, California (8½" plate); University of Kansas; Lincoln Memorial University, Tennessee; Michigan State College; University of Ohio; Oregon State College Diamond Jubilee; Pacific University of Forest Grove, Oregon; Purdue University; Stanford University; Texas State College for Women, first edition, 1953; University of Texas; Stephen F. Austin State College, Texas; and University of Wisconsin. Stanford plate does not have the Vernon Kilns backstamp. Examples are found on page 99; see page 131 for a 1943 company list.

Cups and saucers, both demitasse and regular size, were also produced. To name a few: San Jose State College (now known as San Jose State University), University of Southern California, and U.S. Naval Academy (a demitasse cup and saucer made expressly for Herff-Jones Co., Annapolis.) A creamer and sugar was made for Duke University, and a spoon holder that pictured Campanile Tower was made for the University of Kansas (see page 127).

World War II Commemoratives : These were popular during those years. Mentioned before was the plate picturing General Douglas MacArthur. *Remember Pearl Harbor* is an unmarked Vernon Kilns and is backstamped "Made in U.S.A., Exclusive distributors China and Glass Co., New Orleans, La." (page 95). The artist was Margaret Pearson Joyner. Others commemoratives have the Army Air Corp song or the Navy Oath of Allegiance; both plates were made for Walter S. Mills Co., Ltd.

Religious: Religious groups placed special orders, especially churches. Some were of the Old Cathedral in Vincennes, Indiana; Catholic Churches of the Rio Grande Valley, Texas; Episcopal Churches of the Rio Grande Valley; Denver Messiah Lutheran Church; St. Louis Cathedral, New Orleans; First Presbyterian Church, San Diego; Pioneer Congregational Church, Sacramento; St. Mary's in the Mountain, Nevada; First Presbyterian Church, Fayetteville, North Carolina; and Franciscan Monastery, Washington, D.C. (Capsco backstamp). The Black Hills Passion Play might be in this category.

Forest Lawn Cemetery of Glendale, California, ordered several different items. Demitasse cups and saucers (Melinda shape) and 8½" plates (standard blanks) each pictured one of three different Forest Lawn scenes: The Church of the Recessional, Wee Kirk o' the Heather, or Little Church of the Flowers.

Also, a 14" plate was designed to show the entrance gates to the cemetery, with a fountain and a church in the background. The Forest Lawn items did not carry the Vernon Kilns backstamp (see page 121).

In addition to the Temple plates mentioned before, the Church of Jesus Christ of Latter Day Saints (the Mormon church) ordered a plate commemorating The Relief Society centennial.

Two unusual plates believed to be scarce are Noah and the Ark and Pope Pius XII. The Pope Pius XII plate could also be classified as a Famous People piece (page 121).

Organizations: Plates were made for Masonic and Eastern Star organizations, i.e., El Jebel, Denver, Colorado, dated 1953; Al Malaikah Imperial Council Session, Los Angeles, 1950, picturing the late film star Harold Lloyd, Imperial Potentate (on page 99); Scottish Rite Temple, Guthrie, Oklahoma; Order of the Eastern Star Grand Chapter, Indiana, 75th anniversary, 1874 – 1949; Kansas Order of the Eastern Star, Grand Chapter, 75th Session, 1951.

Other plates were for the Supreme Forest Woodmans' Circle, Omaha, Nebraska; the United Daughters of the Confederacy, Texas Division, dated 1946; Beta Sigma Phi, of Abilene, Texas, an international service sorority; and Sigma Alpha Epsilon, a college fraternity (plate done in purple print). A Chi Omega college sorority demitasse cup and saucer has been reported.

The Rotary Club of Vernon ordered Rotary motif vases, carafes, large platters, and dishware. At least one set of dishes is known to have been made, complete with dinner, salad, and bread plates, fruits dishes, and cups and saucers. These are decorated with the Rotary Club emblem and usually with signatures of members of the city of Vernon Rotary, including Faye G. Bennison and F. B Klinker. These are found on both Melinda and Ultra shapes. Examples are seen on pages 95 and 100. (The report that Mr. Klinker may be the brother of Vernon Kilns artist Orpha Klinker has been disputed.)

Conventions: An example of this type of special order is the large platter for the Republican Convention of 1956, held in the state of California, and given by the host state to the attending delegates (see page 99). Other orders were filled for the American Society of Civil Engineers at Houston, 1951; 46th Convention of Postmasters, St. Louis, 1950; and the 48th Convention of Postmasters, Boston, 1952.

Transportation: Airplane and train 10½" plates are very popular with collectors (pages 107 and 108). Ashtrays with some of the same subjects were also made. Two plates were made for the Chicago Railroad Fair in 1949, which commemorated the "One Hundredth Anniversary of Railroad Progress." One was designed exclusively for Consolidated Concessions, Inc.; the other was made exclusively for Marshall Field & Company. Both are pictured; see pages 105 and 108. Other pieces are *In My Merry Oldsmobile*, for Pig 'n Whistle Gifts, and two turnpike plates, representing the New Jersey and Pennsylvania turnpikes, for Howard Johnson Turnpike Shops.

Advertising and Business: Two editions, 1940 and 1941, were made of the Dorchester, Massachusetts, plate for Walter Baker & Co. The backstamp pictures La Belle Chocolatiere, its famous trademark. The plates are sought by both Baker's Chocolate and Vernon Kilns collectors. See page 109.

In the 1950s, a Coca-Cola bowl was made. It is pictured alongside a figural penguin bottle on page 124. This bottle, made for a brand of sloe gin, has been seen with the original liquor label and federal tax seal still intact.

The Shamrock Hotel in Texas ordered an attractive plate in green print with a shamrock border, designed for them. It is one of the Highlights of Houston plates designed by Mary Petty. Dishes were made for Trader Vic's Honolulu restaurant and are pictured on page 124. Moorman's Feeds of Quincy, Illinois; the Nut Tree Restaurant in Vacaville, California; and "John Pritzlaff Hardware Company, 100th anniversary, 1950" are among the subjects found on plates in this category.

Foreign Countries: Known 10½" picture plates are of Caracas, Venezuela, which pictures Estatua del Libertodor surrounded by city buildings and is backstamped in Spanish, "Disenado por Vernon Kilns, Los Angeles, California"; Republic of the Philippines (unmarked Vernon Kilns), commemorating Independence Day July 4, 1946; Jose Marti, the plate pictures a bust of the celebrated Cuban patriot against shelves of books and the Cuban flag, "1853 – 1953." The backstamp has a date of January 28, 1953, and says "Vernon Kilns." An unmarked Vernon Kilns ashtray, in addition to a plate backstamped "Flota Mercante Grancolombiana, S.A. Venezuela, Colombia, Ecuador," must have been produced for a company; it translates as "Great Colombian Merchant Fleet." *S.A.* (abbreviation for *sociedad anonima,* "anonymous society") is the Spanish equivalent of "Inc." This was previously described in error as having been made for South American countries. (Example are on page 123.) A binational plate for El Paso and Juarez was made. A Rio de Janeiro plate is also known (listed on the 1943 company list, page 134).

Souvenirs: This is a general category which groups national parks and monuments, historical sites, events, state parks, recreational areas, and miscellaneous subjects that were specially ordered specifically to be sold as souvenirs. Many of the plates and items in the preceding categories could be classified as souvenirs as well. Subjects were depicted on hollow ware and flatware of the same dinnerware shapes described under Stock Items.

Some examples of dinnerware short sets are Alaska (page 125) and Yosemite National Park and Lake Tahoe (page 127); other items include after dinner cups and saucers similar to the Scenic America series (*Chief Seattle,* for Frederick & Nelson's, and *Dover Old State House,* ordered by the Delaware D.A.R.); a 4½" miniature plate, "Sugar Bowl Classic for Maison Blanche Company, New Orleans"; an unusual tray in the shape of Lake Tahoe; 8½" Detroit plate for J. L. Hudson, commemorating the 250th year of the founding of Detroit; a Valley of the Moon mug; a mug commemorating the Kerr County, Texas, centennial; an 8½" plate picturing Mt. Rushmore in the Black Hills of South Dakota, for the Burgess Company, Inc; and a 1-pint Ultra Salamina jug with the word "Ketchikan" on the handle (on page 243).

Some 10½" plates were of Boulder Dam, Nevada, for Navi-Hop Trading Post; Franconia Notch and Old Man of the Mountain for the New Hampshire Forest and Recreation Department; Lake Texoma, Oklahoma, for W. J. Baldwin; the Statue of Liberty, two different designs (by different artists), both for James Hill, Bedloe's Island; Tennessee Great Smoky Mountain National Park for Ogle's Crafts, Gatlinburg, and (a different design) for Standard Souvenir and Novelty, Inc.; Tacoma Narrows Bridge for Peoples Store, Tacoma; and Monticello, for the Thomas Jefferson Memorial Foundation, New York City.

The Historic Baltimore series of eight 8½" plates in sepia, blue, or maroon print was made exclusively for Hutzler Brother Company. The plates in the series depict the following: 1. Carroll Mansion, *Homewood*; 2. Baltimore Harbor, 3. University of Maryland School of Medicine, 4. John Hopkins Hospital, 5. Fort McHenry, 6. Court House and Battle Monument, 7. Washington Monument, and 8. Old Shot Tower. See page 122.

The Brulatour Courtyard, New Orleans, was made for Bague Southern Souvenir Mfg. Co., New Orleans, and the Spindletop, Beaumont, Texas, plate, "1901 – 1951," for Smith Ward Jewelry Co. Both are 10½". A cup and saucer and matching plate picturing an Eskimo were made for the Alaska Crippled Children's Association.

A number of Vernon pottery pieces have been seen exhibited. Vernon's Statue of Liberty plate (featured on book cover) is in the statue's historic display at Bedloe Island; the U.S. Naval Air Station plate is in the Naval Air

Museum at Pensacola Naval Air Training Station, in Florida; the Alamo plate is in the Alamo Museum in San Antonio, Texas. The Presidential plate showing Eisenhower and Nixon was acquired by a former vice-presidents museum, and the Virginia Truckee plate was part of the Nevada History Collection. The Coca-Cola bowl was seen in the World of Coca-Cola museum exhibit in Las Vegas. *The Fires of Fredericksburg* plate and the Fredericksburg, Texas, plate are both housed in the Old Church Town Museum in Fredericksburg.

Oddities have been reported, such as a Historic Natchez, Mississippi, plate with two artist signatures, Eugene Derdeyn's in the lower left and Paul L. Davidson's in the upper right, and an Ohio plate signed by both R. Schepe and Cavett.

Vernon Kilns was commissioned to produce special items for the American Ceramic Society of Southern California. One example is the small vase on page 109, picturing a baseball player, a souvenir for the society's Annual Sports Day, July 16, 1955. Annual Chairman's Award plates were sponsored by Vernon Kilns for the ACSSC. Two different plates for the years 1951 and 1954, each of which pictured recipients of awards for Meritorious Service, are pictured on page 126. A third 14" award plate, for 1952 and designed by Biondi, is also described on the same page. A loving cup (Chatelaine sugar bowl) given to the Soft Ball Champions of the ACS, Southern California Section, in 1952 is also pictured.

Company souvenir plates with photos of company employees were given as gifts to individual retirees.

Vernon Kilns office staff members were in a company bowling league and bowled in Huntington Park, located near the city of Vernon. A member of the league was Marie Rogers, who worked from 1952 to 1958 as a keypunch operator processing orders that came into the company. She related the information regarding the league and the trophies.* Examples of trophies are the Vernon Kilns bowling league tumbler (seen on page 109) and the same tumbler with its matching decorated snack tray that has an indent for holding the tumbler (seen in photo on page 104). The indented tray and tumbler are in the San Clemente (Anytime) shape. The snack tray was apparently made for the Tickled Pink pattern, to hold the Tickled Pink tumbler. It is possible that the snack tray was made for other San Clemente (Anytime) patterns.

Of particular interest to collectors, the history of the two Arkansas plates, *Arkansaw Traveler* and *Turn of the Tune,* was furnished by Vernon Carrens of Arkansas. The Vernon Kilns plates were renderings of the original paintings by Edward Payson Washburn (the *Traveler* was painted in 1858). The Historic Arkansas Museum in Little Rock houses the Currier & Ives lithograph print of the famous *Arkansas Traveller* painting. Paul Davidson was the artist of the Vernon plates.

As background for the history of the plates, copies of two postcards are pictured; originals were loaned by Mr. Carrens. The *Traveler* card was postmarked Oct. 30, 1914, and the word *Arkansas* was spelled with a *w*; that was common in an earlier time. In 1881, the state legislature of Arkansas declared the rightful spelling to be A-r-k-a-n-s-a-s and the pronunciation to be Ark-an-saw.

In 1936, Mr. R. E. McCann requested Vernon Kilns produce the two plates. It appears, as Mr. Carrens says, that Mr. McCann had the pictures and some dialogue copied to the plates with the same Arkansa*w* spelling as was on the postcard. In June of 1936, he applied for copyright for each plate.

Mr. Carrens is of the opinion that Mr. McCann had the plates produced for the Arkansas 1936 Centennial Celebration held in Little Rock. He was the owner of a photography company, located at 714 Garrison, Ft. Smith, Arkansas. It is possible he ordered the plates to be given out as advertising in conjunction with the centennial. Unfortunately, Mr. McCann died of a heart attack prior to the celebration.

According to Mr. Carrens's account, a supply of *The Arkansaw Traveler* plates that were ordered by Mr. McCann were found stored in the basement of the McCann family home some years later. The plates were still in the original boxes, most of which had deteriorated from dampness and years of storage. No examples were found of *Turn of the Tune,* the scarcer of the two plates. See page 110 for pictures of plates and postcards.

A rare spoonholder (dinnerware shape) mentioned previously was designed as an invitation, presumably to the buyers attending the summer gift show, and is pictured on page 103. The invitation read "You are invited to meet Mr. and Mrs. Faye Bennison of Vernon Kilns on July 9, 1952 from 4 to 8 p.m. at the Gotham Hotel, Fifth Avenue, New York City. RSVP Zepha Bogert, Gotham Hotel." Bubbles and two champagne glasses decorated the item. It was produced in green on ivory.

Personalized Dishes: These, in the Melinda shape, were available by special order. They included dinnerware sets for yacht owners, plates for family surname coats-of-arms, and plates for individual given names.

Goes to Sea yachting dinnerware was offered in a choice of red and blue (Monterey) or green and yellow (Philodendron) borders with the boat name in rope design or in block letter style. Table settings, according to the company brochure, included plates, cups and saucers, chowders, a creamer, and a pitcher. The Four Winds was designed for a yacht that sailed the Transpacific Yacht Club Race from Los Angeles to Honolulu (year unknown). Additional personalized yachting dinnerware sets known are: Mary Clay, Flamingo, Goose B III (Philodendron),

* *Vernon Views* Summer 2001 issue

Hazel K, Jada, La Osa, Kathleen-Newport, Kipajoge II, Nan Jo, Pompano, Roaring Bessie, Sal-Al III, Slip Away, and Tondeleyo. There may be more. Examples are pictured: The Four Winds cup (page 257), Flamingo and Kathleen-Newport fruit bowls, a Kathleen-Newport 9" bowl, a Kipajoge II sugar bowl (page 259) and a Hazel K bowl (page 127).

Known coat-of-arms plates that were ordered are for Smith, Jones, Brown, and Miller surnames. The Brown and Miller plates are pictured on page 127.

Seen in an old *House Beautiful* magazine by the *Vernon Views* editor was an ad for "name plates," which were described as "dinner plates in warm ivory, banded in dark green and yellow or red and blue, and the facsimile of your signature is copper-etched under permanent glaze on the rim." The ad continued, "Six 10½" plates $9.90. Open stock pieces available."

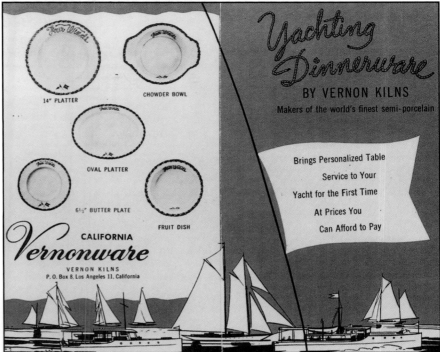

Company brochure advertising Goes to Sea yachting dinnerware produced on the Melinda shape.

THE WORLD'S FINEST SEMI-PORCELAIN

Goes to Sea

Vernonware yachting table service has been proven at sea. Acknowledged by yachtsmen to be a compliment to the finest yachts afloat, it has been proven on the famous but rugged Transpacific Yacht Club Race from Los Angeles to Honolulu. After three months at sea, going through some of the worst weather seen on the Pacific Coast in many years, down through the tropical South Sea Islands, and returning to the Pacific Coast through squalls and rugged weather, not one piece of Vernonware yachting table service was broken, chipped, cracked or crazed—a tribute to the world's finest semi-porcelain.

How often have you wanted a personalized table setting for your yacht—plates, cups, saucers, chowders, cream and pitcher—the whole complement of a fine dinnerware set, complete with the name of your yacht or, if you desire, your house flag and yacht club burgee in full color on each piece.

Heretofore, such sets have been out of the range of most yachtsmen. Now, you can have a complete set of famous Vernonware, guaranteed against crazing—and it is a proven good sailor, too. Made to withstand all yacht service with a choice of beautiful red-and-blue, or green-and-yellow edges, with your boat name copper-etched in rope design and your house flag and club burgee in full color under a permanent glaze.

FOUR WINDS—*for over two years has enjoyed the outstanding beauty and lustre of Vernonware yachting table service.*

An assortment of ashtrays, with prices ranging from $15.00 to $35.00. Frontier Days and Winchester '73 would be at the top of the range.

TOP: Mesa Verde National Park, Colorado, for Jackson Hardware, Inc., Durango, Colorado; Winchester '73 ashtray alongside later Frontier Days, both identical except for the difference in ground color (P.L. Davidson, artist); SWECO, probably advertising.

CENTER: picture map of South Carolina; Lions International Convention, Chicago, 1950, designed exclusively for Northwest Lions Club, Chicago; The San Juan, The Narrow Gauge Capitol of the World, Durango, Colorado; University of North Carolina, picturing the old well, "1789," made exclusively for Danziger's, Chapel Hill, North Carolina.

BOTTOM: Picture map of Florida; California, picturing the state Capitol as multicolor; Georgia map.

Examples of city and state items. Price range is $20.00 – 30.00, multicolor having greater value. Miniature plates, $15.00 – 20.00.

TOP: Mississippi 5½" ashtray; Alaska Husky 4½" mini plate (Orpha Klinker, artist); Oklahoma map portraying famous places; Detroit 5½" ash tray (Orpha Klinker, artist), "Made exclusively for the J. L. Hudson Co."

SECOND ROW: Flint, Michigan, Home of General Motors, "Made expressly for McLogan & Austin, The China Closet," border design of 1950 vintage automobiles; Honolulu, pre-statehood, hand-tinted (Orpha Klinker, artist); Memphis, Tennessee, pictures Colonel Memphis, "Designed for The John Gerber Company."

THIRD ROW: Vermont, Green Mountain State (H. Goode, artist), pictures 30th president, Calvin Coolidge, and Freeman's Oath paragraph backstamp; Omaha's 100th Birthday, "1854 – 1954," hand-tinted picture of places and farm products (Paul L. Davidson, artist), story of Omaha backstamp; Kentucky Blue Grass State, pictures race horse and places of interest.

BOTTOM: Chicago, picturing the Marshall Field clock plus points of interest, "Made exclusively for Marshall Field & Co."; Seattle, Washington (Orpha Klinker, artist), illustrates Seattle's scenic beauty, backstamp states "Seattle founded in 1851...," plate dated 1941; Alaska Commonwealth (prior to statehood),* Bear backstamp reads "...1867...purchased from Russia for $7,200,000."

*Vernon Kilns produced the identical Alaska Bear plate with two other backstamps, one "U.S.A." only, the other "Designed for Wesco Kilns, U.S.A."; neither was marked as Vernon Kilns.

Page 95

Presidents, Civic Clubs, and World War II examples. Prices range from $20.00 to $75.00, with World War II themes in the top of the range and multicolor prints having greater value than plain prints.

TOP: Abraham Lincoln, the 16th president, backstamp gives the dates of his birth and his death and quotes a paragraph from his second inaugural address ("With malice toward none, with charity for all...") (Melinda shape); Lincoln Memorial, 8½" plate (artist Joe C. Sewell), backstamped "Fourscore and seven years ago..." and "the Earthly Pilgrimage of Abraham Lincoln."

SECOND ROW: *The United States in Action* (Goode, artist), hand-tinted print pictures branches of armed forces in combat surrounding central portrait of F. D. Roosevelt, "Commander of Armed Forces," backstamp reads "With confidence in our armed forces — with the unbounding determination of our people — we will gain the inevitable triumph — so help us God..." (From Roosevelt's first war address December 8, 1941, at 12:30 P.M. at a joint session of Congress after the attack on Pearl Harbor), first edition, 1942; presidential plate, emphasis on war time (Cavett, artist), backstamp is paragraph from "Declaration of War Against the Axis"; George Washington, "The Father of His Country 1789-1797" (Cavett, artist), depicts scenes from his life, backstamp gives birth and death dates and has a paragraph from his Farewell Address.

THIRD ROW: Coffee server decorated with Rotary Club International's insignia and signatures of members of Vernon City Rotary Club, circa 1953, backstamp reads "Made for City of Vernon Rotary Club" (see page 100 for other items made for the Vernon Rotary Club); *Presidential Gallery No. 2*, pictures all presidents, includes Dwight D. Eisenhower and Presidential Seal, 1953 (Paul Davidson, artist); *Our Presidential Gallery*, pictures all presidents, George Washington in center, includes Harry S. Truman, 1945.

BOTTOM: *Airborne Division*, portrays a parachute trooper on the ground in combat position and five Airborne Division patches, backstamp paragraph reads "For the men of five Airborne Divisions and the troopers of the unattached Parachute Regiments and Battalions who jumped and glided into combat, charged with savage fury... this plate was designed by David K. Webster and manufactured by Vernon Kilns, Los Angeles, California, 'Yours was the Glory: To battle fear and conquer Fascism,'" (Montecito shape); *Our Presidential Gallery*, first edition, 1942, 12½", "made expressly for Everlast Metal Products Co.," almost identical in design to *Presidential Gallery* above except Mt. Vernon is pictured in place of Truman; "Remember Pearl Harbor, On to Victory" (Margaret Pearson Joyner, artist), not marked Vernon Kilns.

Memento ashtray. Given to visitors to the Vernon factory, it shows both the new, modern plant and the old original building. See the Memento plate on page 109. $40.00 – 50.00.

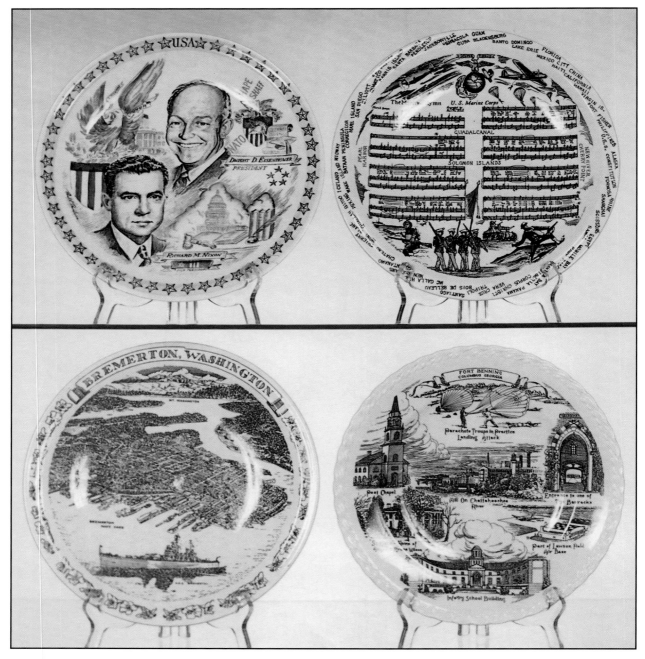

Vernon Kilns' last presidential plate and armed services plates, $35.00 – 75.00.
TOP: *Our President and Vice President* portrays Dwight D. Eisenhower and Richard M. Nixon (Paul L. Davidson, artist); *The Marine Corps* features the "Marines' Hymn" and marines in action, the border design names places where marines have fought or been stationed. Backstamp states, "The Marine Corps Authorized by the Continental Congress at Philadelphia Nov. 10, 1775. For nearly a hundred years the Marines' Hymn has been sung around the world. Designed by Vernon Kilns by Special Permission and Authorization of the United States Marine Corps to Walter S. Mills. Copyright 1929 by U. S. Marines Corps" (Goode, artist).
BOTTOM: Bremerton, Washington, pictures aerial view of Bremerton Navy Yard and the U.S.S. *Bremerton* at sea (L. Hicks, artist); Ft. Benning, Georgia, scenes including parachute troops in practice landing attack, post chapel, and infantry school building (Melinda shape).

School and Organizations. $20.00 – 35.00. Plates executed on Montecito shape, with exceptions noted.

TOP: "Southside High School 25th Anniversary, 1922 – 1947 Alma Mater." Pictures scenes of the school, including stadium, Minuteman Flag, and Calhoun Street entrance. No clue as to school location, but probably somewhere in Massachusetts, green print; "El Jebel, The Temple of the Mountains, Denver, Colorado," signed on back by W. Dale Houston, Illustrious Potentate, 1953 (Paul L. Davidson, artist).

CENTER: "State Headquarters, North Carolina Federation of Women's Club, Raleigh, North Carolina," pictures "...the historic house purchased in January 1951, built in 1911 by General Albert Cox, son of the famed confederate General William Ruffin Cox," as stated in the backstamp (Paul L. Davidson, artist); "Texas Division, United Daughters of the Confederacy, 1896 – 1946, backstamp reads "...organized May 5, 1886 at Victoria, Texas," and "Texas Golden Jubilee," with these last words in a scroll (Orpha Klinker, artist, name found in border).

BOTTOM: "Grand Chapter of Texas, Order of the Eastern Star, 1947 – 1948," pictures Eastern Star Home in Arlington, Texas and worthy grand officers. Backstamp gives history of the chapter, executed on the Melinda shape (Goode, artist); "Beta Sigma Phi" features the sorority's emblem, backstamp states, "Founded April 30, 1931, in Abilene, Kansas," and that the organization "has an international membership of 100,000" and is a "cultural, social, and service sorority, headquartered in Kansas City, Missouri." Plate is on the San Marino shape (Paul L. Davidson, artist).

Page 99
College, Religious, Political, and Fraternal. $25.00 – 50.00. Universities and oversize are at the top of range.
TOP: *El Camino Real*, 14" plate, designed by Annette Honeywell, limited first edition, pictures 21 California missions and their founding dates all on one plate; Franciscan Monastery, Washington, D.C., "Commissariat of the Holy Land," double-marked "A Capsco Product by Vernon Kilns," pictures monastery scenes.
SECOND ROW: "Michigan State College," green print, features campus scenes and college seal (R. Schepe, artist, signature in tree branch), backstamped "Copyright 1941, Pig 'n Whistle Gifts, East Lansing," brief paragraph about the college; "Sigma Alpha Epsilon," rare purple print, shows fraternity insignia and scenes (P.L.D., artist), backstamp paragraph states, "…the first national fraternity to originate in the South, found at University of Alabama, March 9, 1856 …narrowly surviving the War Between the States, it soon flourished again, becoming truly national in the 1890 decade…"; Relief Society of the Church of Jesus Christ of Latter Day Saints centennial commemorative pictures the first Society meeting, "Nauvoo, March 17, 1843," backstamp states that the Society is the "…oldest national women's organization in the United States, organized by Joseph Smith…"
THIRD ROW: "The University of Notre Dame," hand - tinted print, pictures the Rockne Memorial Fieldhouse and halls of learning, backstamp reads, in part, "…founding in 1842" and has the University seal; "The University of Idaho," shows campus buildings and the university seal, backstamp reads "…located at Moscow, established 1889, six months before Idaho was admitted to statehood, Made exclusively for Davids, Inc., Moscow, Idaho"; "Ohio State University" (R. Schepe, artist, signature in foliage), pictures medical center, stadium, and halls of learning, backstamp includes university seal.
BOTTOM ROW: Al Malaikah, Los Angeles, Shrine plate dated 1950, pictures Harold Lloyd (film star), Imperial Potentate, handicapped children, Shrine auditorium and insignia (Erik Sederling, artist); 1956 Republican National Convention 13" hand-painted souvenir plate depicts state seal and message signed by then-governor Goodwin J. Knight. This was presented to attending delegates by the California State Host Committee. The backstamp paragraph reads that the meeting marks the centennial year of the first national convention of the party, whose first presidential candidate was a Californian, John Fremont. This was also the first Republican Party convention to be held in the West. The plate was found in its original cardboard box, which was decorated with a map of California and on which was written, "Welcome to California. We hope you enjoy your visit and take this opportunity to see as much of our Golden State as possible."

Front and back of a 14" University of Southern California chop plate on a standard blank. The inscription on the reverse, hand written under the glaze, reads "To coach Jones. Faye G. Bennison. Vernon Kilns. Vernon, Calif." It is not known whether other examples of this chop plate were ever produced. PND. *Bob Hutchins photos.*

Rotary Club examples, plates have the Melinda shape except as noted. Vases, $35.00 – 65.00. Plates, $30.00 – 45.00.

TOP: 2-handled 9½" vase; 10½" plate dated July 7, 1943 with members signatures, "Made especially for the Vernon Rotary Club"; 9½" ewer vase.

CENTER: 12½" plates, center emblem is in colo. Plate on the right has Ultra shape; otherwise, both have the same design.

BOTTOM: 8" angular handled vase, Casa California decor (see Montecito dinnerware for pattern), mark 12; 8" vase of the same shape, believed to be an earlier version, undecorated and unmarked.

Another version of a Rotary dinner plate, 10½", on a Melinda blank, with signatures both on the rim and inside the well. $40.00.
Bob Hutchins photo.

An ashtray made for the Rotary Club of Southgate/Walnut Park, California, with a dark blue transfer on a Modern California blue 4½" square ashtray. $30.00 – 35.00.
Bob Hutchins photo.

These plates picture famous people and historic plates. A few plates dating from 1936 through 1956 are pictured; some are special orders and some are stock items. $20.00 – 45.00. Multicolored items are always higher.

TOP: *Williamsburg, The Historical City* pictures scenes of the restored village, "Made exclusively for Casey's, Inc."; "The Little White House," features President Franklin Delano Roosevelt, "Made exclusively for the Little White House Souvenir Shop, Warm Springs, Georgia."

SECOND ROW: *Our National Capitol* features the Capitol building with a brief paragraph of historical facts, and the colorful maroon and blue leaf border of the Melinda shape lends itself to a maroon-transfer patriotic color scheme; the symbolic Statue of Liberty represents a land of freedom for all oppressed peoples. Backstamp reads "the New Colossus... This tablet, with her sonnet to the Bartholdi Statue of Liberty engraved upon it, is placed upon these walls in loving memory of Emma Lazarus, born in New York City, July 22nd, 1849, died November 19th, 1887. This plate was made expressly for James Hill, Bedloe's Island, N. Y.," (Orpha Klinker, artist). Another Statue of Liberty plate was designed by Paul Davidson.

BOTTOM: Beloved humorist Will Rogers (1879 – 1935), a stock item, pictures his birthplace, Santa Monica ranch, and memorials (Cavett, artist); General Douglas MacArthur, courageous military leader of World War II, made while he was in command of the United States Far East Forces at age 62, "Made exclusively for Barker Bros." (a Los Angeles furniture store no longer in business), also marked "First edition 5000 plates." The last two plates are very plentiful.

Invitation spoon holder. Given to buyers attending the New York City Gift Show on July 9, 1952, inviting them to meet Mr. and Mrs. Faye Bennison. Rare. PND. *John and Joanne Barrett photo.*

Historic Places. $25.00 – 45.00.

TOP: 14" *New England*, designed by Jack Frost, pictures 19 historic places, including Old Tower, Newport, RI; the Old North Church, Boston; the home of Paul Revere, North Square, Boston; The Old Man of the Mountains, New Hampshire; Fort McClary, Kittery, Maine; and Maple Sugaring, Vermont.

CENTER: Brulatour Courtyard, New Orleans, backstamp reads "Aunt Sally's original Creole praline shop, corner Royal and St. Louis Streets, Scenes of old New Orleans, made exclusively for Bague Southern Souvenir Mfg. Co., New Orleans," backstamp also shows picture of "site of old slave block in 1835"; Spindletop, Beaumont, Texas, 1901 – 1951, anniversary plate, backstamp reads "...50th Anniversary Commission. On the 10th day of the 20th Century a new era in civilization began in Beaumont. The first great oil well in the world — The Lucas Gusher — blew in, at 100,000 barrels per day...produced 800,000 barrels of oil in the nine days it ran wild. Made for Smith Ward Jewelry Co., Beaumont, Texas" (Paul L. Davidson, artist); Fort Defiance, backstamp "1794 – 1944, Defiance, Ohio, built at confluence of Maumee and Auglaize rivers by General Anthony Wayne, during military campaign that established American rule in the Old Northwest." All three plates have the Montecito shape.

BOTTOM: Tacoma Narrows Bridge,* Melinda shape (Erik H. Sederling, artist), "designed exclusively for People's Store, Tacoma's oldest store since 1888, Tacoma, Washington"; San Jacinto Monument, pictures Stephen F. Austin, Father of Texas, and General Sam Houston, hero of San Jacinto, also shows the monument that commemorates the heroes of the Battle of San Jacinto, April 21, 1836. Backstamp reads that the museum at the base of the monument "...depicts the history of Texas from the pre-Spanish era to modern times." Made especially for San Jacinto Museum of History Association (Goode, artist).

* The first Tacoma Narrows bridge collapsed on November 7, 1940.

Page 105
Transportation and other subjects. $25.00 – 60.00. Trains and multicolor have higher value.
TOP: "Chicago Railroad Fair," "Made exclusively for Marshall Field & Company... 1949 commemorating the one hundredth anniversary of railroading," shows the progression from the earliest engines to the streamliner and features 26 railroad logos on its border (Stevan, artist); *In My Merry Oldsmobile*, commemorating the "era of horse-less carriage and the yester-years when motoring was an heroic and adventurous feat... rapid development, in styles and added conveniences, through the untiring efforts of the automotive industry...," "Copyrighted 1950, made for Pig 'n Whistle Gifts, East Lansing" (Hicks, artist).
SECOND ROW: Mark Twain plate commemorating Twain and depicting Twain landmarks (Sederling, artist); Vallejo, California, "Home of Mare Island Navy Yard," backstamped "City was founded in 1849 by General Vallejo and was State Capitol in 1851 for two years."
BOTTOM: "American Society of Civil Engineers," 8½" plate presented at 1951 convention in Houston, Texas; *Colorful San Francisco* (stock item) pictures cable cars, hillsides, and Chinatown. Backstamp states that the "first cable car started on its initial run August 1, 1873 with inventor Hallidie at the grip..." and that "the 1906 earthquake and fire reduced cable facilities to rubble but the pint size cars were back on the job within a few short months."

Bowling League Tumbler and Snack Tray. This trophy was for members of the company bowling team during the 1956 – 1957 season. Tray (mark 27) is 12" x 8", with an indentation for the tumbler. Produced on the San Clemente (Anytime) shape. Rare. PND.

Also known is a streamlined 1-pint pitcher, 5½" tall, with a purple rim on cream ground decorated with a green bowling ball and the block letter words, "For the Vernon Kilns Bowling League, W53, W54." Unmarked. Reported in the *Vernon Views* Summer 2001 issue is a mug owned by former employee Marie Rogers and dated 1958, the last year Vernon Kilns was in business. The mug is white with specks of silver and purple and shows a bowling ball rolling towards two pins.

Page 107

Pictured are 10½" plates that in the 1940s were all special orders, sold in minimum lots of 1000. Today, they are relatively scarce and are prized by train and plane buffs as well as Vernon Kilns collectors. All have the Vernon Kilns U.S.A. mark. $35.00 – 95.00. Aviation and multicolored items have higher values.

TOP: "The San Juan" (Erik Sederling, artist), backstamp states, in part, that this train was "...last of its kind to remind us of the spectacular little trains that once were found running throughout the West..."; "The Galloping Goose" (R. Schepe, artist), paragraph on back reads, "Through the rugged mountains of Southwestern Colorado serving lonely and sparsely settled areas, runs the Rio Grande Southern Railroad..." Shows the Goose as it is today and Engine No. 9 as it was in the 1890s; "The 'Emma Sweeney,' Star of *Ticket to Tomahawk* filmed in Durango and Silverton, Colorado," has statement on back, "Old Engine No. 20 of the Rio Grande Southern... restyled and decorated for *Ticket to Tomahawk* filmed by 20th Century Fox... during the summer of 1949" (Erik Sederling, artist). These three plates have a railroad track border design and are backstamped "Manufactured for Jackson Hardware, Inc., of Durango, Colorado."

SECOND ROW: "U. S. Naval Air Station, Alameda, California," pictures 1940s-era Navy propeller planes and administration building, backstamp includes insignia and reads "The United States Naval Air Station, Alameda, California" (similar plate for the Naval Air Station at Pensacola, Florida); "In the Air — It's Convair," pictures propeller and jet, military and passenger planes. "Made exclusively for Consolidated Vultee Aircraft Corporation, San Diego, California, Ft. Worth, Texas"; "Vultee Get 'em into the Blue," first edition, pictures military and one private plane, the *Stinson Voyager*. A descriptive paragraph on the back of the plate gives a brief history of Vultee Aircraft, founded in 1932.

THIRD ROW: Lockheed Aircraft plate pictures both military and civilian planes of the early 1940s, backstamp gives facts about Lockheed, "...organized in 1926... Howard Hughes used a Lockheed for his record around the world flight," "Designed for Lockheed Aircraft Corp., Burbank, California"; "North American Aviation," company logo and the words "Bombers — Fighters — Trainers Built the North American Way," air view of factory is the background, planes are in the air. Backstamp gives brief history of company, informing that it was founded in 1928, with factories at Inglewood, Kansas City, and Dallas, and that it was "Designed for North American Aviation"; "Douglas, First Around the World" features 1940 military planes set against a Southern California shoreline and has a backstamped paragraph, "The First Twenty Years," and also a backstamp, "Designed for Douglas Aircraft Co., Inc., Santa Monica, California, Sold Exclusively at Henshey's, Santa Monica, California."

BOTTOM: Douglas, Long Beach, California (Margaret Pearson Joyner, artist; this is the only airplane plate with an artist signature), pictures early 1940 Army cargo, B-19, and Flying Fortress planes, and an airview of Douglas, Long Beach. Backstamp boasts, "America's most modern aircraft plant...Made exclusively for Stricklin's, Long Beach"; "Martin Aircraft" pictures — among other planes — the famous China Clipper and B-26, with Maryland coast airview. Backstamps reads "The longest line of military aircraft history is the Martin Bomber" and "Made exclusively for Hecht Brothers, Baltimore, Maryland"; "Curtiss-Wright" features World War II military pursuit planes in combat, including U.S. Army P-40 and RAF Kittyhawk. Backstamp states "Curtiss-Wright, Aviation's Oldest Names... the company was incorporated in New York state in December 1910, the largest producer of aircraft during World War I..." and "Designed for Curtiss-Wright Corporation, Airplane division, Buffalo, Columbus, St. Louis."

Note: Another aircraft company in the Vernon Kilns series was Consolidated Aircraft. A plate was unavailable for photographing at the time of this edition.

Three additional transportation plates. $45.00 – 95.00. Multicolored have higher value.

TOP: "The San Juan" in full color (Erik H. Sederling, artist), same as in picture shown in plain print. (See page 92 for the San Juan ashtray.)

BOTTOM: Boeing plate showing early planes and the B-17 Flying Fortress, backstamp reads "Tomorrow's planes today. Founded in 1918 by William E. Boeing, ... recognized pace-setter in aircraft design and performance ever since" and "Designed Exclusively for Frederick & Nelson, Seattle"; "Chicago Railroad Fair," pictures trains beginning 1831, border features railroad logos, (R. Schepe, artist), backstamp reads "1849 – 1949 commemorating the 100th anniversary... Designed exclusively for Consolidated Concessions, Inc." This plate is one of two different designs made for the fair (see page 105 for the other plate).

Page 109

Events (sports), $45.00+; Christmas items, $35.00 – 55.00; historical and souvenir wares, $25.00+; memento plate, $95.00; Mother Goose plate, $65.00.

TOP: Ye Olde Tymes tea cup and saucer, matches 10½" plate (row 3); Old Faithful after-dinner cup and saucer; special order 5" vase pictures baseball player, made for American Ceramic Society, Southern California Section, Annual Sports Day, July 16, 1955, backstamped "Donated by Vernon Kilns"; Vernon's Christmas Tree cup and saucer, has the same transfer (except for borders) as the two-tier tidbit server pictured on page 112.

SECOND ROW: *The Arkansaw Traveler* 10½" plate (initials "P.L.D."), copyright date 1936, backstamped "R. E. McCann, Ft. Smith, Arkansas"; souvenir salt and pepper shakers picture Half Dome, Yosemite National Park (unmarked); Dorchester, Massachusetts, circa 1773, commissioned by Walter Baker & Co., Inc., to mark its 175th anniversary, pictures the village and mill in which James Baker and John Hannan made the first chocolate in America in 1765. A treasure for Baker's Chocolate as well as Vernon historical plate collectors. Backstamped "First Edition, 1940," has the famous LaBelle Chocolatiere trademark, second edition is dated 1941 and not as deep a blue; scarce 1949 Easter Fires of Fredericksburg, Texas, plate features bunnies preparing eggs for distribution to children, background of church steeples and rooftops of Fredericksburg and Cross Mountain — where Easter fires flare. Backstamped "century old custom based on folklore and tradition." Close-up pictures of Easter Fires of Fredericksburg plate and matching cup and saucer are seen on page 113.

THIRD ROW: Vernon's 10½" Santa Claus plate and matching cup and saucer; Vernon Kilns bowling league 1956 tumbler (San Clemente [Anytime] shape), pictures ball and pins, "Donated by Vernon Kilns" (a close-up view of the bowling league snack set, which is the same bowling tumbler and a snack tray indented to hold it, can be seen on page 104.) 10½" Christmas Series motif "Ye Olde Tymes" plate (special order version). The same plate was made for the Austin Company, entitled "The Austin Children's Christmas Party," (L. Hicks, artist, name is on the mailbox). See page 111 for another version of the scene for "Ye Olde Tymes" plate.

BOTTOM: 8½" plates, French Opera Reproduction #6, *Les Dragons de Villars*; memento plate given to visitors to the Vernon factory, pictures the new modern plant and the old original building, popular dinnerware patterns decorate the border (L. Hicks, artist), backstamp has Faye G. Bennisons signature facsimile; Vernon's Mother Goose plate (Fellepe, artist), pictures nursery rhyme figures and the words "My Own Mother Goose Plate," backstamped "Boys and Girls Plate, designed by Vernon Kilns," circa 1950, scarce.

LEFT TO RIGHT: 10½" plates, *The Arkansaw Traveler* and *The Turn of the Tune.* $25.00 – 35.00. *The Turn of the Tune* is harder to find. *Vernon and Mary Carrens photo.*

The original shipping box containing *The Arkansaw Traveler* plates found after years of storage in the McCann family home basement. The words "WORLD'S LARGEST MAN-UFACTURER OF PICTURE PLATES" appear on the top length of the box; on the lower length is a mission scene and the words "CALIFORNIA, Vernonware [in script], FROM VERNON KILNS – LOS ANGELES – U.S.A." Note that Arkan*sas* was spelled Arkan*saw* on the plates.

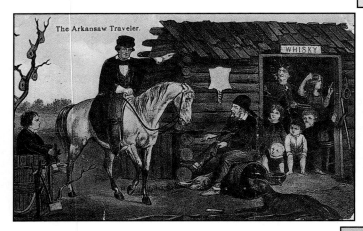

The Arkansaw Traveler postcard. See page 90 for background story.

The Turn of the Tune postcard. See page 90 for background story.

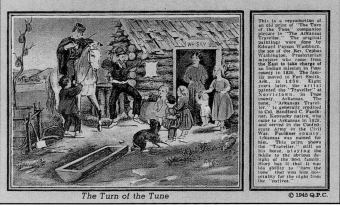

Ye Olde Tymes 10½" plate, Vernon's stock version, which pictures child and lady. Backstamped "Ye Olde Tymes by Vernon Kilns, U.S.A." $35.00 – 45.00.

A 12" Christmas Tree chop plate made from a Montecito blank, with a green rim. The transfer on the chop plate is identical to that on the Christmas Tree dinner plates, in size as well as appearance. The chop plate is the only known Christmas Tree piece with a green rim. The chop plate was specially ordered by Plummer Ltd. in New York City, which had locations at 7 East 35th Street and 695 Fifth Avenue. Plummer Ltd. also specially ordered another Christmas Tree chop plate, almost identical to this piece but with a red rim. $50.00 – 60.00. 10½" Christmas Tree plates, $35.00 – 45.00. *Bob Hutchins photo.*

An undecorated Christmas Tree dinner plate, with a brown transfer on a Montecito blank. $30.00. *Bob Hutchins photo.*

Harry Bird 9½" luncheon plate with a Christmas pattern on a Montecito blank. The plate is marked with a variation of mark 31, without a pattern identification. It is not known whether this plate is part of a complete or partial dinnerware set. $75.00. *Bob Hutchins photo.*

The Christmas Tree two-tier tidbit server with brass fittings. Made from the saucer and 10½" plate. Backstamped "Vernon's Christmas Tree By Vernon Kilns U.S.A.". $75.00. There were also Christmas Tree candleholders that utilized Christmas Tree teacups (Montecito shape) and the same brass fixtures.

$35.00 – 60.00, Alaska items at the top of range.

TOP: 10½" plates: A reproduction painting (Paul Davidson, artist) of the Last Supper scenes from the Black Hills Passion Play of America ("first American performance of the World Famous Luenen Passion Play in 1932… in the Black Hills"), back-stamped "copyright 1953, Janice A. Blue, Spearfish, South Dakota"; *Our West*, first edition, 1942, pictures wagon trains, land clearing, gold panning, and a modern city.

BOTTOM: Cup, saucer, and matching plate, made exclusively for the Alaska Crippled Children's Association, each piece marked. Decorated with dog sleds and an Eskimo portrait, borders picture animals of the far north.

1949 Easter Fires of Fredericksburg, Texas. The 10½" plate to the left, and the after-dinner cup and saucer above (both Montecito shape) feature bunnies preparing eggs for distribution to children, with a background of church steeples and roof tops of Fredericksburg and Cross Mountain, where Easter fires flare. Plate is backstamped "century old custom based on folklore and tradition by Vernon Kilns, U.S.A.," saucer is marked "Easter Fires of Fredericksburg by Vernon Kilns, U.S.A.," and cup is marked "by Vernon Kilns, U.S.A." Plate, $65.00 – 95.00. Cup and saucer, $45.00 – 55.00. The Easter Fires plate and the Fredericksburg plates are both displayed in the Old Church Town Museum in Fredericksburg, Texas.

Colorful 6½" plate (Montecito) with Easter motif. Faint backstamp is believed to be "Multi-Lines" over "T-686" (a mark 33 variation showing initials "G.T."). $75.00 – 85.00.
Kay Bernhard Photo.

Plates are $35.00 – 45.00+, with Alaska items at the top of range.

TOP: Alaska plate features scrimshaw-type art, black print on ivory ground (Robert Mayokok, artist, see page 75 for biography), backstamp reads "...reproduction of an original sketch by Robert Mayokok, an Eskimo of Nome, Alaska. Distributed exclusively by the Alaska Native Industries Cooperative Association"; Santa Fe Trail, striking plate done in colors of turquoise and black on gray ground. Pictures canyon lands of New Mexico, with thunderbird border design.

BOTTOM: "Silverton, Oregon, Centennial, 1854 – 1954," pictures early settler scenes, backstamped "Gateway to Silver Falls State Park," with dates of history from 1846; MoorMan's Feed advertising plate, Quincy, Illinois, backstamped "Quincy Ho, August 11 through October 4, 1952."

Bits 8½" plates and Race Horse examples. Race Horse items are marked "Made by Vernon Kilns, U. S. A." 8½" Bits, $25.00 – 75.00; Bits chop plates, $60.00 – 95.00; Race Horse saucer only, $15.00.

TOP: *Off to the Hunt,* Old South; Old England #4 (value at low end of range); *San Juan Capistrano,* California Missions.

SECOND ROW: *The Cove; Tapping for Sugar;* and *The Old Lighthouse.* All are from the Old New England Bits series.

THIRD ROW: *Stage Robbers* and *Thirst,* both of Old West; *Baking Bread,* of Southwest.

BOTTOM: "Greyhound 1:55¼," 6½" saucer; *Horse Thieves,* Old West 14" chop plate; "Coaltown," 6½" saucer.

Northwest and Middle West plates are harder to find. 8½" Bits, $25.00 – 75.00; Bits chop plates, $60.00 – 95.00.

TOP: *Down on the Levee*, Old South 14" chop plate (San Fernando shape).

CENTER: *Unloading the Nets; Log Jam; Sheep Herder.* These are three examples of the Bits of the Old Northwest.

BOTTOM: *4th of July; River Commerce; Saturday Night.* These are three examples of the Middle West Bits.

Race Horse items. 10½" plates, $75.00; 8½" plates, $65.00. Race horse cups and saucers sell for $35.00.
TOP: "Citation," 10½" plate, backstamped "Citation... best 3-year-old since Man O'War... He won the Triple Crown in the Kentucky Derby, Preakness Stakes, and Belmont Stakes with ease. Bay horse foaled in 1945, owned and bred by the late Warren Wright's Calumet Farms, Lexington, Kentucky."
BOTTOM: "Greyhound 1:55¼," 8½" plate, backstamped "Greyhound 1:55¼, Sep Palin up" (up meaning driver). "The world's champion trotter, grey gelding foaled 1932 by Guy Abbey-Elizabeth... its greatest champion establishing 16 world records"; "Coaltown," 8½" plate, backstamped "Coaltown, outstanding sprinter of 1948, smashing times were climaxed in his Whirlaway Stakes victory that saw him go a mile in 1:34 to establish a new world record... a bay colt, foal of 1945 by Bull Lea-Easy Lass by Blenheim II."

Close-up view of *A Southern Mansion*, Old South.

Pictured are 8½" stock items. Mission plates, $25.00 – 65.00; northern mission plates are harder to find and have the highest value. Top row plates, $45.00 – 65.00.
TOP: "Virginia & Truckee RR, Route to the Comstock," pictures the *Reno*, the old No. 11 engine, backstamp reads "...The Reno was used for passenger service between Reno, Carson City, and Virginia City from 1872, service discontinued in the late 1930s. The No. 11 built in 1872 at a cost of $12,250. On March 1945 sold to MGM Studios where it has been used in the filming of motion picture *Union Pacific*"; Avalon Bay view, Santa Catalina Island.
BOTTOM: San Juan Bautista; San Jose de Guadalupe; and San Carlos Borromeo, Carmel. These are three plates from the Mission series. (Orpha Klinker artist.)

More 8½" stock items. Cocktail Hours, $45.00 – 65.00; French Opera Reproductions, $18.00 – 25.00; Music Masters, $18.00 – 25.00.
TOP: Cocktail Hour — "Singapore Sling," "Bacardi," "Hot Toddy."
SECOND ROW: French Opera Reproductions — No. 6. *Les Dragons de Villars*, No. 3. *Le Barbier de Seville*, No. 1. *Le Pre Aux Clercs*.
THIRD ROW: Music Masters — Frederick Chopin, Ignace Jan Paderewski, Edvard Grieg.

Bits Series: Temples of the Church of Jesus Christ of Latter-Day Saints plates are pictured in this photo. 8½" plates, $25.00+.

TOP: The Los Angeles Temple (an artist's rendering of future temple), "ground broken September 22, 1951, eleventh temple built by the church and will be the largest to date. Cost more than $4,000,000 requiring four years to build, tower of 265 feet"; The Salt Lake Temple, "dedicated April 6, 1893, sixth temple completed by the church at a cost of $3,500,000. Built of solid granite"; the Idaho Falls Temple, "dedicated September 23, 1945, tenth temple constructed by the church, cost of construction approximately one million dollars."

BOTTOM: The Alberta Temple (Canada), "dedicated July 27, 1913, Grecian massiveness with a Peruvian touch, seventh temple to be completed at a cost of one million dollars"; The Arizona Temple, Mesa, "dedicated November 28, 1921, ninth temple called the Lamanite Temple because of its close proximity to the homes of several Indian tribes"; The Hawaiian Temple, Oahu, "dedicated November 27, 1919, built in the shape of a Grecian cross."

World famous Forest Lawn Memorial Park; Bits-style plates are seen in this picture. 8½" plate, $20.00; chop plate, $25.00.

TOP: Entrance Gates to Forest Lawn Memorial Park, Glendale, California. Pictured on a 14" plate, these were described as the largest wrought iron gates in the world, and were in the design of the English Renaissance period.

BOTTOM: Three 8½" plates picturing the churches in Forest Lawn. Wee Kirk O' The Heather is a faithful reconstruction of the church in Glencairn, Scotland, where Annie Laurie prayed for the safety of her sweetheart, William Douglas. Eight stained glass windows in the south wall tell Annie's romantic love story. Little Church of the Flowers was inspired by a little village church at Stoke Poges, England, the scene of Thomas Gray's beloved poem, "Elegy, written in a Country Churchyard"; the Church of the Recessional is a noble memorial to the sentiments expressed in Rudyard Kipling's immortal poem, "The Recessional," and a faithful reproduction of the parish church of St. Margaret, in Rottingdean, England.

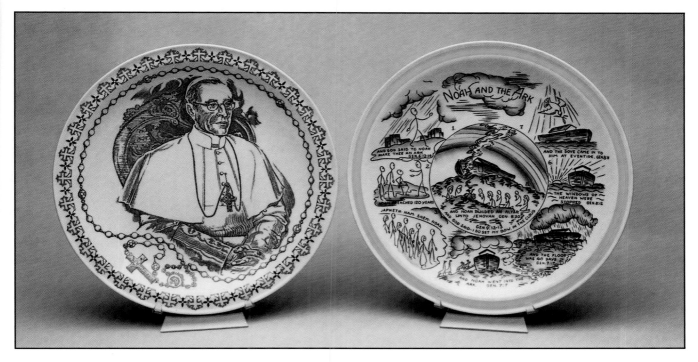

Two plates in the religious category, both 10½".
LEFT: A portrait of Pope Pious XII, backstamped "His Holiness Pope Pious XII, Prayer for Peace." $45.00.
RIGHT: The Noah's Ark plate featured seven multicolor scenes of the Bible story; the ark is in the center, with references to Bible verses. Backstamped "copyright 1953, Gayle Oler, Quinlan, Texas." Both plates are marked "by Vernon Kilns, U.S.A." $85.00 – 95.00.

Scenic America after dinner cups and saucers, pictured in three different available shapes. There were stock items in 24 different scenes. $20.00 – 30.00.
LEFT TO RIGHT: *My Old Kentucky Home* (San Fernando), the Apache Trail, Arizona (Montecito), and Niagara Falls, New York (Melinda). Shapes indicated in parentheses may be seen in the Dinnerware section.

Historic Baltimore Series — four examples from series of eight 8½" plates, in both blue and sepia prints on ivory. Pieces from this series have also been found in maroon. The series was made exclusively for Hutzler Brothers Co., a Maryland institution established in 1858. $30.00 – 35.00.
TOP: No. 8. "Old Shot Tower, built in 1828"; No. 4. "Johns Hopkins Hospital, World Famous medical center."
BOTTOM: No. 7. "Washington Monument, first monument to George Washington"; No. 5. "Fort McHenry, inspiration of the Star Spangled Banner."

Foreign Countries. $25.00 – 45.00. TOP: Ashtray, 5¾", Flota Mercante Grancolombiana, South America. Venezuela, Colombia, Ecuador, pictures scenes, monument, and map of South America. BOTTOM: 10½" plate with portrait of Jose Marti, Cuban patriot, 1853 – 1953 (backstamp is written in Spanish); Republic of the Philippines, backstamp reads "Independence Day July 4, 1946." Plate shows map of the islands, with scenes including Wainwright Tunnel, Corregidor Island, a famous World War II landmark.

Huge spectacular map of the United States formed of commemorative plates, a part of Vernon Kilns pottery that was displayed in an exhibit entitled Eats: An American Obsession at the Track 16 gallery in Santa Monica, California, April 15 – September 1, 1995. Edward J. Fischer, the last president of Vernon Kilns, is standing in foreground. *Jean Fischer Volner photo.*

Advertising. Coca-Cola 10" bowl, circa 1950, designed to hold six bottles and crushed ice, mark 22; penguin figural decanter, 9½", circa 1933. Has been reported as a bottle for a brand of sloe gin and was seen with federal tax seal and label still intact. Coca-Cola bowl, $500.00 – 600.00. Penguin bottle, $85.00; with label, $100.00.

Trader Vic items. 9½" plate, "Designed Especially for Me, Trader Vic (signature facsimile)"; 8½" Mai Tai glass, figure and decoration in high relief, made for "Trader Vic's, Ltd., Honolulu, Hawaii." Plate, $85.00+; Mai Tai, $95.00 – 125.00.

Royal Hawaiian cup and saucer. A beautifully embossed design of hibiscus and camellia blossoms on the Montecito shape. The set is believed to be experimental. Backstamped "Ceremetal Process over banner mark with Royal Hawaiian," on both cup and saucer, indicating 1950s period. Other marks penciled under glaze, "Brown A #2" is on the bottoms of both pieces. Could this have been intended as restaurant ware for the Royal Hawaiian hotel? PND. See page 280 for "Ceremetal Process" mark.
Al Albertts collection.

Alaska plates, $20.00 – 45.00; hollow ware, $25.00 – 75.00; Trader Vic 6½" plates, $35.00; egg cup, $85.00. Alaska and Trader Vic dishware are all on Ultra shape.

TOP: 8½" plate features husky face; 12½" chop plate pictures scenes that appear on the rest of the set. Both plates have brief Alaska history along with the backstamp (Orpha Klinker, artist).

CENTER: Creamer, scenes of gold panning in the historic Yukon and on Mt. McKinley; 1-pint jug pictures a husky on one side and a boy with a pup on the other, totem on handle; cup depicts Columbia Glacier and steamer; saucer, St. Michael's cathedral, Sitka; sugar bowl, boy with pup and Mendenhall Glacier scenes on reverse.

BOTTOM: 6½" plate pictures tropical shore, marked "Designed for Me, Trader Vic [in script]"; egg cup and 6½" plate, both feature tropical scene and a building believed to be the restaurant. Plate "Designed Especially for Granny Abbott [script signature] of Trader Vic's Ltd., Honolulu, Hawaii, by Vernon Kilns." Egg cup has a similar mark, but does not say "Honolulu, Hawaii."

Awards and mementos. Award plates, $75.00 – 125.00; event souvenirs, $25.00 – 45.00; memento ashtray, $45.00 – 50.00.
BACK ROW: Two 14" plates. On the left, the 1954 Chairman's Award, Southern California section, for American Ceramic society, names 1954 awardees, honor roll members for years 1950, 1951, 1952, 1953, and pictures presentee, (marked "Sponsored by Vernon Kilns." On the right, 1951 Chairman's Award for meritorious service, picturing all recipients. On the back, 1950 and 1951 honor roll member names are listed and there are pictures of the early and later factory buildings (the same as are on the memento plate and ashtray).
FRONT LEFT: Saucer (San Fernando shape), demi size, for Southern California Potters' picnic July 14, 1956, backstamp reads "Donated by Vernon Kilns."
CENTER: "Softball Champions, Southern California section, A.C.S., 1952 Beer Bust, Lakewood Country Club," executed on Chatelaine sugar resembling a loving cup, "Donated by Vernon Kilns" on bottom.
FRONT RIGHT: Memento ashtray, gift to visitors of the factory, shows pictures of the early factory and the present day (at that time) factory.

Harvey Duke photo.

So. Calif. Section 1951 Awards by Clark Sutherland (seated extreme right) went to (standing l. to r.) Joe Biondi, Ed. Dietterle, Hal Lamb, John Wurtz, Dick Iander, Dick Haecker, Ralph Martin, Joe Taylor, Mitch Simons and Ad Hawley; (seated, l. to r.) Ed. Kunzman, Corena Sherrill and Mel Jontz. Annual award of plates is sponsored by Vernon Kilns. Inc. Plates this year carried recipients' pictures.

    Noteworthy is the design or theme of the Chairman's Award plates. The 1954 *Westward Ho* plate pictures a scene of covered wagon (as found in the Winchester '73/Frontier Days pattern.) Style (Ultra pattern) decorates the border of the 1951 plate. The 1952 14" plate (not pictured) has an all-over design of Palm Brocade (Melinda pattern), with a cameo photograph in the center. Ten names in block letters encircle the narrow orange rim. The back view shows the factory buildings and, between the buildings, reads "Designed for Vernon Kilns by Biondi." Underneath the buildings it reads "All Good Wishes, Sincerely, Faye G. Bennison [name in script], President." (For Biondi's dinnerware backstamp as seen on the Palm Brocade pattern, see mark 49 in Evolution of Marks.)
    Among those who received awards in 1951 was Joe Biondi. Was this possibly the same Biondi?
    Yet to be reported are plates for 1950 and 1953 or for years following 1954.

A Miller Coat-of-Arms plate, from a 10½" Melinda blank.
Bob Hutchins photo.

Yachting and Heraldry examples, Melinda shape, special order items. Vegetable bowl is personalized "Hazel K," backstamped "Made especially for the Hazel K. by Vernon Kilns"; 12" plate has the Brown Coat of Arms and *"Est-Concordia-Fratrum,"* backstamped "Vernon Kilns, U.S.A." Yachting, $25.00 – 45.00; Heraldry, $25.00 – 35.00.

Another special order item that has been reported on the Melnda shape is a 10½" plate with the backstamp "M.C.A.S. Officers' Mess EL TORO BY VERNON KILNS, U.S.A." The plate has the Marine Corps aviation insignia at the top in maroon and a maroon border stripe. It is possible this is part of a dinnerware set. El Toro, an air base in Orange county, California, was closed in 1999.

Assortment of souvenirs. Demitasse cups and saucers, $20.00 – 30.00; miniature plates, $15.00 – 20.00; spoon rests, $35.00+; mugs, $20.00+; teapots, $65.00+; creamers and sugars, $45.00; map-shaped tray, $45.00+.
TOP: U.S. Naval Academy demitasse cup and saucer; Yosemite teapot picturing Mirror Lake. Both have the Melinda shape.
CENTER: Sugar Bowl, Louisiana 4½" miniature plate; *Valley of the Moon* mug; Duke University creamer and sugar. All items have the Montecito shape.
FRONT: Spoon rest pictures Campanile Tower at the University of Kansas; Lake Tahoe map-shaped tray; spoon rest of Brookdale Lodge, California.

Three Melinda-shape 1½-pint pitchers with state seal transfers — Arizona, Illinois, California. $45.00 – 50.00. *Bob Hutchins photo.*

Yosemite National Park examples from short set dinnerware. Plates, $20.00 – 45.00; teapot, $75.00; creamer, $20.00; sugar, $25.00; pitcher, $50.00.
BACK ROW: 10½" and 8½" plates, same design (Montecito shape).
FRONT ROW: "Mirror Lake" teapot; "Bridal Veil Falls" creamer; "El Captain" sugar; "Wawona" 1½-pint pitcher (Melinda shape).

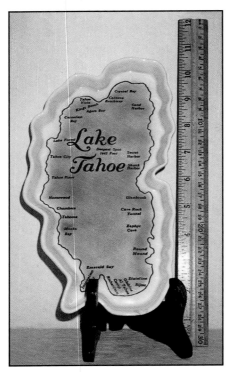

Close-up view of Lake Tahoe 10" map-shaped tray. $45.00+.

Yosemite ashtray pictures Half Dome. $20.00.

Children's dishes. It is not known whether these were stock or special order items. Bowls, $35.00 – 45.00+; 7½" plates, $45.00 – 65.00; Mugs, $65.00 – 75.00.
TOP: 7½" plate, #792, pictures a frog sitting on mushroom, smoking a pipe; unmarked mug pictures a Scottie. Both are on Ultra shape.
BOTTOM: Little Miss Muffet 7½" plate; Bubbles mug (Bubbles is pictured on reverse); Playmates mug (Little Miss Muffet is on reverse); Bubbles 6" bowl. All items except bowl have the Montecito shape; it has the Ultra shape. Designed by Amanda Owens. Mark 9.

Child's 6" bowl picturing a bunny, #790, Ultra shape. This series was hand painted with an airbrush. Mark 19 variation. $35.00 – 45.00+.

Four more plates, also believed to have been designed for children's dishes. 6½" Montecito shape. Artist initials B.L.O., backstamped mark 13. $50.00 – 60.00.

This section of the book has only touched upon the many hundreds of pictorial wares made by Vernon Kilns. A few representative examples have been pictured and cited. Without a doubt, there is much more to be learned regarding the extent of the company's pottery production. The historical significance of pictorial wares is now becoming apparent; values will only increase in the years ahead.

The following list shows specialty plates and the retail stores that sold them. The information was taken from a list sent by Vernon Kilns, in 1943, to a collector.

City Picture Plates	Where They Could be Purchased
Abilene, TX	Lester's Jewelers, Abilene, TX
Albuquerque, NM	Maisell's Trading Post, Albuquerque, NM
Alexandria Bicentennial	Alexandria Bicentennial Commission, Alexandria, VA
Alexandria, LA	C. A. Schnack Co., Alexandria, LA
Anniston, AL	Couch's Gift Shop, Anniston, AL
Asheville, NC	Bon Marche, Asheville, NC
Athens, GA	W. A. Capps Co., Athens, GA
Atlanta, GA	Davison Paxton Co., Atlanta, GA
Atlanta, GA	Rich's, Atlanta, GA
Augusta, ME	R. B. Herrick Specialty Co., Augusta, ME
Augusta, GA	J. B. White & Co., Augusta, GA
Austin, TX	Ellison Photo Co., Austin, TX
Avalon, Catalina Island	The Treasure Shoppe, Catalina Island (Avalon), CA
Baltimore, MD	Lycett, Inc., Baltimore, MD
Bay City, MI	C. E. Rosenbury & Sons, Bay City, MI
Bedford, VA	Auto Service & Elect. Co., Bedford, VA
Birmingham, AL	Odum, Bower & White, Birmingham, AL
Birmingham (Vulcan)	Bromberg Galleries, Birmingham, AL
Boston, MA	Filenes, Boston, MA
Bradenton, FL	The Blossom Shop, Bradenton, FL
Bremerton, WA	The Treasure Chest, Bremerton, WA
Bristol, VA	Dr. Guy C. Richardson, State & Moore Sts., Bristol, VA
Burlington, IA	Wyman & Rand, Burlington, IA
Caracas, Venezuela, S.A.	George Alfredo Wolf, Caracas, Venezuela
Carlsbad City, NM	McCoy Jewelry Co., Carlsbad, NM
Cedar Rapids, IA	The Killian Co., Cedar Rapids, IA
Central Florida	Yowell, Drew, Ivey Co., Orlando, FL
Charleston, SC	Adams, Ortman & Co., Charleston, SC
Charleston, SC	Kerrison's, Charleston, SC
Charlotte, NC	J. B. Ivey & Co., Charlotte, NC
Charlottesville, VA	Brown's Gift Shop, Charlottesville, VA
Chattanooga, TN	Miller Brothers, Chattanooga, TN
Cheyenne, WY	Skaggs Self Service Drugs, Cheyenne, WY
Cincinnati, OH	S. & H. Pogue Co., Cincinnati, OH
Cleveland, OH	The Higbee Company, Cleveland, OH
Colorado Springs, CO	Kaufman's, Colorado Springs, CO
Columbia, SC	Belk's Department Store, Columbia, SC
Columbus, GA	Max Rosenberg Co., Columbus, GA
Columbus, MS	Loeb Furniture Co., Columbus, MS

City Picture Plates	Where They Could be Purchased
Corpus Christi, TX	Litchenstein's, Corpus Christi, TX
Dallas, TX	A. Harris & Co., Dallas, TX
Danville, VA	Belk Legget Co., Danville, VA
Daytona Beach, FL	Lauch's Jewelry Co., Daytona Beach, FL
Deming, NM	J. A. Mahoney, Inc., Deming, NM
Denver, CO	Carson Crockery Co., Denver, CO
Des Moines, IA	Younker Brothers, Des Moines, IA
Detroit, MI	The J. L. Hudson Co., Detroit, MI
Douglas, AZ	The Gift Box, Douglas, AZ
Durham, NC	Balk Leggett Co., Durham, NC
El Paso, TX	The White House, El Paso, TX
Ellensburg Rodeo	Button Jewelers, Ellensburg, WA
Estes Park, CO	The Aspen Shop, Estes Park, CO
Excelsior Springs, MO	Ye Olde Colony, Excelsior Springs, MO
Fayetteville, NC	Hatcher's Jewelry Store, Fayetteville, NC
Flagstaff, AZ	Flagstaff Pharmacy, Flagstaff, AZ
Flagstaff, AZ	Navajo Hopi Trading Co., Flagstaff, AZ
Flint, MI	McLogan & Austin, Flint, MI
Fort Worth, TX	The Fair Co., Ft. Worth, TX
Franciscan Monastery	Capitol Souvenir Co., Washington, D.C.
Ft. Worth Centennial	W. C. Stripling Co., Ft. Worth, TX
Galveston, TX	Robert I. Cohen Inc., Galveston, TX
Grand Canyon	Fred Harvey, Indian Dept., Albuquerque, NM
Grand Canyon	Verkamp's, Grand Canyon, AZ
Greensboro, NC	Belk's Dept. Store, Greensboro, NC
Greenville, SC	Meyers Arnold Co., Greenville, SC
Gulfport, MS	Joseph K. Fasold, Gulfport, MS
High Point, NC	Alexander's, High Point, NC
Hot Springs, AR	Valley Curio Store, Hot Springs, AR
Houston, TX	Texas Lamp & Oil Co., Houston, TX
Huntsville, AL	Rose Jewelry Co., Huntsville, AL
Indianapolis, IN	L. S. Ayres & Co., Indianapolis, IN
Jackson, MS	Century Electric Co., Jackson, MS
Jamestown and Newport News, VA	The China Palace and Gift Shop, Newport News, VA
Junction City (Ft. Riley), KS	Eunice C. Starck Jewelry Co., Junction City, KS
Kannapolis, NC	The Jewel Shoppe, Kannapolis, NC
Kansas City, MO	Hall's, Kansas City, MO
Key West, FL	Frank Johnson, 604 Duval St., Key West, FL
Knoxville, TN	Anderson, Dulin, Varnell Co., Knoxville, TN

City Picture Plates	Where They Could be Purchased
Lake Arrowhead, CA	Lake Arrowhead Gift Shop, Lake Arrowhead, CA
Laguna Beach, CA	La Solana Pottery, Laguna Beach, CA
LaJolla, CA	Cole's of LaJolla, CA
Las Cruces, NM	The Myers Co., Las Cruces, NM
Las Vegas, NV	W. M. Davis & Co., Las Vegas, NV
Lexington, VA	The Dutch Inn, Lexington, VA
Lincoln, NE	Miller & Paine, Lincoln, NE
Little Rock, AR	Gus Blass Company, Little Rock, AR
Little Rock, AR	Pfeifer's, Little Rock, AR
Long Beach, CA	The China Shop, Long Beach, CA
Louisville, KY	J. Bacon & Sons., Louisville, KY
Lynchburg, VA	Millner's, Lynchburg, VA
Macon, GA	The Belk Matthews Co., Macon, GA
Mason City, IA	Damon's, Mason City, IA
Mesa, AZ	Strauch's, Mesa, AZ
Memphis, TN	Lowenstens, Memphis, TN
Memphis (Historical), TN	Goldsmith Bros., Memphis, TN
Miami, FL	Burdines, Miami, FL
Minneapolis, MN	The Dayton Co., Minneapolis, MN
Mobile, AL	Gayfer's, Mobile, AL
Monterey, CA	Lucky Boy Market, Monterey, CA
Montgomery, AL	Montgomery Fair, Montgomery, AL
Nashville, TN	Gain Sloan Company, Nashville, TN
Natchez, MS	Dixie Furniture Co., Natchez, MS
New Iberia, LA	The Evangeline China Market, New Iberia, LA
New Orleans, LA	Hausmann's Inc., New Orleans, LA
New York City, NY	Bloomingdale's, New York City, NY
New York City, NY	Dennison Mfg. Co., 411 5th Avenue, New York City, NY
New York City, NY	Macy's, New York City, NY
Norfolk, VA	Ames & Brownley, Norfolk, VA
Norfolk, VA	D.P. Paul Co., Newport News, VA
Oklahoma City, OK	Harbour Longmire Co., Oklahoma City, OK
Palm Springs, CA	Reid Pottery, Palm Springs, CA
Pasadena, CA	F. C. Nash Co., Pasadena, CA
Pasco, WA	Gregg's Pasco, WA
Pensacola, FL	Elebash Jewelry Co., Pensacola, FL
Peoria, IL	Bergner & Co., Peoria, IL
Philadelphia, PA	Strawbridge & Clothier, Philadelphia, PA
Philadelphia, PA	Wanamaker's, Philadelphia, PA
Pittsburgh, PA	Kaufman Dept. Store, Pittsburgh, PA
Portland, OR	Lipman Wolfe Co., Portland, OR

City Picture Plates	Where They Could be Purchased
Portsmouth, VA	Cooper's, Portsmouth, VA
Prescott, AZ	Sam Hill's, Prescott, AZ
Raleigh, NC	Taylor's, Raleigh, NC
Reading, PA	Bechtel, Lutz & Jost, Reading, PA
Reno, NV	Payless Drug Store, Reno, NV
Richmond, VA	Miller & Rhodes, Richmond, VA
Richmond, VA	Thalheimer's, Richmond, VA
Rio De Janeiro, Brazil, S.A.	Polimercante de Brazil, Rio de Janeiro, Brazil
Roanoke, VA	H. Heironimus Co., Roanoke, VA
Roanoke, VA	Thurman Boone Co., Roanoke, VA
Rome, GA	Wyatt's, Rome, GA
Roswell, NM	Central Hardware Co., Roswell, NM
Saginaw, MI	Morley Brothers, Saginaw, MI
Salem, MA	Daniel Low & Co., Salem, MA
Salem, OR	George E. Allen Hardware Co., Salem, OR
San Angelo, TX	Cox, Rushing, Greer Co., San Angelo, TX
San Antonio, TX	Joske Brothers, San Antonio, TX
San Antonio, TX	The Vogue, San Antonio, TX
San Bernadino, CA	Arthur's, San Bernadino, CA
San Diego, CA	Whitney & Co., San Diego, CA
San Jose, CA	Collins, Groth & Johnson, 1355 Market St., San Francisco, CA
San Pedro, CA	Phillips Furniture Co., San Pedro, CA
Santa Barbara, CA	Ott Hardware Co., Santa Barbara, CA
Santa Cruz, CA	Irwin M. Smith Pottery, Santa Cruz, CA
Santa Fe, NM	S. Spitz, Jeweler, Santa Fe, NM
Santa Rosa, CA	Hardisty's, Santa Rosa, CA
Sarasota, FL	The Blossom Shop, Sarasota, FL
Savannah, GA	Leopold Adler Co., Savannah, GA
Scranton, PA	Scranton Dry Goods Co., Scranton, PA
Seattle, WA	Frederick & Nelson, Seattle, WA
Sheridan, WY	Totman's, Sheridan, WY
Shreveport, LA	Hearne Dry Goods Co., Shreveport, LA
Silver City, NM	Paul R. Gantz, Silver City, NM
Sonoma, CA	Mission Hardware Co., Sonoma, CA
Spartanburg, SC	Montgomery & Crawford, Spartanburg, SC
Spokane, WA	Spokane Dry Goods Co., Spokane, WA
St. Augustine, FL	W. J. Harris Co., St. Augustine, FL
St. Louis Map	Mrs. M. Vangelder, St. Louis Chamber of Commerce, St. Louis, MO
St. Louis Map	Stix, Baer & Fuller, St. Louis, MO
St. Louis, MO	Scruggs, Vandervoort & Barney, St. Louis, MO
St. Paul, MN	Schuneman's, Inc., St. Paul, MN
St. Petersburg, FL	Maas Brothers, St. Petersburg, FL

City Picture Plates	Where They Could be Purchased
Staunton, VA	Holt's, Staunton, VA
Tacoma, WA	Peoples Store, Tacoma, WA
Tallahassee, FL	W. W. Putnam, Tallahassee, FL
Terre Haute, IN	Root Dry Goods Co., Terre Haute, IN
Tombstone, AZ	H. F. Ohm, Tombstone, AZ
Tri City (Davenport, Moline & Rock Island)	Petersen Harned Von Maur, Daveport, IA
Tucson, AZ	Thunderbird Shop, Tucson, AZ
Tulsa, OK	Brown Dunkin Dry Goods Co., Tulsa, OK
Vallejo, CA	Cooper's, Vallejo, CA
Vicksburg, MS	O'Neil McNamara Co., Vicksburg, MS
Vicksburg, MS	Z. M. Davis, National Park Store, Vicksburg, MS
Virginia Beach, VA	Denton's, Virginia Beach, VA
Warm Springs, GA	Mrs. J. M. Rothrock, Warm Springs, GA
White City, NM	White City Curio Shop, White City, NM
Wichita, KS	Hinkel Dry Goods Co., Wichita, KS
Williams, AZ	Petty's Curio, Williams, AZ
Williamsburg, VA	Bozarth of Old Williamsburg, Williamsburg, VA
Williamsburg, VA	Casey's Inc., Williamsburg, VA
Williamsburg, VA	The College Shop, Williamsburg, VA
Williamsburg & Yorktown	The China Place, Williamsburg, VA
Winston Salem, NC	Electric Service Co., Winston Salem, NC
Winston Salem, NC	Salem Book Store, Salem, NC

State Picture Plates	Where They Couould be Purchased
Alabama	Bromberg Galleries, Birmingham, AL
Arizona	Posten's, Douglas, AZ
Arizona	Dorris-Heyman Co., Phoenix, AZ
Arkansas	Dougherty's, Fayetteville, AR
Arkansas	McCan's, Ft. Smith, AR
California State Map	Could write to Vernon Kilns, 2310 E. 52nd, Los Angeles, CA
Colorado	Carson Crockery Co., Denver, CO
Delaware	Harold B. Budd, 166 5th Ave., New York City, NY
Florida	Blossom Shop, Bradenton, FL
Florida	Carribean Shop, Coral Gables, FL
Florida	China Mart, Orlando, FL
Georgia	Book & Gift Shop, Albany, GA
Georgia	Mary Eliza Shop, McIntosh, GA
Georgia	Wm. Schweigert Co., Augusta, GA
Hawaii	Margaret's Gift Shop, Honolulu, HI
Idaho	Idaho Candy Co., Boise, ID

State Picture Plates	Where They Could be Purchased
Illinois	A. C. McClurg & Co., 333 E. Ontario St., Chicago, IL
Indiana	A. C. McClurg & Co., 333 E. Ontario St., Chicago, IL
Iowa	A. C. McClurg & Co., 333 E. Ontario St., Chicago, IL
Kansas	Newman Dry Goods Co., Arkansas City, AR
Kansas	Sayers Hardware Co., Independence, KS
Kentucky	Belknap Hardware Co., Louisville, KY
Louisiana	C. A. Schnack Jewelry Co., Alexandria, LA
Louisiana	Gift Mart, Lake Charles, LA
Louisiana	Heyman Lieberman, Baton Rouge, LA
Louisiana	Masur Bros., Monroe, LA
Maine	C. T. Bodwell, Franconia Associates, Littleton, NH
Maryland	Lycett, Baltimore, MD
Massachusetts	McClennan Stores Co., Hyannis, MA
Massachusetts	McClennan Stores Co., Plymouth, MA
Minnesota	A. C. McClurg & Co., 333 E. Ontario St., Chicago, IL
Missouri	A. C. McClurg & Co., 333 E. Ontario St., Chicago, IL
Montana	John J. Moore, Gardiner, MT
Montana	The Paris of Montana, Great Falls, MT
Nevada	Bartlett Bros. Hardware Co., Las Vegas, NV
New Mexico	Chas. Ilfeld Co., Albuquerque, NM
New York	Harold B. Budd, 166 5th Ave., New York City, NY
North Carolina	Belk Brothers Co., Charlotte, NC
North Carolina	I.X.L. Stores, Inc., Asheville, NC
North Dakota	Mann's, Devils Lake, ND
North Dakota	R. B. Griffith Co., Grand Forks, ND
Ohio	A. C. McClurg & Co., 333 E. Ontario St., Chicago, IL
Oklahoma	Kerr's, Oklahoma City, OK
Oregon	Meier & Frank Co., Portland, OR
Oregon State Map	Holt Berni Merchandise Mart, Portland, OR
Pennsylvania	Bechtel, Lutz & Jost, Reading, PA
Rhode Island	The Shepard Co., Providence, RI
South Carolina	Belk's Dept. Store, Columbia, SC
South Dakota	Shriver Johnson Co., Sioux Falls, SD
Texas	Texas Lamp & Oil Co., Houston, TX
Texas	Walgreen's, Wichita Falls, TX
Utah	Holt Berni Merchandise Mart, Portland, OR
Vermont	C. T. Bodwell, Franconia Associates, Littleton, NH
Virginia	Miller & Rhoads, Richmond, VA
Washington	Margaret's Gift Shop, Chehalis, WA
Washington	Dayton Hardware Co., Dayton, WA
West Virginia	Robert Cales, Chimney Corner Gift Shop, Gauley Bridge, WV
Wisconsin	A. C. McClurg & Co., 333 E. Ontario St., Chicago
Wyoming	Dan S. Parks Co., Cheyenne, WY

Miscellaneous Picture Plates	Where They Could be Purchased
Alligator Farm	St. Augustine Alligator Farm, St. Augustine, FL
Appalachian Mountain Club Huts	Gorham, NC
Bellingrath Gardens	C. J. Gayfer Co., Mobile, AL
Bok Singing Tower (Mountain Lake Sanctuary)	Lake Wales, FL
Boulder Dam	Nava Hopi Trading Post, Boulder City, NV
Brookdale Lodge	Brookdale, CA
Broulator Court	Bagur's, New Orleans, LA
Brownsville Centennial	Brownsville Historical Assoc., Brownsville, TX
Brunswick & St. Simons Island	Ligeur's, Brunswick, GA
California Centennial	Barker Brothers, Los Angeles, CA
Carlsbad Caverns	White City Curio Shop, Carlsbad, NM
Cherokee Indian Reservation	Standard Souvenir & Novelity Co., Knoxville, TN
China Town, San Francisco	Collins, Groth & Johnson, 1355 Market St, San Francisco, CA
Christmas Tree	Bullocks, Los Angeles, CA
Corn Palace	Dan Grigg Enterprise, Mitchell, SD
Deep in the Heart of Texas	Foley's, Houston, TX
Ellensburg Rodeo	Button Jewelry Co., Ellensburg, WA
Estes Park	The Aspen Shop, Estes Park, CO
Famous Shrines of Virginia	Miller & Rhoades, Richmond, VA
Farmers Market	China House, 3rd & Fairfax, Los Angeles, CA
Fisherman's Wharf	Brannan's, 2795 Taylor St., San Francisco, CA
Flume Reservation	Flume Reservation, Franconia, NH
Fort Benning	Post Exchange, Fort Benning, GA
Fort Defiance	Defiance Chamber of Commerce, Defiance, OH
Fountain of Youth	Fountain of Youth Gift Shop, St. Augustine, FL
Franciscan Monastery	Capitol Souvenir Co., Washington, D.C.
Gateway to the Grand Canyon	Petty's Curio, Williams, AZ
Grace Episcopal Church	Mrs. Camilla Leake Barrow, St. Francisville, LA
Great Smoky Mountains	Standard Souvenir & Novelty, Knoxville, TN
Historical Liberty County	Mary Eliza Shop, Hinesville, SC
Hot Springs National Park	Chas. Weaver, Hot Springs N.P., AR
Indian Head, White Mountains	Indian Head, Franconia Notch, NH
Inland Empire	Northwest Supply Co., Spokane, WA
Jackson, Andrew	Jefferson Davis Shrine, Biloxi, MS
Jackson, Stonewall	Jefferson Davis Shrine, Biloxi, MS
Jefferson Davis Shrine	Jefferson Davis Shrine, Biloxi, MS
Johnston, Gen. Albert Sidney	Jefferson Davis Shrine, Biloxi, MS

Miscellaneous Picture Plates	Where They Could be Purchased
Knott's Berry Farm	Knott's Berry Farm, Buena Park, CA
Lee, Robert E.	Jefferson Davis Shrine, Biloxi, MS
Let 'er Buck	Taylor's Hardware Co., Pendelton, OR
Liberty Plate	Strasmick's, Ardmore, OK
Lincoln, Abraham	Drach Restaurant, Springfield, IL
Lincoln, Abraham	Myers Brothers, Springfield, IL
Lookout Mountain	Lively's Lookout Museum, Lookout Mountain, TN
Marineland	Marine Studio, Marineland, FL
Mayo Clinic	The China Hall, Rochester, MN
Monticello	Monticello, Charlottesville, VA
Monument Terrace	J.P. Bell Co., Lynchburg, VA
Mount Rushmore Memorial	Martin W. Morris, Deadwood, SD
New Hampshire Aerial Tramway	Franconia Notch, NH
Norris Dam	Standard Souvenir & Novelity Co., Knoxville, TN
Nut Tree	The Nut Tree, Vacaville, CA
Old Man of the Mountains	New Hampshire Forestry & Recreation, Franconia Notch, NH
Old Vincennes Cathedral	Old Vincennes Cathedral, Vincennes, IN
Ortman Clinic	The Gift Shop, Canistota, SD
Our West	New State Hardware Co., Ardmore, OK
Palo Duro Canyon	The Prairie Dog, Amarillo, TX
Patio Vieux Carre	Chopin's, New Orleans, LA
Petrified Forest	Rainbow Forest Lodge, Holbrook, AZ
Philippines	Doan's Dept. Store, Manila, Philippines
Presidential Gallery	Jefferson Davis Shrine, Biloxi, MS
Redwood Highway	Redwood Service Craft, Eureka, CA
Relief Society	Relief Society (Latter Day Saints), Salt Lake City, UT
Rogers, Will	Murphy's, Claremore, OK
Roman Nose National Park	Jaycee Jills, Watonga, OK
Roosevelt, F. D.	Star China Co., Anderson, IN
Roosevelt, Theodore	Star China Co., Anderson, IN
Rosalie	D.A.R., Natchez, MS
Salmon Derby	Ernst Hardware Co., Seattle, WA
San Jacinto Monument	San Jacinto Monument & History Assoc., San Jacinto, TX
Ski	Frederick & Nelson, Seattle, WA
Sportsman's Paradise	J. S. Casper Co., Milwaukee, WI
St. Louis Cathedral	St. Louis Cathedral, New Orleans, LA
Statue of Liberty	Statue of Liberty Shop, Bedloe Island, NY
Sugar Bowl Classic	Maison Blanche Co., New Orleans, LA
Supreme Forest Woodmen	Supreme Forest Woodmen Circle, Omaha, NE

Miscellaneous Picture Plates	Where They Could be Purchased
Texas Battleship	Foley's, Houston, TX
This is the Place	T. Ray Kingston, Murray, UT
Tops in Texas	Foley's, Houston, TX
Utah Centennial	T. Ray Kingston, Murray, UT
Vincennes Cathedral	Vincennes Cathedral, Vincennes, IN
Washington, George	Star China Co., Anderson, IN
Wilson, Woodrow	Star China Co., Anderson, IN
Ye Olde Colony	Ye Olde Colony, Excelsior Springs, MO
Yosemite National Park	Yosemite Park & Curry Co., Yosemite Park, CA

College Picture Plates	Where They May be Purchased
A&M College	Creech's, Stillwater, OK
Alma College	Mrs. Roy Hamilton, 619 W. Center, Alma, MI
Bessie Tift College	Forsythe, GA
Flora MacDonald College	Red Springs, NC
Girard College	Philadelphia, PA
Howe Military Academy	Howe, IN
Iowa State College	Florence Langford Gift Shop, Ames, IA
Mississippi State College	Columbus, MS
Notre Dame	Ohio China Co., Monroe, MI
Oklahoma Baptist University	Kib Warren, Shawnee, OK
Oregon State College	Whiteside's, Corvallis, OR
Southeast Missouri State College	Cape Girardeau, MO
Southern Methodist	Titche-Goettinger Co., Dallas, TX
State College of Washington	David's, Moscow, ID
University of Chicago	University Book Store, Chicago, IL
University of Idaho	David's, Moscow, ID
University of Illinois	Topper's, Champaign, IL
University of Michigan	Roberts Gift Shop, Ann Arbor, MI
University of Minnesota	Powers Mercantile Co., Minneapolis, MN
University of New Hampshire	New Hampshire
University of North Carolina	Danziger Candy Shop, Chapel Hill, NC
University of Oklahoma	Varsity Book Shop, Norman, OK
University of Oregon	Quackenbush & Co., Eugene, OR
University of South Dakota	Sletwold Flower Shop, Vermillion, SD
University of Southern California	YWCA, Los Angeles, CA
University of Virginia	Brown's Gift Shop, Charlotte, VA
University of Washington	B. F. Connelly Co., Seattle, WA
West Georgia College	Horton's Book Store, Carrollton, GA
Whitman College	Drumheller Co., Walla Walla, WA

⚮ Dinnerware ⚮

Mr. Bennison recounted that in the 1933 earthquake, most of the old Poxon and Vernon China wares toppled from the shelves, fell to the cement floors, and shattered. Mr. Bennison then immediately ordered his employees to remove the broken pottery (which was carried out in cartloads) and to get on with business. The disaster no doubt changed the company's course. It prompted the design of new molds, and led to production of the company's first and most popular shape, Montecito.

As previously mentioned, Gale Turnbull was hired in early 1935 as art director. Mr. Bennison hired famous artists to work under Turnbull's direction. Turnbull was also responsible for new shapes and designs. He left Vernon Kilns around 1942, but his creative influence endured for the lifetime of the company.

Harry Bird, who was on the scene prior to Turnbull's arrival, was already producing truly beautiful designs and had an exclusive Vernon-patented process.

Royal Hickman, too, was employed by Vernon Kilns. He designed the Melinda shape, which the company introduced in 1942. He is also well known for his Swedish glass, Heisey animals, and Royal Haeger pottery.

In 1952, designer Elliott House headed the art department. He remained until the close of business in 1958. He is credited with the design of the San Clemente* (Anytime) shape. In the 1950s, two artists — Sharon Merrill and Jean Ames — designed the attractive patterns* Chatelaine and Sun Garden, respectively.

Dinnerware was sold in better stores throughout the United States and Canada. Ads in national magazines like *House Beautiful, Life, Good Housekeeping, Fortune, Sunset,* and others attested to Vernon's superior quality, durability, and light weight compared to the heavier pottery of most contemporary manufacturers. An ad in the April 1955 *House Beautiful* read, "guaranteed for 25 years against crazing or crackling, completely underglazed, oven proof and detergent proof." It has passed the test of time.

The dinnerware chapter has been organized according to shapes and in chronological order: Montecito, Coronado, Ultra,** Melinda, San Fernando, San Marino, Lotus,** Pan American Lei variation, Chatelaine, San Clemente* (Anytime), and Transitional* (Year 'Round). Company names for shapes are given when known. It has been reported that in 1936 a complete alphabetical list was published of all American dinnerware shapes by name. For Vernon Potteries, Ltd., the shapes named were Coronado, Montecito, Sierra, and Wilshire. To date, there is no information indicating which shapes were Sierra and Wilshire.

An index of all known patterns by name, number, or both is provided at the end of each shape section.

A word of warning — not all pieces were made in every pattern, and sizes may vary from the measurements given.

The early decal wares are not included in this section examples can be seen on pages 23 – 26.

*Recent research by Michael E. Pratt has revealed the company names for these previously author-named shapes. In all instances throughout this book, the company's shape names will be given, with previous name in parentheses.

Mr. Pratt is the author of *Mid-Century Modern Dinnerware: Ak-Sar-Ben Pottery, Denwar Ceramics, Iroquois China Company, Laurel Potteries of California, Royal China Company,* and *Stetson China Company,* from Schiffer Publishing Ltd., 2002.

**These shape names are author-designated names in lieu of unknown company name.

Montecito ∞

This is believed to be Vernon Kilns' first original shape. Recognized by the indented concentric rings, the flatware rim is of medium width, with one ring at the rim's outer edge, two at the rim's inner edge, and another within the flat surface of the plate, directly beneath the flat rim. In the later years of the company, the rings were much less distinct, the result of redesign. Some rings do not appear at all on later pieces. The earliest Montecito hollow ware shapes and handles were angular, with the outer ring on some pieces (such as tumblers) creating a banded effect, or collar.

Montecito pieces bearing only mark 8 have been found with decals. The production of these pieces probably occurred prior to the creation of the Early California pattern. Examples of these early patterns executed on Montecito shape may be seen in the pictures on pages 24 and 26. Early California was the first line of solid colors to be introduced with the angular shape. Modern California with pastel colors followed, and appeared on the later version with rounded handles. Nevertheless, a few Modern California pieces can still be found on the angular shape, too. Later on, Early California was also produced in the rounded shape.

Specific examples of the Montecito angular and, later, rounded shapes are seen in the butter trays with covers and the 1-pint bowls. The earlier butter tray has the Hamiltons' Rippled tab handles, and its cover has defined angles and a knob finial. The redesigned tray with slightly rounded sides and plain tab handles has a rectangular finial on its cover. The early 1-pint bowl is angular, as compared to a later round shape. The butter trays with covers and the two versions of the 1-pint bowl are pictured on pages 144 and 145. Another example of the different styles of Montecito can be found in the large salad bowl. Harry Bird's 13" Fish and 15" Painted Pig angular bowls can be seen on page 161. The round salad bowl can be seen on page 145.

Slight variations are sometimes seen in the sizes and shapes of some Montecito pieces. The 7½" or 8½" round serving bowl, which is 2½" deep, might easily be confused with the flat rim soup, which a company price list described as 8½". The soup bowl, however, measures only 1½" deep.

Solid-colored Coronado was a variation of the Montecito shape that was sold as premium ware. Montecito itself had the longest lifetime of all company shapes and was still in use in 1958. Harry Bird and Gale Turnbull used both versions of this design in their decorating. Hand-painted and transfer patterns were done in great numbers.

Early California ∞ Vernon Kilns' first solid color pattern, Early California, was introduced about 1935 on angular hollow ware in the Montecito shape. The pattern was later produced on the rounded shape Montecito. In 1937, colors used were yellow, turquoise, green, brown, dark blue, light blue, ivory, orange, and pink. A 1946 company price list showed only the colors blue, green, peach, turquoise, and yellow. Though not found listed, maroon and white were added colors. Early California has a high, or glossy, glaze that distinguishes it from Modern California's satin finish. The production dates of these two colors are not known, and Early California pieces in maroon an white are considered scarce. An orchid item has been reported, but it could be a mismarked Modern California piece. Beginning in 1950, Early California was not in company price lists.

A list entitled "Early California Colors, Montecito," from Vernon Potteries, Ltd. and dated May 28, 1935, was printed in the Fall issue of *Vernon Views*. In addition to the usual dinnerware items, the following were listed: ashtrays, regular and individual; 7" baker, buffet (grill) trays, covered cigarette box, coaster; covered and uncovered cream soup cup; coffee server #1, wood handled; coffee server #2, cast handled; coffee, after dinner; 4" fruit, 7" nappie, oatmeal, pickle, plates (4", 5", 6", 7", 8"), 6" coupe; 6 oz. tumbler, unhandled; and 3-way relish dish. In an early company brochure, a 6" bowl that looks like an oversized fruit was identified as a cereal bowl. Some examples of these early Montecito shapes in Early California are seen in pictures to follow.

In the mid-1930s, cups and saucers were 40¢, tumblers were 30¢, a coffee server was $1.75, plates were from 25¢ to 40¢; chowder bowls were 40¢, with the cover at 15¢; a muffin tray was 75¢, with the cover at 75¢; a 17" chop plate was $3.00, a footed comport was $1.50, a covered casserole was $2.00, a 6-cup teapot was $1.50, a nest of five mixing bowls was $2.00, an individual 2-cup coffee pot was $1.65, a 20-piece set was $4.80, a 22-piece set was $5.95, a 32-piece set was $8.55, and a 22-piece Rainbow (assorted colors) set was $5.00. Orange pieces and sets were "slightly higher."

A NEW IDEA
IN COLORED POTTERY...
Soft Pastels

Vernon's "Modern California"

Its lovely glaze, satin-like texture, and modern design offer new ways to create smart and distinctive table settings like the one above, arranged by Barker Brothers, Los Angeles. Now featured by leading stores, "Modern California" is available in azure, orchid, pistachio, straw, sand and gray, in open stock and by the set. A dinner, luncheon or buffet supper table is equally effective in a single shade or in any of many harmonizing color combinations. Typical prices: 7-inch Plate, 45c; Tea Pot, $1.75; Coffee Server, $1.95; Cup and Saucer, 50c; 22-Piece Set, $6.90; 32-Piece, $9.70.

Free Booklet Shows Other Designs
Send for your copy - it shows many of the original patterns that have made Vernon Pottery so outstanding in artistic and authentic design, color and craftsmanship.

Phone to Find
WHO SELLS IT
SEE LAST PAGE

Authentic
VERNON
CALIFORNIA
POTTERY

Vernon Kilns
2300 E. 52nd Street • Los Angeles

Below - typical pieces in Vernon's "Native American" series.

Above - "Organdie," a striking new design by famed Vernon Artist, Gale Turnbull; in 2-tone combinations of green, brown, blue and pink-and-gray. Below - some of Mr. Turnbull's Marines and Coastlines.

Full page company ad showing a Modern California table setting with the Phoenix Bird centerpiece, and the Organdie, Native American, Coastline, and Marine series. Possibly an earlier ad than the 1938 *Sunset* magazine advertisement on the following page.

FROM ONE GIFT PACKAGE

COME 45 PIECES OF CALIFORNIA COLOR

SERVICE FOR EIGHT—ONLY $14.95!

Imagine the thrill of opening this exciting gift box and lifting out piece after piece of delicate, pastel dinnerware...Vernon "Modern California" pottery...in azure, pistachio, straw, and orchid. The package itself is adorned with typical California designs...and the pottery it contains is the finest ware made, every piece flawless, durable and craze-proof.

A SPECIAL GIFT PACKAGE AT A SPECIAL PRICE

Just think—for only $14.95 you get eight 9½-inch plates, eight 7½-inch plates, eight chowders, eight cups and saucers, a 12-inch chop plate, a large vegetable dish, covered sugar bowl and cream pitcher. Each of the forty-five pieces is individually packed without messy cut paper or excelsior, making your gift even more fastidiously perfect!

The Vernon Gift Package solves the problem of the perfect wedding, birthday, or Christmas gift for the truly smart woman, and also makes it possible for you to start your own new pottery service at a real saving of money.

If you prefer gay, vivid colors—for the same price you can buy a 45-piece Gift Package set of Vernon "Early California" ware in green, orange, turquoise, brown and other brilliant tones. At the left are just a few of the many exquisite hand-decorated lines made by Vernon, which blend so well with the solid colors of Modern and Early California.

A beautifully illustrated folder in full color showing these and many other distinctive patterns will be sent to you without cost upon request. Address Vernon Kilns, 2300 East 52nd Street, Dept. 11-S, Los Angeles, California.

VERNON
AUTHENTIC CALIFORNIA POTTERY

Phone to Find
WHO SELLS IT
SEE LAST PAGE

Ad from a 1938 *Sunset* magazine.

The next photographs show early examples of Early California. All bear mark 13, with exceptions noted in parentheses.

TOP CENTER: 1½ qt. tankard pitcher (mark 10).
CENTER: 1 pt. bowl; jam jar with notched cover (mark 10); 9" muffin tray and cover; 2 qt. ice-lip disk jug (jug interchangeable with Ultra).
BOTTOM: ¼ lb. butter tray and cover (mark 10), tray handles have same Rippled design of the Hamiltons' dishes; fast-stand sauce boat; pepper and salt shakers (mark 9); and three oval platters, 8½" relish, 12", and 14".

TOP: 11" grill plate (grill plates have been found decorated with floral decals and stamped with mark 8); 7½" covered casserole, somewhat like an old-fashioned 2 lb. sugar bowl; 9½" plate.
CENTER: Lug chowder; cup (mark 10); saucer; 2-cup individual coffee pot (mark 10); 6-cup angular teapot; three bulb mugs with applied handles, in brown (mark 10), ivory (mark 9), and orange.
BOTTOM: Mug with metal clip Bakelite handle (mark 10, no. 3 tumbler without clip); orange creamer and dark blue sauce boat (mark 10); stacked 5½" fruit (unmarked), 6½" plate, and 7½" plate; demitasse cup (unmarked) and saucer; round shape creamer.
Note: The grill plate pictured above has also been found bearing the backstamp "Sunset Pottery, Made In California, U.S.A." Pieces on both Montecito and San Marino blanks have been found bearing the Sunset mark. There seems to be little doubt among collectors that these were by Vernon Kilns. See page 312 for further information.

Except for the early sticker label, mark 5, marks are not indicated in the pictures that follow.

TOP: Chowder with cover; butter tray and cover (Ultra cover, Montecito tray with plain handles, interchangeable with Ultra); teapot; demitasse cup and saucer; pint bowl.

CENTER: 12" salad bowl; group of early egg cups featuring seven colors.

BOTTOM: All are examples of early shapes and are considered scarce. Pitcher with original sticker (mark 5); butter cover with knob handle and tray with Rippled handles; 13½" x 10½" grill plate, indented to hold style no. 1 tumbler; early chowder, applied pierced handles, also with original sticker (mark 5); angular pint bowl (compare to round bowl on top shelf).

Note: The early chowder measures 6" when it has the applied pierced handles, and 4¼" when it does not.

TOP: Two styles of ashtrays, three individual 3" square and one 4½" round (square ashtrays were also made in larger size); Four styles of tumblers, identified by description of shape and by number: No. 1 has a banded rim and base, 4½" tall; No. 2 has concentric rings midway beneath a bulge top, 4½" tall; No. 4 has flared top, 5" tall (interchangeable with Ultra); No. 3 has bulbous base, 4" tall. (No. 5 is the later straight-sided Montecito shape on page 187. No. 2 with clip handle is pictured in Organdie on page 187. No. 3 is pictured on page 144. These are shown with clip handle or applied handle. Both styles with clip handles were used as mugs.)

BOTTOM: Set of five graduated sizes of mixing bowls.

Shown is an example of an early tumbler, 4" high and 3¼" diameter. Although unmarked, it is believed by Bill Stern (author of *California Pottery: From Missions to Modernism*) to be the 6 oz. tumbler on the 1935 company price list for the following reasons: it was one of group that came with an early angular Early California carafe, the base is identical to the Vernon (white clay showing through the dry foot), it has the same cobalt glaze as is found on an after dinner cup that has a foil label (see example of foil label on a creamer on the following page), and it holds the same amount of liquid as was listed for the tumbler in the 1935 price list. *Bill Stern collection and photo.*

Rare green Early California 5½" lemon server with applied center handle. Not marked. *Brent and Sandra Purdom photo.*

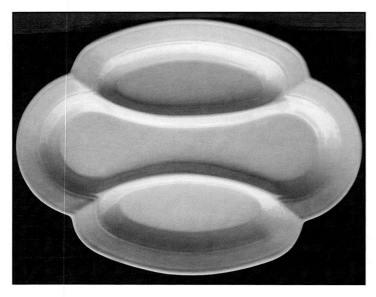

Scarce 3-way relish as described in the aforementioned 1935 list, 10" x 7", in white. Backstamped with mission bell (mark 8). A blue relish has been found unmarked. May be seen decorated with Harry Bird Incienso and Bird's Eye on page 153. *Brent and Sandra Purdom photo.*

Close-up of a surviving Early California sticker on the early angular creamer.
Dennis Donnal photo.

Early California 5" jam jar in the scarce maroon.
Brent and Sandra Purdom photo.

2-cup coffee pot, 6¼", and after dinner cup and saucer (unmarked) in rare peach color (circa 1946).

Contrast No. 1 pattern grill plate, 11", designed by Turnbull, marked with mark 33 and the pattern name. *Brent and Sandra Purdom photo.*

Modern California ⟳ This pattern is characterized by its satin-finish pastels. A 1938 *Sunset* magazine ad specified color choices of Azure (blue), Pistachio (green), Straw (yellow), and Orchid. An undated company brochure in the mid-1930s specified six lovely soft pastel shades (the gray Mist and the beige Sand were the two new colors), and a September 1937 advertisement mentioned gray. Ivory and a deep yellow have also been found. In the first picture, all have mark 14 except as noted in parentheses. Compare the rounded hollow ware here with the angular Early California. A seldom-seen blue Modern California two-handled casserole is known to exist, but was unavailable for photographing.

As mentioned earlier, some Modern California was also produced in the angular shape. Examples are seen in the group photo and close-up views on the following page.

The brochure also stated the pattern could be purchased in "Rainbow" sets of assorted shades, which would blend with any floral decoration and offer a striking contrast when used on a solid color tablecloth "now so much the vogue." Typical prices were: plates, from 25¢ to 50¢; cup and saucer, 50¢; chop plates, $1.25, $1.95, and $3.25; platters, 65¢, $1.25, and $2.00; jug pitcher, $1.35; tea pot, $1.75; coffee server, $1.95; covered chowder, 65¢; coffee mug, 50¢; 22-piece set, $6.90; 32-piece set, $9.70.

Early California and Modern California have been introduced first in this section in order to familiarize collectors with the history and development of Montecito. These pages serve as a prelude to the designs of two artists, Harry Bird and Gale Turnbull, and to those of all subsequent patterns.

TOP: Pistachio coffee server with matching Bakelite handle; 9½" plate; 12½" platter; 10" vegetable bowl; 9½" comport (comport is the label given by the company), scarce.
CENTER: Cup; saucer; muffin tray and cover; early mug (no. 3 tumbler shape) with clip Bakelite handle, mark 10; sauce boat; teapot; demitasse cup (unmarked) and saucer; mug with applied handle.
BOTTOM: Covered lug chowder; 3" ashtray.

Marks are not indicated for the pieces in this photograph.
TOP: 11" grill plate and three different versions of pint bowls.
CENTER: Nest of five mixing bowls, shown separately.
BOTTOM: Large 4½" square ashtray; individual sugar and creamer (note oval shape of the individual-size hollow ware); butter tray and cover (knob finial, Rippled-handled tray); scarce double-handled bowl sitting in saucer, thought to be a bouillon or an alternate style sugar bowl; egg cup; covered vegetable bowl; butter cover only (this is a later version showing different finial and cover shape).

Angular gravy, Modern California Azure (blue).
Bill Stern photo.

Angular 1-pint bowl, Modern California Mist.
Bill Stern photo.

Harry Bird Designs ∝ It is believed that Harry Bird preceded Gale Turnbull at Vernon Kilns during their overlapping period of employment. To read more of Bird's background, see page 60. Bird's designs must have been some of the very first patterns. As previously mentioned, the backstamps identifying his work were either his signature (mark 30) or his personal bird trademark (mark 31) over "Vernon Kilns," as seen in Evolution of Marks on page 8. His patterns were identified by a name or number preceded by a *B*, and sometimes with neither.

He had a unique, patented method of applying colored glaze. He used a silver-tipped syringe to form a design that would achieve an embossed effect once fired with a clear satiny glaze. This process was designated "inlaid glaze." Ads from 1936 and 1937 for Vernon pottery featured designs by Harry Bird. One ad pictured Spectrum — a series of geometric designs, each in a different combination of colors — and described it as a "new design by famed artist Harry Bird... an exclusive Vernon creation — the bright glaze is inlaid-handwork." Specific colors were not mentioned. Spectrum prices were listed: 4" plates, 35¢; 7" plates, 55¢; covered muffin plate, $2.25; 22-piece set, $9.50; and 32-piece set, $13.20.

Another ad described the Harry Bird dull matte color glazes in two-tone effects and also offered a group of fine pastels. Also in the Bird line were other groups of inlaid glazes; bright California flowers and gay tropical fish were two. Particularly appealing was an ad featuring the Harry Bird line of birds, which included scarlet tanagers, parrots, and the "bird ring," with appropriate decorations in contrasting colors. The Birds and Flower series prices were advertised as follows: 7" plate, $1.00; cup and saucer, $1.25; 22-piece set, $17.45; and 32-piece set, $24.35.

Multi-Floral and Trellis patterns used vibrant Early California colors. Pieces could be combined for color harmony and pattern contrast in the same setting.

Movie star Delores Del Rio was pictured in an ad holding pieces of Vernon Olinala ware. The ad stated, "old when found by Cortez, Miss Del Rio rediscovered the Aztec ware and commissioned Harry Bird to re-create it in faithful reproduction..." Designs were in soft blue, green, yellow, or rose on a warm background. A 22-piece set sold for $21.30, 32-pieces sold for $29.70, a cup and saucer was $1.50, and a 7" plate was $1.25. Montezuma-Aztec, similar to Olinala-Aztec, was another design.

What a delight to possess a mixed or matched dinnerware set in any of these vibrantly colored patterns or pastel designs: animals, fish, birds, flowers, or colors. Examples are seen in the pictures to follow. Marks are not indicated but are generally either mark 30 or mark 31, with or without the Vernon Kilns name. "Bird Pottery," in block letters, is also a mark.

Olinala-Aztec and Montezuma-Aztec.
TOP: Montezuma saucer; 9½" plate; coffee carafe.
CENTER: Olinala chowder with cover; 10½" orange plate (orange was not mentioned in ad); 9½" plate.
BOTTOM: Olinala creamer; footed 10" comport; carafe without stopper.

Olinala-Aztec.
TOP: 4½" coaster (also used as a cup warmer/cover); cup and saucer; early style mug.
BOTTOM: 12" oval platter; covered 9" vegetable bowl.

Matte colors in two-tone. Coffee carafe and cups and saucers, Pomegranate (pink).

Shown are examples of all the two-tone matte colors in the series except Pomegranate.
TOP: Bridal Satin 6" plate; Evening Star 3" candlestick; Evening Star demitasse cup and saucer and covered chowder; beige (may not be this series) cup and saucer.
BOTTOM: Golden Maple 8½" plate; Avocado 6" plate and covered chowder; After Glow and Tangerine 6" plates.

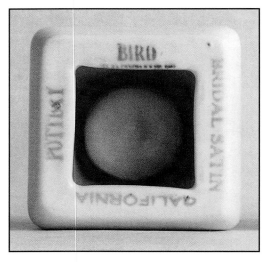

Backstamp.

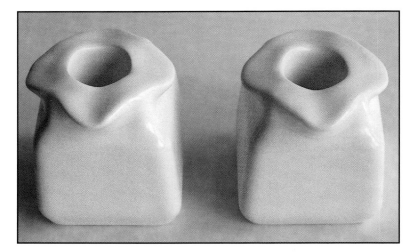

Close-up view of pair of Bridal Satin candlesticks, 2¾" high. Marked "Bird Pottery, Bridal Satin, California," in block letters.

One brochure mentioned that a dozen or more flowers were depicted in the Bird series. Twenty-seven different flowers are in the pictures that follow. An example of Larkspur was not available. Larkspur on a pink background has also been reported. Imagine a complete mixed or matched dinner set in any of these!

This picture also features some hollow ware with Bird's flowers.
TOP: Iris, Guatomote, both 6½" plates; Columbine coffee carafe above a Columbine center-handled 5½" lemon server; Petunia, Lupin, both 6½" plates.
CENTER: Begonia, 9½" plate; Lady Slipper, 7½" plate; and Fiddleneck, 9½" plate.
BOTTOM: Bird's Eye 3-part relish, 10" x 7"; Bird's Eye cup and saucer (cup marked only "Bird Pottery, Pat. Pend.," in block letters); Incienso 3-part relish.

TOP: Lily Blue and Checker Bloom, 14" plates.
CENTER: Mariposa Tulip and Wild Pink, 10½" plates.
BOTTOM: Water Lily and Phacelia, 10½" plates.

TOP: Lily Orange and Desert Poppy, 10½" plates.
CENTER: Desert Mallow and Chinese Lantern, 10½" plates.
BOTTOM: Cassia and Birds Eye, 10½" plates.

TOP: Geranium and Nasturtium, 10½" plates. (A blue geranium was done on blue ground also.)
CENTER: Lion's Tail and Golden Brodiaea, 10½" plates.
BOTTOM: Trumpet Flower and Morning Glory, 10½" plates.

Backstamp.

Eucalyptus plate, size unknown. *Tim and Linda Colling photo.*

Bird's Eye angular coffee server with six no. 1 tumblers, 4½" high.
Phil Shirley photo.

Three Desert Mallow coasters, 3¾", marked "Bird Pottery."
John and Joanne Barrett photo.

Incienso 13" bowl. Flowers are "planted" in the bottom of the bowl. *Dennis Donnal photo.*

Floral (unidentified) on Golden Maple ground, 10½" plate.
John and Joanne Barrett photo.

Iris on Avocado ground, 9½" plate, mark 31.
Museum of California Design photo.

Fiddleneck on Avocado ground, 9½" plate, mark 31.
Museum of California Design photo.

Mariposa Tulip on Avocado ground, 9½" plate, mark 31.
Museum of California Design photo.

Blooming Cactus, 7½" plate. *Dennis Donnal photo.*

Two Bird plates in the Flower series have been found on Baurer "ring" plates. Examples may be seen in the pictures below:

Bird's Eye on Bauer 11" plate. *Dennis Donnal photo.*

Mariposa Tulip on Bauer 8" plate. *Dennis Donnal photo.*

Another series of patterns, identified only by two letters and a number, incorporates both a band of color and flowers from the preceding series. The first letter is a *B* for Bird, and the second letter indicates the band color (e.g., *B* for blue, *Y* for yellow, etc). The numbers 1 through 6 indicate the flowers and colors. In lieu of a pattern name, the author has elected to refer to the pattern as "Banded Flower." Examples of it are seen in the next photograph.

TOP: BP-1 chowder, fruit, and 8½", 10½", and 6½" plates (P-pink).
CENTER: BP-5 cup and saucer; BB-2 sugar; BG-5 12½" chop plate (G-green).
CENTER FOREGROUND: BG-3, BY-2, and BY-5 demitasse cups. (Y-yellow, B-blue.)
BOTTOM: BP-3 and BP-6 10½" plates.

This coffee server appears to be Banded Flower BP-1.
Tim and Linda Colling photo.

Close-up views of two Banded Flower 10½" plates.

BG-3, green band, small yellow flower.
Dennis Donnal photo.

BY-3, yellow band, small pink flower.
Dennis Donnal photo.

159

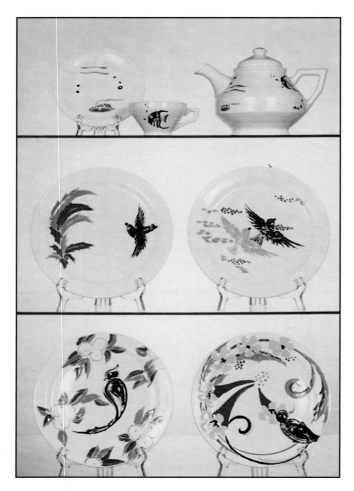

Bird's Tropical Fish and Birds are seen in this picture. The beauty of these rare pieces is beyond description, particularly that of the last two in the bottom row.

TOP: Tropical Fish cup and saucer and teapot.

CENTER: Two Bluebird 9½" plates. Left plate is B-353 Bluebird, right plate is a Bluebird with no number or pattern name.

BOTTOM: Two plates, one picturing a crested bird amidst foliage (left) and one showing a bird sipping nectar from a cluster of trumpet flowers (right).

Ring of Birds 9½" plate. *Dennis Donnal photo.*

15½" angular bowl. An exotic orange bird with a long orange and green tail, perched on a flat bowl. Mark 31. B number is not known. *John and Joanne Barrett photo.*

Three large bowls are featured in this photograph. They were probably salad bowls.

TOP: Tropical Fish 13" flat rim bowl.

BOTTOM: Tropical Fish and Painted Pig 15" bowls. These were done on angular bowls with double-scalloped rims, not on the Montecito shape.

10½" dinner plate, inlaid glaze. The only backstamp is "FANTAIL."

Lug chowder bowl and lid. Bowl is backstamped "TROPICAL FISH" in black, and has mark 31.
John and Joanne Barrett photo.

Spectrum series.
TOP: B-300 creamer below a Polychrome A demitasse cup; B-310 footed comport; B-300 10½" plate.
BOTTOM: B-305 9½" plate; B-305 demitasse cup in a Vert saucer; Vert 10½" plate. Vert has been found with a cobalt blue border on light blue ground.

Two 17" chop plates. Spectrum series. On the left is B-305, and on the right is B-304.
John and Joanne Barrett photo.

The items in this picture are also thought to be Spectrum patterns because of their numbers. Multi-Flori California and B-327 are identical, except Multi-Flori California is monochromatic — a single color on ivory, in tones of green, brown, yellow, orange, or maroon (rose) — and B-327 is polychromatic — all colors together in a single pattern.
TOP: Two Multi-Flori California 6½" plates, one in rose and the other in brown, alongside a B-327 polychromatic 6½" plate.
BOTTOM: 9½" yellow plate, Multi-Flori California; B-327 1-quart jug; 9½" green Multi-Flori California plate.

Tahiti C is a striking pattern similar to Multi-Flori California but it is more detailed. It is known to exist in soft rose and ivory, also. There are probably Tahitis A and B, soft rose being one of these.

This 12½" chop plate features the Tahiti C pattern. Note the curve to the plate rim, typical of chop plates, as opposed to the flat rim of the smaller plates.

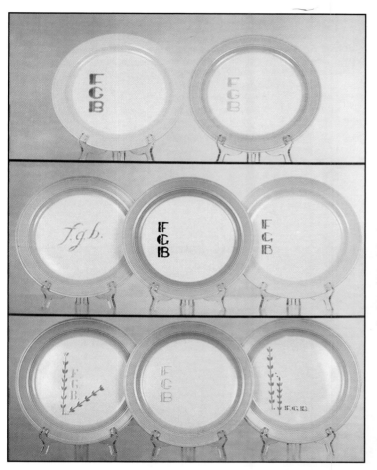

This photograph features eight plates with different color combinations and different style monograms. The initials were those of Vernon Kilns owner and president, Faye G. Bennison. Another monogram plate with the initials *RAM* is pictured in a following photograph. Ralph Martin was a long-time employee and was the superintendent of production for many years, and perhaps the plate was his.

Coffee server. William H. (Harry) Bird monogram.
Museum of California Design photo.

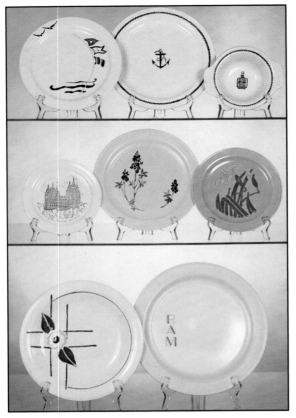

A varied assortment of Bird items is pictured here.
TOP: Nautical motifs. Flags, 9½" plate; Anchor 10½" plate; Lantern chowder.
CENTER: Mormon Temple (Salt Lake City) 7½" plate (backstamp states "dedicated 1893"); B-156 10½" plate; B-102 8½" plate.
BOTTOM: Spectrum B-325 12½" chop plate; monogram "RAM" 14" chop plate.

Harry Bird's Nautical pattern. Each piece of dinnerware is backstamped with its descriptive name and mark 30; teacups, embossed with mark 10, show no descriptive name.
BACK ROW: Life Saver 9" bowl; Anchor 10½" plate; Wheel 6½" plate.
MIDDLE ROW: Lantern chowder.
FRONT ROW: Sextant cup and saucer; Flag 8½" plate. Another 8½" plate named Square Knot has also been reported.

Examples of polychrome, Nautical, Tropical Fish, and monogram.
TOP: Three polychrome plates: 9½" B, 9½" E, and 10½" A (there are probably polychrome C and D plates as well); Flags 12½" chop plate; Tropical Fish 9½" plate.
BOTTOM: "B" monogram salt and pepper shakers (Ultra shape).

Corset 4" vase. Mark on this piece does not have the Vernon Kilns name. **$50.00.** *Judi Thompson photo.*

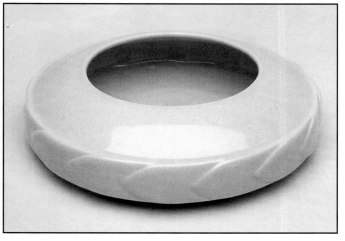

The only flower bowl by Bird seen thus far. It has a 6½" diameter and does not carry the Vernon Kilns name. **$40.00.**

Small Harry Bird pitcher, 3½". *Museum of California Design photo.*

Pictured is a Vernon Kilns Montecito pitcher with an interesting history. As told to Bill Stern of the Museum of California Design, Harry Bird's son, Lincoln, and Lincoln's wife, Mary, both worked for Wallace China in the early 1940s. Harry's wife, Matty, went to work there in 1945. Since it has a Wallace backstamp one would assume that this Vernon Kilns pitcher is a consequence of the Bird/Vernon/Wallace relationship.

The 1-pint bulb pitcher appears to be decorated with Spectru B-300. It is backstamped "WALLACE CHINA" in green ink, and has a date code that appears to be from 1944. *Museum of California Design photo.*

Gale Turnbull's Montecito Period ⟶ Gale Turnbull's peasant-style art was the result of French influence (from Turnbull's years of study in France) upon Vernon Kilns' motifs. Most of Turnbull's patterns were named, but many were identified only by number; some patterns had both number and name. A number preceded by *T* indicated a Turnbull design. His backstamps appeared either with his signature (marks 33 and 34) or with just initials (see Evolution of Marks on page 8). Two shapes were used by Turnbull: mostly the round Modern California version of Montecito, but he also created a few designs on Ultra (see page 223 – 228).

The Native American design was advertised in the "Window Shopping" column of *House Beautiful*, in the December 1937 issue. The ad stated, "From California and the Vernon Kilns of California comes this essentially native product, very aptly called 'Native American.' Gale Turnbull, its designer, is inspired by the carefree existence of California in old Mission days." The ad specified ten designs "you can buy mixed or all alike…" with a variety of scenes. It is now believed there are many more than ten designs, since a number of patterns are now known that fit the Native American description. (Two patterns have been found marked "made for Barker Bros." There may be others.) Subjects were done in yellows, greens, and browns. The designs depicted people in native dress, missions and little mission houses, cacti, and scenes in old California. One called *Arizona* pictured saguaro, the state flower of Arizona.

The aforementioned ad showed two plates, one identical to the Pedro and Conchita 7½" plate seen in a photograph on page 174, and the other depicting Pedro and Conchita standing before a mission house. A coffee carafe in the advertisement also pictured Pedro and Conchita.

Even the company packing boxes, which contained 45-piece place settings, were decorated with Turnbull's art. In the ad the coffee server was priced at $3.00; the 7" plates, 60¢; the chowder, 55¢; a 22-piece set, $9.50; and a 32-piece set, $13.20. What a bargain for hand-painted ware!

The following photographs show examples of Native American patterns by Turnbull. For a list of all Native American patterns known so far, see page 214.

TOP: Little Mission 10½" plate; matching carafe on sand-colored background.
CENTER: *Smoke Tree* (no. 1 style) tumbler; matching 10½" plate.
BOTTOM: *Sentinels* 10½" plate; matching carafe.

Little Mission 13" salad bowl, overhead view.
Joanne and John Barrett photo.

Two sizes of plates and the company box are shown in this picture.
TOP: Solitude 10½" plate; Palm Springs 9½" plate; Arizona 10½" plate.
CENTER: T-620 Totem 9½" plate; original company box still intact after almost 60 years. (Note the Turnbull art on the box.)
BOTTOM: Mountain Mission, Going to Town, and Cabanas Chico 10½" plates.

Guerrillas, Native American 10½" plate, mark 33.
Sean Meredith photo.

Little Mission plate, ivory ground, yellow band on rim. Size not known.

Las Palmas, fruit bowl, 5½", ivory ground, green band on rim.

Pepita 10½" plate, sand ground, rim band appears to be black.
Cindy Anderson photo.

A rare find. Native American patterns decorate three early Montecito tumblers.

Sentinels tumbler, no. 1 shape, 4½" tall.
Tim and Linda Colling photo.

Little Mission tumbler, no. 2 shape, 4½" tall.
Tim and Linda Colling photo.

Unidentified pattern tumbler, no. 2 shape, 4½" tall.
Tim and Linda Colling photo.

Still Life. Both pattern and comport are considered scarce.
Cindy Anderson photo.

The next three pictures are believed to be part of Marine series.

Man O' War. 10½" plate, sand ground. *Ann Brady photo.*

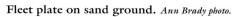

Fleet plate on sand ground. *Ann Brady photo.*

Fleet chowder bowl, backstamped with Turnbull's mark 33.

More Native American patterns on sand ground.
TOP: Barbary Fig cup and saucer, 9½" plate, and covered creamer and sugar.
CENTER: Still Life covered chowder, 9½" plate, and teapot.
BOTTOM: Banana Tree cup and saucer (matching carafe on page 174); Peppers 9½" plate, tumbler (no. 1 style), and cup and saucer.

Barbary Ho 14" chop plate. Identical to Barbary Fig on preceding page except that it is on ivory ground. *Josephine Morse photo.*

Indian jars are featured in this T-623 pattern. This pattern appeared in an article in the July 1938 issue of *House and Garden*. T-622 has been reported as having a similar design, picturing one jar and cactus instead of the two jars seen in T-623. Three sizes of plates, the cup and saucer, and the creamer and sugar of the T-623 pattern are shown here. *Norvelle Weeks photo.*

Coastline and Marines were two other series of Turnbull's unusual designs. A sales brochure described the Marine series as consisting of faithful reproductions of old windjammers, spouting whales, etc. Marine series colors run to blues, greens, and browns on ivory ground. Some items pictured in the Marine series were part of a collection called the Whaling service. The Porthole items are in this group as well.

The Coastline designs adapted the pictures of actual coastlines of the Atlantic and Pacific shores, Lake Michigan, and the Gulf of Mexico for use as dinnerware decorations. The sales brochure stated, "Imagine the thrill the youngsters will get out of learning geography from their dinner plates." Coastline colors are in blue and black on ivory ground. Prices were listed as follows: plates, 35¢ – 80¢; cup and saucer, 85¢; pitcher, $1.75; coffee server, $3.50; and chop plates, $1.75 – 5.00.

Two covered creamers or individual tea pots from Turnbull's Marine and Coastline series. Porthole (left) and Coastline Gulf of Mexico (right). Both are backstamped with a variation of mark 33. *John and Joanne Barrett photo.*

Porthole 8½" plate, mark 33, initials only. *Phil Shurley photo.*

This photo features Native American series and Coastline examples.
TOP: Banana Tree coffee server (matching cup and saucer shown on page 171). Center: Coastline 9½" plate, map from Santa Barbara to San Diego, California; Michigan Coastline 12" chop plate; Coastline 10½" plate, California coastline from San Francisco to San Luis Obispo.
BOTTOM: Native American Little Mission 9" vegetable; Pedro and Conchita 7½" plate; Cottage Window 9" vegetable, a Turnbull design but bears strong resemblance to the four plates on page 130 that are initialed "B.L.O."

All pieces in this photograph are Coastline.
TOP: 5½" fruit, New England map of Bridgton, Dover, Georgetown, Washington and Baltimore; carafe, Michigan Coastline, map of Marquette and Sault Sainte Marie; sugar bowl, map of Florida, showing Tampa, Sarasota, and Everglades on the Gulf of Mexico.
CENTER: 12" chop plate, New England coast map of Portland, Maine, to Cape Cod and New Bedford, Massachusetts; clip-handled mug, map of Marquette and Sault Sainte Marie; 12" chop plate, Louisiana from New Orleans to Abbeville on the Gulf.
BOTTOM: Michigan Coastline 5½" fruit, 9½" plate, and cup and 6" plate.

The 1942 Culinary Arts Institute's *Breakfast and Brunch Cook Book* pictured a Coastline 9½" plate (Southern California). Also, a Moby Dick plate was shown in the New England breakfast recipe section of the cookbook.

Coastline subjects and pieces known in the series are:

Fruit, 5½"	New England, Michigan
Plate, 6½"	New England, Michigan
Plate, 7½"	New England
Plate, 9½"	California, Michigan
Plate, 10½"	California
Plate, chop, 12"	New England, Michigan, Gulf of Mexico
Plate, chop, 14"	Gulf of Mexico
Plate, chop, 17"	Michigan
Cup	California, Michigan
Saucer	California
Sugar	Gulf of Mexico
Salad, 13"	Subject not known
Carafe	Michigan
Ashtray	Gulf of Mexico
Tumbler	Michigan
Creamer	Gulf of Mexico

Examples pictured are from the Marine and Fish series.
TOP: Three different Fish 9½" plates, pattern named on back of each.
CENTER: Marine series plates — Porthole, 10½"; Whaling service, Windjammer, 9½".
BOTTOM: Whaling service, spouting whale and shore scene 9½" plates.

This is No. 4 of the colorful Turnbull Fish series plates. Marked "Hand Painted Under Glazes by Gale Turnbull, Vernon Kilns, California." *John and Joanne Barrett photo.*

Although not in the Marine series, another Turnbull marine plate. The scene, which looks very much like Glacier Bay, is marked "To Alaska with the Schreibers August 23, 1937" on the reverse. *Bob Hutchins photo.*

Casa California and Casa California Hermosa patterns are typical of Turnbull's peasant-style art. Casa California ("California Homes") was described in a company brochure as "a modern adaptation of a primitive style of decoration, reminiscent of the ancient Indians of Mexico and country potters working today in Italy." The description stated that there were six patterns in the line in either blues and greens or browns and yellows, "each employing a variety of vivid colors to complement any decorative scheme." T-629 and T-632 patterns were pictured. The brochure listed items ranging from tiny coasters to 17" chop plates, from individual sugar bowl to salad bowl. Typical prices: plates, 30¢ – 65¢; cup and saucer, 70¢; chop plates, $1.50 – 4.25; 1-quart pitcher, $1.65; covered chowder bowl, 75¢; sets from $7.20.

Casa California Hermosa was described as basically the same as Casa California, only "more elaborate," peasant ware with "the crude, primitive, and artistically sound" informality of the "early California haciendas." Prices were slightly higher than those listed for Casa California. Patterns pictured were T-630, T-631, T-669, T-670, and T-673. Examples are seen in the following photographs.

TOP: T-631 8" mixing bowl; T-632 12" chop plate; T-631 9½" plate.
BOTTOM: T-630 muffin tray and cover; T-630 9½" plate; T-680 multi-aster jug/pitcher, not Casa California, though pictured here.

T-631 tumbler, early Montecito no. 3 shape, 4" tall.

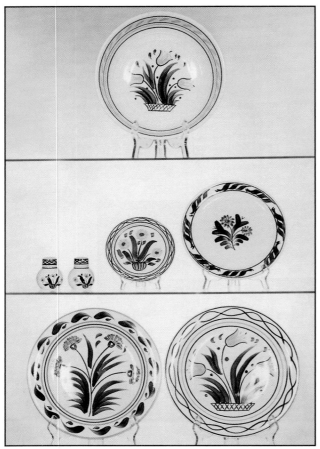

All items in this picture are believed to be Casa California Hermosa except where noted.

TOP: T-670 11½" salad bowl.

CENTER: T-669 salt and pepper shakers (marked "Made in U.S.A." only); matching T-669 6½" plate; Casa California T-629 9½" plate.

BOTTOM: T-673 and T-670 12½" chop plates.

T-671 plate, mark 10. The pattern has a splash border similar to that of T-673 and a floral similar to that of T-670.
Tim and Linda Colling photo.

Close-up view of the T-669 17" chop plate.
John and Joanne Barrett photo.

Two other groups described in the same brochure were Blue Glazes and Decorated Pastels. When discussing these, the brochure stated, "for the first time in pottery history, underglaze decorations have been successfully placed under a colored glaze producing an interesting new effect — an exclusive Vernon process." With a soft blue background and darker blue borders, T-651 Constellation (previously called "Blue Star" by author) and T-659 Blue Bow were the examples of Blue Glaze shown in the brochure.

The Decorated Pastel series was described as another "new departure in pottery making." The brochure described this grouping, which offered hand-decorated underglaze designs on soft pastel colors, and pictured T-657 and T-655. T-653, T-654, and T-656 are more patterns fitting the description and numerical sequence of this series.

In the photograph are examples of the two groups.
TOP: Constellation T-651 individual creamer and sugar on either side of T-652 Blue Feather coffee server.
CENTER: Constellation T-651 12" chop plate; Decorated Pastel T-657 12" chop plate.
BOTTOM: Decorated Pastel T-655 and T-653 9½" plates.

In this photograph are two colorful coffee servers. The one on the left, a Casa California Hermosa T-631 2-cup coffee pot, illustrates the stylized shape of early Montecito. On the right is an unidentified Decorated Pastel (unmarked) coffee server, with bright blue decoration and light pink glaze (neither T-number nor pattern name is known; it may be T-656).

Blends ∽ The Blends, as the name implies, are patterns with two contrasting colors, or the same color in different intensity, that blend from rim to center, light to dark. Known Blend pattern numbers go from 1 to 19; some numbers in this range are left out, but there are probably still Blend patterns for these. Some Blends are seen in the picture to follow, as are some Blue Glaze examples.

TOP: Blend No. 10 9½" plate; T-659 Blue Bow, 10½" plate; Blend No. 4 9½" plate.
BOTTOM: Blend No. 10 cup and saucer; Blend No. 4 4½" tumbler (style no. 1); T-652 Blue Feather, 8½" plate; Constellation T-651 individual creamer; unmarked Blend (possibly No. 1) creamer with cover, serves a dual purpose as an individual teapot.

TOP: Blend No. 5. A striking blend of colors seen in the coffee server, creamer, and sugar.
BACK CENTER: 12" chop plates, Blends Nos. 1 and 5.
FRONT CENTER: Creamer (not numbered, appears to be No. 5); No. 2 6" plate; creamer (not numbered, believed to be No. 4).
BOTTOM: Blend No. 9 8½" plate; chowders, Blend Nos. 1, 4, and 19.
Note: Because colors vary in intensity within the same pattern, can be difficult to identify a pattern if it is not marked.

Carafe, another Blend; the number is not known. Purple shades to a deep maroon. *Tim and Linda Colling photo.*

This is a close-up view of an individual sugar and a demitasse cup and saucer, Blend No. 6, yellow shading to gray. Note the oval shape of the individual sugar bowl, typical of the Montecito individual creamers and sugars of this time period.

Duo-Tone ~ This series was pictured and described in a company brochure as "formal enough for 'state occasions' yet sufficiently colorful to avoid monotony." The 11 color combinations in the series were lavender and gray (T-633), golden brown and pink (T-634), yama green and gray (T-635), black and pink (T-636), turquoise green and red-brown (T-637), blue and yellow (T-638), yellow and walnut (T-639), red-brown and blue (T-640), yellow and yama green (T-641), pink and yama green (T-642), and yellow and gray (T-643).

Prices were somewhat less for this series of patterns than for many others: plates, 25¢ – 45¢; cup and saucer, 60¢; covered muffin tray, $1.75; and coffee server, $2.25. Examples of Duo-Tone are seen in the picture below.

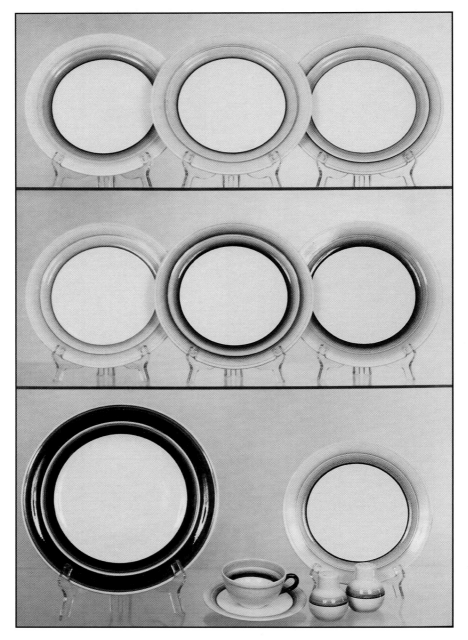

The items shown are Duo-Tone 9½" plates, exceptions noted, and one example of Two-Some, a very similar design.
TOP: T-636; T-635; T-634.
CENTER: T-633; T-637; yellow and walnut plate (probably T-639).
BOTTOM: Two-Some (a very similar design to that of Duo-Tone) T-698 12" chop plate; Duo-Tone T-638 cup and saucer and pair of salt and pepper shakers.

The following photographs show examples of other interesting Gale Turnbull designs done in his inimitable style.

Garden Plates.
TOP: Pea pods 12" chop plate.
BOTTOM: Asparagus and Onion 10½" plates.
Other items known in this series, believed to be a short set of dinnerware, are Celery, Ear of Corn, Artichoke, Pepper, and Beet, all 6½" plates, and a 13" salad bowl decorated with three stalks of celery. All are marked Garden Plates and are in sepia tones on ivory ground.

Zodiac.
TOP: Cancer and Leo, both 10½" plates.
BOTTOM: Taurus 14" chop plate.

Close-up view of Elephants 9½" plate of the Noah's Ark series.

Noah's Ark; all are 10½" plates.
TOP: Ark; Geese and pelicans.
CENTER: Noah's three sons, Ham, Shem, and Japhet; Noah; Mrs. Noah.
BOTTOM: Sheep; Giraffe.

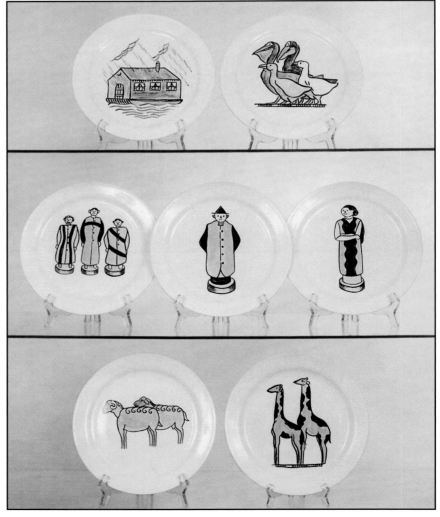

184

Organdie Group ∽ About the same time the Native American series was introduced, an early plaid group produced on the Montecito shape made its debut. The first plaid patterns in different color combinations were numbered only, all under the heading of Organdie. Thus far there are no records for the numbers, but known numbers start at 504 and may or may not be preceded by a *T.* A September 1937 ad in *Homes of the West* described the group colors as two-tone combinations of green, brown, blue, and pink-and-gray. A 1937 ad for the group described it as having the "bold, gay patterns of crisp organdie, subdued and mellowed by undertones of contrasting color and design." The ad stated that the plaid patterns were painted under glaze by hand, each piece bearing Mr. Turnbull's signature mark and available in sixteen different attractive color combinations on a neutral background. Colors were not given. Generally, the pattern number was under Turnbull mark 33 (see Evolution of Marks).

Yet another ad pictured Coronation Organdy (note the different spelling of *organdy*), stating that colors of this pattern were gray and rose. The Coronation Organdy pattern number is T-508. The Coronation Organdy ad listed a coffee server at $2.95 and a muffin dish at $2.25. At the present time, starting with number 504, 23 different patterns have been identified; only sixteen were mentioned in the ad (see Montecito pattern index, page 208).

These first plaids were the forerunners of the six popular Plaids of the 1940s and 1950s: Calico, Gingham, Homespun, Organdie, Tam O'Shanter, and Tweed. The Plaids were one of Vernon's most popular and successful pattern groups of all time. Sometimes the hand-painted patterns were displayed and sold in combination with boldly colored Early California or subdued, pastel Modern California.

Some early plaids.
TOP: T-607 demitasse cup and saucer; T-607 coffee server.
CENTER: Believed to be T-509 6½" plate; Organdie T-512 4" coaster; T-507 6½" plate.
BOTTOM: Unnamed Montecito 9½" plate, mark 8; Organdie T-506 12½" platter.

Another example of a plaid in the early Organdie group. T-605 fast-stand gravy boat.
John and Joanne Barrett photo.

An early egg cup. Unmarked, but believed to be T-513. *Bob Hutchins photo.*

Plaids ∽ The next several pages will feature the six plaids and some of the items that may be found in this group. An entire collection of Organdie was loaned for some of the pictures in this book. For this reason, and in order to show representative pieces found in the Montecito dinnerware line, most of these pictures are of Organdie pieces.

The Organdie pattern, as it is known today, was originally the No. 511 pattern in the early Organdie group. The numbers were eventually dropped, and the brown and yellow plaid combination was assigned the Organdie name. Items that are numbered 511 would indicate an earlier production piece. This pattern had the longest run of any plaid and perhaps the largest production of any dinnerware pattern. It has been said that Homespun was the all-time favorite during its days of production and continues to be a favorite today.

TOP: Coffee server on its own wrought iron stand.
CENTER: Coffee mug and style no. 5 tumbler (both are later styles); Organdie decorated disk pitcher (scarce); early style and rare no. 2 tumbler with a clip handle.
BOTTOM: Organdie coaster, 3¾" (note ridges in center); No. 511 coaster, 4½", also used as a cup warmer.

TOP: Comport (unmarked), pre-World War II.
CENTER: Trio buffet server, 11" across, 2½" deep (late 1950s, interchangeable with other lines); candlesticks, converted tea cups with brass fittings. Trio buffet server is extremely rare in any pattern other than the Transitional (Year 'Round) shape patterns.
BOTTOM: Organdie No. 511 covered muffin tray.

The Vernonware dealer display sign. *Tim and Linda Colling photo.*

An array of Organdie, mostly 1950s production pieces; exceptions are indicated.
TOP: Small round 7½" vegetable bowl; 9½" oval vegetable (early, pre-1950); 3½" pepper mill and salt shaker.
CENTER: 3½" chicken pie, stick handle; 5½" individual salad bowl; drip-cut top syrup; 3½" egg cup (early cupped shape); 3½" egg cup (later style); 3½" individual casserole.
BOTTOM: Spoon holder; 2½" butter pat; 3" diameter custard.

Homespun 10½" salad bowl and two 5½" individual salad bowls.
Bob Hutchins photo.

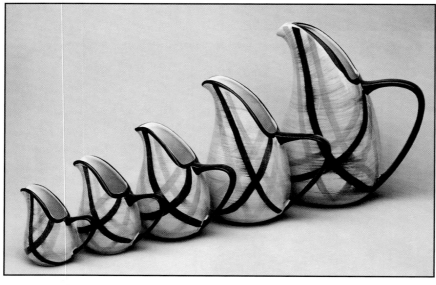

Streamline pitchers in five graduated sizes. Montecito patterns in the 1950s production period were interchangeable with those of the San Marino lines.
LEFT TO RIGHT: 4" ¼-pint, 5" ½-pint, 6" 1-pint, 8½" 1-quart, and 11" 2-quart.
Note: Small sizes of pitchers (especially ¼ pints) are hard to find.

A kerosene lamp has been reported in the Homespun pattern having hardware identical to Vernon's 1860 lamp pictured on page 266. The purchase price was $80.00. The collector was told that it had been originally purchased in the 1950s and that the hardware, along with the teapot, could once be purchased at the Vernon plant.

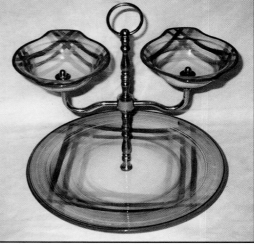

An unusual tidbit in Homespun. The bottom piece is a 14" chop plate. The style of the brass fixtures is the same as that of fixtures found on other company pieces. *Bob Hutchins photo.*

Three graduated sizes of flower pots (saucers are missing from the two smaller sizes) were produced in some 1950s Montecito patterns and were interchangeable with those in the San Marino lines. They are often found with the saucers missing.
LEFT TO RIGHT: 3", 5", and 4" diameter pots.

Four sizes of cups and saucers are pictured.
TOP: Jumbo cup and saucer.
CENTER LEFT: Tea cup and saucer.
BOTTOM: Demitasse cup and saucer.
CENTER RIGHT: Colossal cup and saucer. Colossal cup and saucers were also produced in the San Marino line.

The Colossal cup is a 4-quart version of the tea cup. A January 1953 price list stated that it was "ideal as a collector's item, or for display, salad, punch, fruit, popcorn, planting, and flower arrangement." It was also pictured in a company brochure as an ice bucket. The cup measures 9⅜" in diameter and is 5⅞" deep. The saucer measures 15". The Colossal cup and saucer is considered scarce and was made only for a brief period in the 1950s. The Jumbo cup and saucer are only slightly larger than the tea cup and saucer. The Jumbo cup is 4½" in diameter and the saucer is 6¾". In June 1955, the $12.95 Colossal cup and saucer was the most expensive item in a pattern; a regular tea cup and saucer was just $1.75.

Oddities in Homespun.
TOP: 9½" platter (San Clemente [Anytime] shape); gravy or batter bowl (Transitional [Year 'Round] shape).
BOTTOM: Divided vegetable bowl (Transitional [Year 'Round] shape); covered butter dish (San Marino shape); ring-handled cruet tray (San Clemente [Anytime] shape).
Bob Hutchins photo.

Two Homespun pieces (a 5" mixing bowl and a chicken pie server) with labels intact. The labels read: "Vernon-ware can be used as OVENWARE if used with reasonable care. Do not place on open burner or in preheated oven."
Bob Hutchins photo.

Homespun mug with an unusual mark. Generally, the banner mark (22) is found on mugs. *Bob Hutchins photo.*

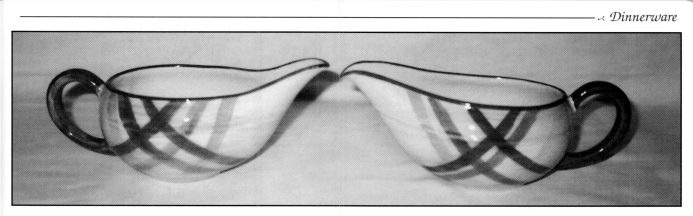

Two versions of the late, streamline-style Montecito sauce boat in Homespun. The spout on the boat at the left is taller and more narrow than on the boat on the right. *Bob Hutchins photo.*

America's Finest Dinnerware

Company brochure for Calico.

Examples of the six Plaids.
TOP: Tam O'Shanter stick-handled chicken pie server; Gingham 8" rim soup; Gingham lug chowder.
CENTER: Tweed creamer; covered casserole; teacup with Jumbo saucer.
BOTTOM: Calico salt and pepper shakers; Homespun tea cup and saucer, Organdie cup warmer is sitting on cup; Home-spun covered oblong ¼ lb. butter; Organdie 1-quart jug and 1-pint jug.
Note: A Calico 1-pint bulb pitcher with a script "Kellogg's" logo has been reported. "Kellogg's" appears under the glaze on both sides of the upper part of the pitcher. Apparently an advertising item and rare. Mark 21.

In 1953, table accessories were added to complement the Montecito and San Marino lines. These were black wrought iron dish holders, complete with glass candle warmers. There were three: Coffee Hot, Casserole Hot, and Casserole Round-Up. The Round-Up was designed to hold a covered casserole and six 4" individual casseroles or chicken pies.

A wrought iron tray to hold two rows of tumblers with pockets for the matching coasters has also been reported. Whether this was made specifically for Vernonware is not known.

Tam O'Shanter pieces. Covered casserole with Casserole Hot, and coffee server with Coffee Hot. *Tim and Linda Colling photo.*

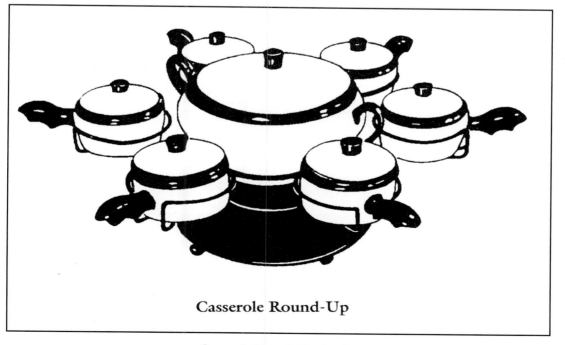

Casserole Round-Up

Casserole Round-Up sketch.

Company photo picturing Mr. Bennison with employees at a table setting of Plaids.
LEFT TO RIGHT: Ruth Penney of the Bogerts Advertising team; Bill Barber, national sales manager; E. V. Bogert, president of the Bogert Advertising Agency; Faye G. Bennison, president of Vernon Kilns; and Zepha Bogert, vice president of Bogerts.
Photo by Lydon Lippincott.

Organdie look-alikes.
LEFT TO RIGHT: Metlox Butterscotch 10½" plate; cup marked "Brown Plaid, Japan"; Colossal-sized cup and saucer marked "Cleminson."

An unmarked cup in a Brown Eyed Susan look-alike pattern, and a Jumbo-sized cup and saucer in a pattern apparently inspired by Homespun, marked "A CALIF CREATION BY ANGELES U.S.A. 'Highlander.'"
Tim and Linda Colling photo.

VERNON'S Tam O'Shanter

Fresh as Highland Heather

...and warm as a Scottish brogue! Diffused stripes of rust, chartreuse
d deep green combine to create an effect that is perfect with provincial,
delightful with Early American and yet...at the same time...sleek
and modern! You'll find Tam O'Shanter serving pieces are designed
for many uses, functional as well as decorative.

his delightful Vernon plaid pattern is hand-painted under the glaze...
guaranteed for 25 years against crazing or crackling...will not fade,
mar or wash off in the dishwasher or with years of use.

Available at:

A.

12-52

VERNON'S Tam O'Shan

OPEN STOCK	LIST PRICE	OPEN STOCK	LIST PRICE
Bowl, 1 Pt.	$1.15	Coffee Server, 10-Cup	$4.30
Butter Tray and Cover	2.95	Coffee Server Stopper	.70
Butter Tray	1.20	Creamer	1.85
Butter Cover	1.75	Custard Cup, 3"	.95
Butter, Ind., 2½"	.55	Egg Cup, Double	1.35
Casserole, Cov'd. 8"	5.75	3" Flower Pot & Saucer	1.50
Casserole, Cov'd., Ind. 4"	1.95	3" Flower Pot only	1.00
Casserole, Open, Ind. 4"	1.20	4" Flower Pot & Saucer	1.75
Chicken Pie, Cov'd., Ind. 4"	2.25	4" Flower Pot only	1.20
Chicken Pie, Open, Ind. 4"	1.50	5" Flower Pot & Saucer	2.00
12" Chop Plate	2.50	5" Flower Pot only	1.40
14" Chop Plate	4.25	Fruit	.65
Chowder	1.00	Lapel Plate, with Pin	1.00
Coaster, 4"	.65	Mug, 9 Oz.	1.35
Coffee Cup & Saucer, Jumbo	2.40	Pepper Mill	8.15
Coffee Cup, Jumbo	1.60	1 Pt. Pitcher	2.00
Coffee Saucer, Jumbo	.80	1 Qt. Pitcher	3.15
Coffee Cup and Saucer, A.D.	1.55	2 Qt. Pitcher	5.25
Coffee Cup, A.D.	1.00	6½" Plate	.65
Coffee Saucer, A.D.	.55	7½" Plate	.80
Coffee Server & Stopper, 10 Cup.	5.00	9½" Plate	1.05
		10½" Plate	1.30

A 1952 company brochure advertisement for Tam O'Shanter.

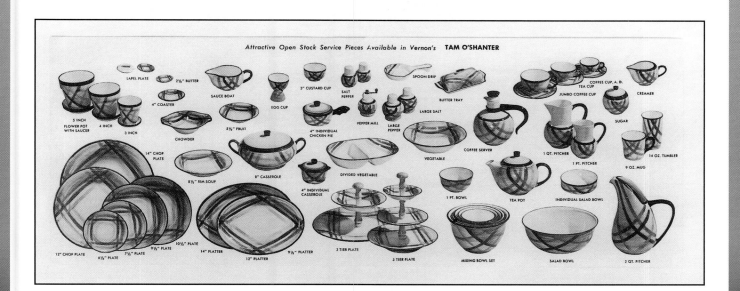

Brown Eyed Susan ∽ Equally popular as the Plaids was hand-painted Brown-Eyed Susan. The pattern has been found backstamped "838" on the Ultra shape, but it was generally produced on the Montecito shape.

Hand-painted patterns similar to Brown Eyed Susan (No. 838) are Linda (No. 836), No. 837 (name unknown), and Meadow Bloom (number unknown, but it may be in sequence). The four patterns all have similar floral motifs. The differences in each are in the color and the floral blossom. Other variations in these patterns are found in the manner in which the floral decorates the flatware; Linda's floral spray covers the center of the plate, Brown-Eyed Susan's goes across the top, 837 has an encircling floral ring, and Meadow Bloom's floral runs across the top. Except for Meadow Bloom, examples of the plates are seen in pictures following. The only example of Meadow Bloom is the creamer pictured on page 199. Again, as in the Organdie group, the pattern numbers of Brown-Eyed Susan and Linda were eventually discontinued in favor of a pattern name. Note that the blossom sprays in the earlier 836 Linda pattern were fuller. The later Linda had simpler floral sprays.

Michael Pratt furnished the author with a copy of an ad for the California Pottery Guild that appeared in an April 1942 issue of *Crockery and Glass Journal*. The black and white copy pictured what appears to be the Linda pattern, described as "Named for Los Angeles' famous tourist attraction, 'Olvera' is the newest decoration on Vernonware's popular Montecito shape. A vivd modern adaptation of gay Mexican designs, it features Loganberry Red, Iris Blue, and Hunter's Green." Items pictured were a coffee server, a mug, an oval serving bowl, a butter tray with an angular lid, and dinner and chop plates.

Occasionally, one will find decorated Brown Eyed Susan glassware that was done by Imperial Glass on their Continental line, identified in their 1953 catalog as 176/Dec. Susan. Seven oz. sherbets, 12 oz. goblets, and 14 oz. tumblers were hand painted. According to the catalog information, there were as many as 17 different items decorated in the pattern. Some were still available as late as 1958.

Plaid-decorated glassware also is sometimes found. Although there are no known Vernon Kilns records to substantiate, this decorated glassware may have been the product of the Gay Fad Studio. According to columnists Ralph and Terry Kovel (King Features Syndicate), Gay Fad Studio in Lancaster, Ohio, decorated glass to match popular ceramic dinnerware patterns. Their column states that the company was founded by Fran Taylor, who opened her factory in 1945. The factory closed in 1965.

Brown Eyed Susan and more Plaid items are seen in this photo. All have mark 21 unless noted.
TOP: Organdie creamer (mark 22), note difference in spout compared to Meadow Bloom creamer in photo on page 199; Brown-Eyed Susan sugar bowl (mark 22); Organdie 10½" salad bowl (an individual 5½" salad bowl is shown on page 188 and in the company brochure on page 195).
CENTER: Gingham 7½" round vegetable; Brown-Eyed Susan sauce boat (mark 22); 10" oval vegetable; Organdie No. 513 9½" plate (mark 33); Brown-Eyed Susan 838 Ultra shape (mark 19).
BOTTOM: Tam O'Shanter chowder; Homespun butter pat or lapel pin (marked "Vernonware, Calif. U.S.A." only); Brown-Eyed Susan 9" round vegetable; Tam O'Shanter 4¼" coaster or cup warmer; Organdie 8½" rim soup.

Two sugar bowls with very similar hand-painted blossom patterns.
LEFT: Vernon's 837.
RIGHT: Linda 836.
Tim and Linda Colling photo.

Floral Wreath (author's name for pattern) was a pattern produced by Vernon Kilns for Frederik Lunning, Inc., New York, under the Lunning trade name (see page 310). There are striking similarities of the Lunning pattern to Vernon's 837, but differences can be observed upon closer examination. The main difference appears to be in the shape of the leaves in the floral ring. This may be noted in the pictures below.

Vernon's 837 plate alongside Lunning's Floral Wreath plate. Both plates are 14". *Tim and Linda Colling photo.*

Some scarce Brown Eyed Susan items and some with additional Plaids; all have mark 22 unless otherwise noted.

TOP: Brown Eyed Susan 4" pepper mill (unmarked); Gingham 1-pint bowl; Calico large pepper shaker (unmarked), shown on Calico saucer (mark 21).

CENTER: Organdie 8" covered casserole (actually measures 11" including handles; 8" is inside diameter and is size listed in company price lists); Tam O'Shanter 11½" double vegetable (mark 21); Organdie T-512 saucer (mark 33, initials only); Brown Eyed Susan 3" regular size salt shaker (unmarked); Tweed wood-handled 14" serving tray (mark 21).

BOTTOM: Organdie chamberstick (saucer with aluminum fittings, base covers mark); Organdie butter tray and cover; Brown Eyed Susan saucer chamberstick (with brass fittings, base covers mark). Both chambersticks are scarce.

Candlesticks were also made from tea cups with brass fittings, and a chandelier utilizing tea cups was also made.

Featured on the cover of Carnation's 1954 *Mary Blake Favorite Recipes* were Homespun mugs and salt and pepper shakers in color. Two different Betty Crocker cookbooklets had, to illustrate breakfast recipes, color photographs that included Brown Eyed Susan (not shown).

All patterns pictured up to this point have been hand painted. The next photographs will show examples of transfer patterns as well as additional hand-painted patterns.

In the picture below, there is an example of Blossoms T-704 (top center). Blossoms T-704 (blue flowers, yellow center) has two alternate color combinations: T-702 (pink flowers, black centers) and T-703 (yellow flowers, brown centers). See an example of T-702 in the second picture below.

TOP: Blossoms T-704 10½" plate; Duo-tone T-638 9½" plate. Both plates have mark 33.
BACK CENTER: Victoria transfer print 9½" plate, mark 16; Linda 836 14" chop plate, mark 19; 707 14½" oval platter, mark 19.
FRONT CENTER: 707 teapot, mark 19; Gingham 10½" platter, mark 21; Dainty transfer sugar without lid, mark 16, same as Victoria but a different color (counterpart patterns Trailing Rose and Dame shown in first photograph on the next page.)
BOTTOM: Meadow Bloom creamer, mark 21; 707 8½" platter, mark 19; Organdie spoon holder, mark 21; ceramic card-holder dealer sign, unmarked; Mexicana creamer and saucer, mark 21.

Blossoms T-702 with pink blossoms. *Tim and Linda Colling photo.*

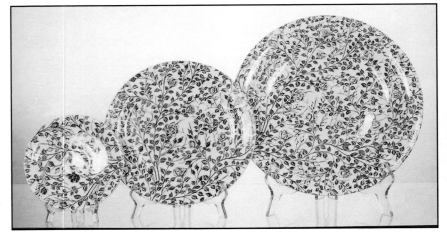

Vernon Kilns chintz-style transfer patterns.
LEFT TO RIGHT: Dame 6" saucer; Victoria 9½" plate; Trailing Rose 12" chop plate. The counterpart, Dainty, is in the picture on the preceding page.

Blossoms T-704 with blue blossoms. Early Montecito tumbler shape no. 3, 4" tall.
Tim and Linda Colling photo.

Another floral counterpart series by Turnbull (perhaps named after the members of a family).
BACK ROW: 9½" luncheon plates in Hadley (hand tinted on blue transfer), Thom (hand tinted on brown transfer), and Marie (hand tinted on maroon transfer). Plain print, untinted pieces in all three colors share the name June.
FRONT ROW: June saucers with blue, maroon, and brown transfers. The mark is a variation of mark 33.
Bob Hutchins photo.

Winchester '73 ⟶ In 1950, the Winchester '73 pattern was designed at Vernon Kilns. Heisey Glass Company of Newark, Ohio, matched it with their etched barware, also called Winchester '73. The dinnerware and stemware were tied in with the promotion and introduced simultaneously as Universal International's motion picture *Winchester '73*, starring James Stewart and Shelley Winters. The movie opened at the Paramount theatre in New York on June 7, 1950, and was released throughout the country during July, August, and September. Theatres were eager to show which stores in their respective areas handled the Winchester '73 pattern.

A company brochure described the pattern: "All the romance of the winning of the west is in this attractive new pattern… designed with a particular eye to masculine taste… for casual dining anytime, anywhere. Winchester '73 has he-man appeal with its bold Western scenes, cowboys, covered wagons… in dramatic colors on a soft green background." (It has been noted that background colors are not consistent and vary from creamy to grayish to soft green.) Faye Bennison informed the author that the design had originally been made for 500 coffee mugs presented to employees and guests at a Winchester Arms convention. One could speculate that perhaps these mugs were identical to those mugs sold with the sets. At any rate, no mugs of this type with a corporate logo are known to have been found.

By January of 1953, the pattern name was changed to Frontier Days due to a conflict with the Winchester Arms company over the use of its name.

Paul Davidson did the artwork and almost every piece carries his signature, sometimes humorously obscured in the artwork. For example, the vegetable bowl pictures the "Davidson's saloon" and its "proprietor, P. L. Davidson." Collectors will be delighted to learn this pattern has many extra pieces.

In the next two photographs are examples of the Winchester '73 or Frontier Days transfer print pattern. (See Evolution of Marks, page 8, for either mark 42 or 43.)

TOP: 14" chop plate; 10½" dinner plate; cup and saucer.
BOTTOM: 9" round vegetable; 6½" plate; 10" oval platter; covered creamer; 7½" plate.
Notes: Variations in the 14" chop plates have been found. The rifle picture was produced on both the Ultra and Montecito shapes. A different picture of a cowboy on a bucking horse appeared on both the Melinda and the Montecito shapes. Examples of the Melinda and Montecito plates are shown.

TOP: Pepper grinder and salt shaker, wood is inlaid with the patterned pottery (unmarked); 8" flat rim soup; stick-handled chicken pie server.
CENTER: 14" chop plate (Melinda shape); two tumblers (style no. 5) that show scenes on either side; two mugs showing scenes on either side.
BOTTOM: Three of a set of five nested mixing bowls.

The unmarked Montecito 10½" plate shown here is a rare Till Goodan artist-signed piece. The western scene is that of a cowboy roping a steer.

1950 company photo of sales representatives, a Frontier Days promotional.
LEFT TO RIGHT: Max May, Arizona; Nort Meyer, Texas; Walter Songster, Colorado; Jay Sutton, Colorado; and Bill Barber, company sales manager.

Vernon WINCHESTER '73

Open Stock

Item	List Price	Item	List Price
Ash Tray	$1.25	2 Qt. Pitcher	5.95
Bowl, 1 Pt.	1.40	6½" Plate	1.00
Butter Tray and Cover	3.40	7½" Plate	1.20
Butter Tray	1.40	9½" Plate	1.65
Butter Cover	2.00	10½" Plate	1.95
8" Casserole, Covered	6.45	12" Platter	3.25
12" Chop Plate	3.25	14" Platter	4.50
14" Chop Plate	4.75	16" Platter	5.95
Chowder	1.50	8½" Rim Soup	1.50
4" Coaster or Ash Tray	1.00	5½" Salad Bowl,	
Coffee Cup and Saucer,		Individual	1.40
Jumba	2.75	10½" Salad Bowl	5.25
Coffee Cup, Jumbo	1.65	Sauce Boat, Reg.	2.95
Coffee Saucer, Jumbo	1.10	Shaker, Pepper	1.15
Coffee Cup and Saucer,		Shaker, Salt	1.15
A.D.	2.05	Sugar, Covered	2.95
Coffee Cup, A.D.	1.20	Tea Cup and Saucer	2.25
Coffee Saucer, A.D.	.85	Tea Cup	1.30
Coffee Server and		Tea Saucer	.95
Stopper, 10 Cup	5.45	Tea Pot, Covered, 8 Cup	5.95
Coffee Server, 10 Cup	4.75	14 Oz. Tumbler	1.35
Coffee Server Stopper	.70	Vegetable Dish, Divided	5.50
Creamer	2.25	10" Vegetable, Oval	1.95
5½" Fruit	1.00	9" Vegetable, Round	1.95
9 Oz. Mug	1.50	4 Pc. Mixing Bowl Set	8.35
Pepper Mill	9.50	Special Retail Price	7.95
Salt Cellar	6.50	5 Pc. Mixing Bowl Set	12.10
1 Pt. Pitcher	2.25	Special Retail Price	10.95
1 Qt. Pitcher	3.95		

STARTER SET (16 pcs.) List Price 20.80
SPECIAL RETAIL PRICE 15.95

VERNON KILNS • VERNONWARE • Los Angeles 58, Calif.

Please send me_____ Starter Sets Winchester '73 @ $15.95
per 16 pc. set.

Cash_____ Charge_____ C.O.D._____

Name_____

Address_____

City_____ Zone_____ State_____

CREATED BY CALIFORNIA VERNONWARE

Company literature for Winchester '73.

Coronado ∽ This solid-colored pattern and variation of the Montecito shape was available as premium ware from about 1936 to possibly as late as 1939 or 1940. The pattern may have been sold in retail stores as well. In the eastern states, it was reportedly obtained at gas stations. In Southern California, it was offered at a major supermarket chain. Nationwide, it was available with a label from Lynden Chicken Fricassee, as seen in the pictured *Sunset* magazine ad of April 1938, found on page 207.

The Lynden ad stated that the dish colors available were blue, orange, green, and yellow, which were the same colors used for Early California. Exclusively Coronado colors were light green, light blue, peach, and pink (not the same as the Early California pink). These pastels are scarce and desired by collectors. Turquoise, white, and brown, all Early California colors also, have been found as well, making a total of eleven known colors for Coronado. Much of this ware is unmarked, but when it is, mark 10 or mark 11 is the most commonly seen. Less commonly found marks are mark 6 and mark 12.

As is shown in the photos, Coronado is easily recognized by its angular handles and the cubist band about half an inch below the rims of the hollow ware and on the rims of the flatware and the tumblers. The angular sugar bowl had two handles and came without a lid. It is believed that some pieces were redesigned in or after 1938; namely, the creamer, the sugar with lid, and the cups and saucers. The redesign placed the cubist band at the base of the hollow ware. The saucer was redesigned with about a ¼" wider indent that would hold the wider-based cup. Salt and pepper shakers were apparently introduced with the later redesign. Maverick Organdie-decorated shakers are pictured. The disk pitcher, standard in Ultra and Montecito shapes but not part of the Coronado line, has been found in the Coronado light green shade. Coronado pink was used on the 129 bowl (page 77).

Coronado was a short set; items known to have been produced are 6½" and 9½" plates, a 5½" fruit, a 7½" soup, a 9" serving bowl, tumblers, a 12½" platter, a carafe and stopper, salt and pepper shakers, a sugar bowl (angular without lid), a sugar bowl with lid (later), and a creamer. Some angular pieces have dry feet, whereas the redesigned pieces have glazed feet. Coronado is generally on the low end value-wise, except for hard-to-find items or colors (pastels or white).

All Coronado items pictured are unmarked, except as noted. Sometimes they will be found marked only "Made in U.S.A."

TOP: 12½" oval platter; sugar bowl with cubist band at base; 9" vegetable, mark 10.
CENTER: Coffee server, cubist band encircles middle; 6½" plate, mark 11; saucer, mark 11; cup, mark 10; tumbler; 7½" flat rim soup, mark 10; two 6½" plates.
BOTTOM: Creamer, mark 10; cup with band at base; 5½" fruit; creamer with band at base.

Two styles of sugar bowls.
LEFT: Redesigned lidded sugar bowl with its lid, cubist band at base.
RIGHT: Earlier sugar bowl (not lidded), cubist band at top.

Coronado orange carafe and stopper; a green Coronado tumbler, transformed into a mug with a clip-on wood and metal handle. *Bob Hutchins photo.*

Coronado pastel pieces: peach tumbler, light green redesigned creamer, pink redesigned sugar bowl with lid, and light blue shakers.
Bob Hutchins photo.

Coronado shakers with Organdie decoration, marked "Hand Painted Underglaze Pottery," in block letters. The early Romeo and Juliet decal has also been found decorating the shape. See page 25. *Bob Hutchins photo.*

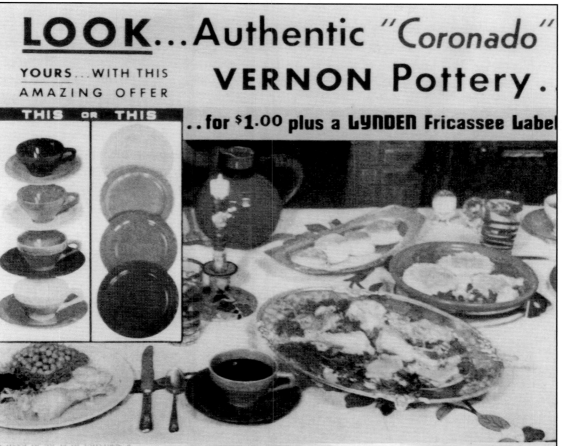

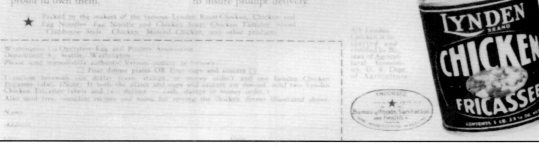

A full page color ad from the April 1938 issue of *Sunset* magazine. Lynden was offering partial sets of Coronado dinnerware for $1.00 and a label from its Chicken Fricassee can.

Montecito Pattern Index

The following are all known patterns on the Montecito shape. All are hand painted and on ivory ground unless otherwise specified. "S.O." designates a special order, and quotation marks around a pattern name indicate that it is not an official company name, merely a label provided by the author to aid reference.

Name	Description	Approx. Period of Production	Artist
After Glow	Matte color. Two-tone yellow and ivory.	1935 – 1937	Bird
Anchor	Nautical series. Simple anchor design.	1935 – 1937	Bird
Arizona	Native American series. Saguaro cacti and purple hills.	1937	Turnbull
Autumn Ballet	Hollow ware only. See Ultra for description.	1941	Disney
Avocado	Matte color. Two-tone green and ivory.	1935 – 1937	Bird
Aztec	Authentic Aztec designs, Montezuma and Olinala.	1935 – 1937	Bird
Banana Tree	Native American series. Banana tree, ivory or sand background.	1937	Turnbull
"Banded Flower"	See BB, BG, BP, BY series. First letter indicates Bird, second is code for color, number is flower.	1935 – 1937	Bird
Barbary Fig	Native American series. Prickly pear cactus.	1937	Turnbull
Barbary Ho	Native American series. Same as Barbary Fig, except sand ground.	1937	Turnbull
Barrel Cactus	Native American series. Cacti, mountain scene. For Barker Bros. (Los Angeles furniture store no longer in business).	1937	Turnbull
Begonia	Floral series.	1935 – 1937	Bird
Beige	All over beige color.	1935 – 1937	Bird
Bird Series	Series picturing birds, including Scarlet Tanager, Parrots, Blue Birds, Bird Ring. Only one has been found with pattern number, B-353.	1935 – 1937	Bird
Bird's Eye	Floral series.	1935 – 1937	Bird
Bird's Solid Colors	See Matte colors.	1935 – 1937	Bird
Blend Series	Contrasting or same colors in different shades blended from center to outside rim. Numbers begin at 1 and go up to 19, but some numbers are missing. There may be other color combinations for missing numbers.	1938	Turnbull
Blend No. 1	Russet in center to pale yellow to deep yellow rim.		
Blend No. 2	Two shades of blue.		
Blend No. 4	Bright yellow to green.		
Blend No. 5	Golden yellow to black.		
Blend No. 6	Gray to yellow.		
Blend No. 9	Pale pink to dusty pink.		
Blend No. 10	Pink to green.		
Blend No. 12	Reported to be yellow to orange to lime.		
Blend No. 19	Cherry to slate gray.		

Name	Description	Approx. Period of Production	Artist
Blooming Cactus	B-321, roly-poly barrel cactus and prickly pear cactus border design. May be in Spectrum series.	1935 – 1937	Bird
Blossoms	Scattered blossoms decorate the pattern. T-702, pink blossoms, black centers. T-703, yellow blossoms, brown centers. T-704, blue blossoms, yellow centers.	1937 – 1938	Turnbull
Blue Glazes	Soft blue glazes with darker blue designs. The blue glazing was an exclusive Vernon process. See T-651 Constellation, T-652, T-659.	1937 – 1938	Turnbull
Bridal Satin	Matte color. All over ivory.	1935 – 1937	Bird
Brown Eyed Susan	See 838. Yellow daisies, green leaves. Meadow Bloom has similar design.	1942 – 1958	
B-100	Lily blue on blue ground.	1935 – 1937	Bird
B-102	Iris in shades of blue on blue ground.		
B-103	Eucalyptus. Unusual cup-shaped yellow flower with orange center and black stamens, green leaves, dark color stem.		
B-118	Phacelia on Golden Maple ground.		
B-119	Unidentified floral on Golden Maple ground.		
B-?	Trumpet Flower on Golden Maple ground – not numbered.		
B-138	Iris on Avocado ground.		
B-139	Mariposa Tulip on Avocado ground.		
B-140	Fiddleneck on Avocado ground.		
B-148	Floral on yellow ground is reported. Yellow may be After Glow.		
B-156	Blue floral, yellow ground.		
B-202	Border design of varying sizes of color splashes large yellow to small green, sand ground.		
B-300	Spectrum series. Geometric design of orange and green ¼" dots spaces and separated by narrow wavy yellow line forms border design.		
B-304	Spectrum series. Border design of pencil-thin lines in red, blue, yellow, green, spaced horizontally on rim only.		
B-305	Spectrum series. Bright green tubular flowers, yellow stamens connected by curving line forms border design.		
B-310	Spectrum series. Geometric triangular border design in vivid multicolors.		
B-313	Spectrum series. All-over geometric design is all that is known.		
B-321	See Blooming Cactus. Roly-poly barrel cactus and prickly pear cactus border design. May be Spectrum.		
B-325	Pictured in company booklet as Spectrum. Off center floral.		
B-327	Spectrum series. Polychromatic stylized all-over petal outline. Same as Multi Flori California except B-327 is multicolored.		

Name	Description	Approx. Period of Production	Artist
B-353	Bird series. Lone blue bird in flight, green foliage offside.		
B-?	Bird series. Lone bird perched on shallow bowl, brightly feathered in orange and yellow and having a long orange and green tail.		
B-?	Bird series. Two blue birds in flight amid sprigs with orange berries.		
B-?	Bird series. Orange-crested blue bird, long tailed, touch of orange and yellow feathers, perched on large orange blossom, and green leaves.		
B-?	Bird series. Round-bodied blue bird with long curving tail feathers, sipping nectar from flowers.		
B-?	Bird series. Bird ring, design of birds encircle rim.		
BB-1,2,6	"Banded Flower." Wide blue border, #1 cobalt blue flower in center, #2 blue flower in center, #6 blue and orange flower.		
BG-5, 3	"Banded Flower." Wide green border, #5 pink flower in center, #3 yellow flower.		
BP-1, 3, 5, 6	"Banded Flower." Wide pink border, #1 pink flower, #3 yellow flower, #6 dark blue flower. Flowers may differ.		
BY-2, 3, 4, 5	"Banded Flower." Wide yellow border, #2 blue flower, #3 rose flower, #4 yellow flower, #5 pink flower.		
Cabanas Chico	Native American series. Couple in native dress, yellow mission, palm trees, mountains.	1937	Turnbull
Calico	Plaid group. One of six later patterns. Pink and blue with blue rim.	1949 – 1954 S.O. 1955	
Casa California	Company brochure state six patterns but only pictured T-629 and T-632. (See numbers.) Described as provincial peasant floral designs in browns and yellows, and blues and greens.	1938	Turnbull
Casa California Hermosa	Described as elaborate peasant ware design. In pinks and greens, browns and yellows, and blues and greens. See T-630, T-631, T-669, T-670, T-671, and T-673.	1938	Turnbull
Cassia	Floral series.	1935 – 1937	Bird
Checker Bloom	Floral series.	1935 – 1937	Bird
Chinese Lantern	Floral series.	1935 – 1937	Bird
Cholla	Native American series. Pictures cactus.	1937	Turnbull
Coastline Series	Map outlines of coastal regions of Atlantic, Pacific, Gulf of Mexico, Lake Michigan. Blue, black outlines.	1937 – 1942	Turnbull
Columbine	Floral series.	1935 – 1937	Bird
Constellation	Blue glaze. See T-651. Previously named "Blue Star."	1938	Turnbull
Contrast No.1	Hand-painted narrow bands of orange, green, and brown on rim.	1937	Turnbull
Coronado	Name of shape and pattern. A variation of the Montecito shape. Early design had cubist band at top rim of angular hollow ware. Later redesigned, cubist band was at base of rounded hollow ware. Solid colors: dark blue, brown, yellow, orange, blue, turquoise, pink, peach, white, light green, light blue. Sometimes found decorated with decals, such as Mexican "Romeo and Juliet" scene. Mostly sold as premium ware.	1936 – 1939	

Name	Description	Approx. Period of Production	Artist
Coronation Organdy	Early plaid group. See T-508.	1937	Turnbull
Cottage Window	Pictures window with tie-back curtains and potted plant on sill.	1937	Turnbull
Country Side	Green transfer print, touches of red. Rural scenes of farmland and village. Unmarked Vernon Kilns. Backstamped da Bron.	1950	Davidson
Dainty	Pink hand-tinted transfer print. Tiny roses and leaves in all-over design. Counterpart patterns are Dame, Trailing Rose, Victoria.	1939	
Dame	Blue hand-tinted transfer print. Tiny roses and leaves in all-over design. Counterpart patterns are Dainty, Trailing Rose, Victoria.	1939	
Decorated Pastels	Series is described in company booklet as underglaze designs on soft, pastel colors of lavender, mauve, pink. Dainty conventional designs. See T-653, T-654, T-655, T-656, T-657. Missing numbers must be other patterns in series.	1937	Turnbull
Desert Mallow	Floral series.	1935 – 1937	Bird
Desert Poppy	Floral series.	1935 – 1937	Bird
Duo-Tone Series	Border design of two contrasting color bands, 11 in series. See T-633 through T-643.	1938	Turnbull
Early California	Solid colors. Pre-1946, orange, dark blue, pink, brown, turquoise, blue, ivory, green, maroon. 1946 colors: green, blue, peach, turquoise, and yellow.	1935 – 1950	
Eucalyptus	Floral series. B-103.	1935 – 1937	Bird
Evening Star	Matte color. Two-tone blue and ivory.	1935 – 1937	Bird
Fairyland	Hollow ware only. See Ultra for description.	1941	Disney
Fantail	Tropical fish design.	1935 – 1937	Bird
Fantasia	Hollow ware only. See Ultra for description.	1941	Disney
FGB	Monograms.	1935 – 1937	Bird
Fiddleneck	Floral series.	1935 – 1937	Bird
Fish	May not be a dinnerware pattern. Only plates have been seen; they are marked "FISH."	1938	Turnbull
Flags	Nautical series. Simple flag design.	1935 – 1937	Bird
Fleet	Sailing ships on sand ground. Believed to be part of Marine series.	1937	Turnbull
Floral Series	Each pattern features the flower named. Design may vary slightly from piece to piece. To date, flowers are Begonia, Bird's Eye, Cassia, Checker Bloom, Chinese Lantern, Columbine, Desert Mallow, Desert Poppy, Eucalyptus, Fiddleneck, Geranium, Golden Brodiaea, Guatomote, Incienso, Iris, Lady Slipper, Larkspur, Lily Blue, Lily Orange, Lion's Tail, Lupin, Mariposa Tulip, Morning Glory, Nasturtium, Petunia, Phacelia, Trumpet Flower, Water Lily, Wild Pink.	1935 – 1937	Bird

Name	Description	Approx. Period of Production	Artist
"Floral Wreath"	Author's name for Frederik Lunning, Inc., NY, unnamed pattern. Hand-painted teal blue and yellow blossoms spaced encircling wreath of leaves.	1940	
Frontier Days	Brown hand-tinted transfer print. Western scenes. Originally named Winchester '73. (See Winchester '73.)	1953 S.O. 1954	Davidson
Garden Plate	Believed to be a short set of dinnerware. Items known are Celery, Pea Pods, Onion, Corn, Artichoke, Pepper, Beet, Asparagus. In sepia on ivory ground.	1938	Turnbull
Geranium	Floral series.	1935 – 1937	Bird
Gingham	Plaid group, one of six patterns. Green and yellow with green rim.	1949 – 1958	
Going to Town	Native American series. Couple in native dress strolling (towards left).	1937	Turnbull
Golden Brodiaea	Floral series.	1935 – 1937	Bird
Golden Maple	Matte color. Two-tone light orange-brown and ivory.	1935 – 1937	Bird
Guatomote	Floral series.	1935 – 1937	Bird
Guerrillas	Native American series. Pictures a group of banditos.	1937	Turnbull
Hadley	Floral series. Hand decorated on blue transfer. Counterpart patterns are June, Marie, and Thom.	1937	Turnbull
Homespun	Plaid group, one of six patterns. Green, rust, and yellow plaid with rust border.	1949 – 1958	
Incienso	Floral series.	1935 – 1937	Bird
"Indian Jars"	Native American series. See T-623 and T-622. Colorful Indian jars and cacti motif.	1937	Turnbull
Iris	Floral series.	1935 – 1937	Bird
Jaune	Spectrum series. Small yellow leaves connected by single yellow line encircles rim. Same as Vert except for color.	1935 – 1937	Bird
June	Floral series. Found in blue, maroon, and brown transfers. Counterpart patterns are Hadley, Marie, and Thom.	1937	Turnbull
Lady Slipper	Floral series.	1935 – 1937	Bird
Lantern	Nautical series. Simple design of ship's lantern.	1935 – 1937	Bird
Larkspur	Floral series.	1935 – 1937	Bird
Las Palmas	Native American series. Pueblo scene on ivory or sand ground.	1937	Turnbull
Life Saver	Nautical series. Simple lifesaver design.	1935 – 1937	Bird
Lily Blue	Floral series.	1935 – 1937	Bird
Lily Orange	Floral series.	1935 – 1937	Bird
Linda	See 836. Blue and maroon floral, maroon rim.	1942 – 1950	
Lion's Tail	Floral series.	1935 – 1937	Bird
Little Mission	Native American series. Scene of mission and palms. Ivory or sand ground.	1937	Turnbull

Name	Description	Approx. Period of Production	Artist
Lupin	Floral series.	1935 – 1937	Bird
Man O' War	Sailing ships scene. Sand ground. Believed to be part of Marine series.	1937	Turnbull
Marie	Floral series. Hand decorated on maroon transfer. Counterpart patterns are Hadley, June, Thom.	1937	Turnbull
Marine Series	Nautical motifs of windjammers, spouting whales, and portholes. Also marked "Whaling Service." Outline colors of blues, greens, and brown.	1937	Turnbull
Mariposa Tulip	Floral series.	1935 – 1937	Bird
Matte Colors	Two-tone combining colors with ivory to white. Matte finish. Hollow ware lined with color, outer side is ivory; lids and flatware have color on top and ivory on bottom. Patterns in series are After Glow, Avocado, Bridal Satin (all ivory), Evening Star, Golden Maple, Pomegranate, and Tangerine.	1935 – 1937	Bird
Meadow Bloom	Rose and blue flowers, brown shaded border. Same as Brown Eyed Susan, different colors.	1942	
Mexicana	Bands of color on border in shades of deep yellow to rust to dark brown. See San Marino. In a 1950 price list, a pencil notation indicated this pattern was on the Montecito shape. It was pictured in a 1951 company catalog on the San Marino shape.	1950 S.O. 1954	
Michigan Coastline	Map outlines of Lake Michigan decorate each piece. May be found marked "Coastline."	1937 – 1942	Turnbull
Milkweed Dance	Hollow ware only. See Ultra for description.	1941	Disney
Modern California	Solid colors. From 1937: Azure, Orchid, Pistachio, Straw, Sand, and Mist. Sand and Mist no longer produced after 1946. Ivory and a deeper yellow have also been found.	1937 – 1949	
Monograms	WHB, FGB, RAM, BB (BB on Ultra may not be Bird).	1935 – 1937	Bird
Montecito	Both shape and pattern name. Some early pieces have backstamp with name Montecito, mark 8.	1935	
Montezuma-Aztec	One of two Aztec patterns. Leaf border design. Known colors: rose, yellow, deep blue and green on warm beige ground.	1937	Bird
Morning Glory	Floral series.	1935 – 1937	Bird
Mountain Mission	Native American series. Yellow mission and pueblo, mountain.	1937	Turnbull
Multi-Aster	T-680. Simple yellow blossom, yellow rim.	1937	Turnbull
Multi-Flori California	Spectrum series. Monochromatic stylized overall petal outline in green, brown, blue, yellow, rose, or orange. May be backstamped "Made expressly for Barker Bros." Same pattern as B-327 (polychromatic).	1935 – 1937	Bird
Multi-Lines	T-686. Hand-painted Easter motif.	1937	Turnbull

Name	Description	Approx. Period of Production	Artist
Nasturtium	Floral series.	1935 – 1937	Bird
Native American Series	Series of patterns, all depicting desert and scenes of old California. Includes: Arizona, Banana Tree, Barbary Fig, Barbary Ho, Barrel Cactus, Cabanas Chico, Cholla, Going to Town, Guerrillas, Indian Jars (T-622 and T-623 author's designation), Las Palmas, Little Mission, Mountain Mission, Palm Springs, Pedro and Conchita, Pepita, Peppers, Pueblo, Sentinels, Smoke Tree, Solitude, Southwest, Still Life, Totem (T-620), T-621. Ivory, sand, or blue ground.	1937	Turnbull
Nautical	Each item in the pattern is named for its nautical theme: Anchor, Flags, Lantern, Life Saver, Sextant, Square Knot, Wheel. Colors are blue and red on ivory ground.	1935 – 1937	Bird
Noah's Ark	May not be a dinnerware pattern. Each plate portrays a different subject: Ark, Noah, Mrs. Noah; Ham, Shem, Japhet (sons); Giraffes, Geese and pelicans, Sheep, Elephants.	1937	Turnbull
North Wind	Two-color combination of wide dark green band and lime green center. May have been experimental.	Not Known	
Olinala-Aztec	One of two Aztec patterns. Floral and geometric band. Soft blue, green, yellow, rose, or orange on beige ground.	1935 – 1937	Bird
Organdie	Plaid, brown and yellow. One of later six Plaids. Originally T-511 in the Organdie Group.	1936 – 1958	Turnbull
Organdie	The early plaids were introduced under the group heading Organdie in about 1936. An ad stated that there were 16 different color combinations. However, more than 16 are listed in this pattern index, starting with T-504. These are all the early plaids that have been reported. See T-numbers.	1936	Turnbull
Organdy, Coronation	See T-508, one in early group, different spelling.	1936	Turnbull
Painted Pig	Design featuring several animals — may not be a dinnerware pattern.	1935 – 1937	Bird
Palm Springs	Native American series. Mountain and palm tree. The pattern has also been found marked "for Barker Brothers."	1937	Turnbull
Pedro and Conchita	Native American series. Man and woman in native dress.	1937	Turnbull
Peppers	Native American series. Multicolor peppers on ivory or sand ground.	1937	Turnbull
Pepita	Native American series. Pictures girl standing in front of pueblos. Similar to Pueblo pattern.	1937	Turnbull
Petunia	Floral Series.	1935 – 1937	Bird
Phacelia	Floral Series.	1935 – 1937	Bird
Plaids — Early	See T- numbers beginning with T-504.	1937	Turnbull
Plaids — Late	Six different plaid combinations: Calico, Gingham, Homespun, Organdie, Tam O'Shanter, Tweed. See individual pattern for description and time period.		

Name	Description	Approx. Period of Production	Artist
Polychrome	A, B, C, D, and E identify the different color combinations for this part of the Spectrum series. Border design of blocks resembling tiles of various color and sizes. Possibly Spectrum. A: Largest block is orange. B: Largest block is green. C: Largest block reported to be yellow. D: Unknown. E: Largest block is lime green.	1935 – 1937	Bird
Pomegranate	Matte color. Two-tone pink and ivory.	1935 – 1937	Bird
Porthole	Marine series.	1937	Turnbull
Pueblo	Native American series. Similar to Cabanas Chico. Scene of lady balancing pot on head, three-level cabana, mountains. Ivory or sand ground. Also reported with blue ground.	1937	Turnbull
RAM	Monogram. Not known if part of a dinnerware set.	1935 – 1937	Bird
Sentinels	Native American series. Desert rock formations, mesas, and cacti. Ivory or sand ground.	1937	Turnbull
Sextant	Nautical series. Simple design of instrument which determines latitude and longitude at sea.	1935	Bird
Smoke Tree	Native American series. Smoke tree bush (a shrub that bears minute flowers suggestive of smoke) and desert.	1937	Turnbull
Solitude	Native American series. Desert scene, lone saguaro and hills. Similar to Arizona.	1937	Turnbull
Southwest	Native American series. Pictures pueblos.	1937	Turnbull
Spectrum Series	Geometric design: B-300, B-304, B-305, B-310, B-313, B-325, Vert, Jaune, possibly B-321, B-327, Multi-Flori California, Polychrome A, B, C, D, E.	1935 – 1937	Bird
Spice Island	Light brown hand-tinted transfer print. Sailing ships, spices, and maps, words "East Indies and West Indies." Unmarked Vernon Kilns. Backstamped "dā Bron."	1950	Davidson
Square Knot	Nautical series. Simple design.	1937 – 1937	Bird
Still Life	Native American series. Pictures fruit assortment, pineapple, bananas. Sand ground.	1937	Turnbull
Tahiti	Similar to Multi-Flori, but more detailed. A: Unknown. B: May be soft rose and ivory. C: All-over ivory blossoms on deep blue ground. Also known to be on soft rose ground.	1935 – 1937	Bird
Tam O'Shanter	Plaid group. One of six later patterns. Rust, chartreuse, and green plaid, with green border.	1952 – 1958	
Tangerine	Matte color. Two-tone orange-red and ivory.	1935 – 1937	Bird
Thom	Floral series. Hand decorated on brown transfer. Counterpart patterns are Hadley, June, Marie.	1937	Turnbull
Totem	Native American series. T-620. Totem figure.	1937	Turnbull
Trailing Rose	Plain transfer print (not tinted) in red, green, or blue. An all-over pattern of tiny roses and leaves. Counterpart patterns are Dainty, Dame, Victoria, all hand tinted.	1939	

Name	Description	Approx. Period of Production	Artist
Trellis	Criss-cross lattice forms wide border design. Pictured in brochure with Multi-Flori. May be Spectrum series.	1935 – 1937	Bird
Tropical Fish	Gaily colored tropical fish decorate each item.	1935 – 1937	Bird
Trumpet Flower	Floral series.	1935 – 1937	Bird
Tweed	Plaid Group. One of six later patterns. Gray and yellow.	1949 – 1954 S.O. 1955	
Two-Some	See T-698 and T-701.	1938	Turnbull
T- numbers	Many patterns had only a T- number, some had name and number. Known numbers are listed, and some colors (as have been reported) are listed.	1937 – 1938	Turnbull
T-504	Gray and pink, gray rim.		
T-505	Black and yellow plaid, black rim.		
T-506	Cinnamon and blue plaid, blue rim.		
T-507	Gray and pink plaid, pink rim.		
T-508	Coronation Organdy, rose and gray plaid.		
T-509	Yellow and cinnamon plaid.		
T-510	Green and black plaid.		
T-511	Yellow and brown. Forerunner of later Organdie. Had the longest run of any pattern (1937 – 1958).		
T-512	Deep rose and forest green plaid, green rim.		
T-513	Yellow and lime green plaid.		
T-515	Two shades of green, dark green rim.		
T-516	Two shades of green plaid.		
T-519	Green and gray plaid.		
T-593	Teal blue and gray plaid.		
T-594	Gray and pink plaid, gray rim.		
T-600	Cherry and butterscotch plaid.		
T-601	Lavender and orange plaid has been reported.		
T-602	Green and cinnamon plaid, green rim.		
T-604	Medium blue and cinnamon plaid, cinnamon rim.		
T-605	Black and cinnamon plaid, black rim.		
T-607	Brown and cinnamon, dark brown rim.		
T-612	Blue, one shade.		
T-615	Dark green, one shade.		
T-620	Native American series. Totem.		
T-621	Native American series. Full-figured standing woman, large Indian jar on ground.		
T-622	Native American series. "Indian Jars," one jar with cactus.		
T-623	Native American. "Indian Jars," two jars with cactus.		

Name	Description	Approx. Period of Production	Artist
T-629	Casa California. Blue and green colors, less elaborate floral, splash border.		
T-630	Casa California Hermosa. Elaborate peasant floral, browns and yellows.		
T-631	Casa California Hermosa. Elaborate floral and vase, blues and greens.		
T-632	Casa California. Provincial floral, browns and yellows.		
T-633	Duo-Tone. Lavender and gray.		
T-634	Duo-Tone. Golden brown and pink.		
T-635	Duo-Tone. Yama green and gray.		
T-636	Duo-Tone. Black and pink.		
T-637	Duo-Tone. Turquoise green and red-brown.		
T-638	Duo-Tone. Blue and yellow.		
T-639	Duo-Tone. Yellow and walnut.		
T-640	Duo-Tone. Reddish brown and blue.		
T-641	Duo-Tone. Yellow and yama green.		
T-642	Duo-Tone. Pink and yama green.		
T-643	Duo-Tone. Yellow and gray.		
T-651	Blue glaze. Constellation (previously named "Blue Stars" by author).		
T-652	Blue glaze. Blue feather on soft blue glaze ground.		
T-653	Decorated Pastel. Stylized orchid, wide pink and mauve border bands.		
T-654	Decorated Pastel. Lavender floral, mauve border.		
T-655	Decorated Pastel. Stylized tulip, lavender ground, ivory ground.		
T-656	Decorated Pastel. Deep blue leaf spray, flower with touch of yellow, deep blue border rim on pink ground.		
T-657	Decorated Pastel. Plume of ivory feathers, blue bow, pink ground, ivory border.		
T- ?	Decorated Pastel. Possibly T-656 or 658. Deep blue leaf spray, touch of yellow, deep blue border similar to T-631 border. Pink glaze.		
T-659	Blue glaze. Large deep blue bow on ribbon band encircling rim, soft blue glaze.		
T-669	Casa California Hermosa. Yellow ruffled flower, green spike leaves, blue bowl, intertwining lines form border design.		
T-670	Casa California Hermosa. Yellow tulip, green leaves, basket. Intertwining lines and yellow splashed border design.		
T-671	Casa California Hermosa series. Yellow tulip-like flower, small blue blossoms and brown spike leaves, border of blue splashes within narrow yellow and blue lines.		
T-672	Reported to be a cinnamon and brown Plaid, but not confirmed.		
T-673	Casa California Hermosa. Pink carnations, green leaves, green splashed border.		

Name	Description	Approx. Period of Production	Artist
T-680	Multi-Aster. Simple yellow blossom, yellow rim.		
T-686	Easter motif design. Hand-painted scene of bunnies, colorful Easter egg, lavender flower, yellow rim. Probably not part of a dinnerware set. Also has indistinct mark believed to read "Multi-Lines."		
T-690	Concentric pencil thin brown lines form outer and inner border design.		
T-698	Two-Some. Two wide brown shaded bands form border design.		
T-701	Two wide shaded yellow to orange bands for border design.		
T-702	Blossoms. Scattered pink blossoms, black centers.		
T-703	Blossoms. Scattered yellow blossoms, brown centers.		
T-704	Blossoms. Scattered blue blossoms, yellow centers.		
Vert	Spectrum series. Small green leaves connected by a single green line encircles rim. Same as Jaune except for color. Also cobalt blue on light blue ground	1935 – 1937	Bird
Victoria	Green hand-tinted transfer print. Tiny roses and leaves in all-over design. Counterpart patterns are Dainty, Dame, and Trailing Rose.	1939	
Water Lily	Floral series.	1935 – 1937	Bird
Whaling Service	Marine series.	1937	Turnbull
Wheel	Nautical series. Simple design of ships wheel.	1935 – 1937	Bird
Wild Pink	Floral series.	1935 – 1937	Bird
Winchester '73	Brown hand-tinted transfer print. Western scenes. Name changed to Frontier Days in 1953.	1950 – 1953	Davidson
Zodiac	Not known if this is a dinnerware pattern. Each piece is decorated with a Zodiac sign.	1937	Turnbull
707	Elaborate colorful floral, bright yellow rims.	1942	
836	See Linda. Earliest pieces were numbered only.	1942	
837	Pattern name unknown. Hand-painted design. An encircling wreath of rosy red flowers with yellow centers and green leaves. Deep blue rim. Design similar to Lunning "Floral Wreath."	1942	
838	See Brown Eyed Susan.	1942	

Montecito and Coronado Values

Not all items will be found in all patterns. The color orange was always priced slightly higher in the solid colors on the old company price lists. Elaborate patterns, especially those that are hand painted, will always be priced higher than simpler designs. Values are based upon mint condition. Coronado was a short set with value in the low end. Dimensions may vary.

Ashtrays, 3" square, individual ....$12.00 – 20.00

    4½" square, regular..$12.00 – 20.00

    5½" round ....$12.00 – 20.00

Bowls, 5½" fruit ....$6.00 – 12.00

    *5½" salad, individual ....$15.00 – 20.00

    6" cereal (early shape same as fruit, only slightly

        larger, may be mistaken for oversized fruit) ....$12.00 – 15.00

    6" chowder, angular, open, with applied pierced handles ....$15.00 – 20.00

        covered (measures 4½" not including handles) ....$35.00 – 40.00

    6" lug chowder, round, open, tab handles ....$12.00 – 18.00

        covered ....$25.00 – 35.00

    8¼" rim soup, 1½" deep* ....$12.00 – 20.00

    8½" coupe soup (Mexicana only)...$10.00 – 12.00

    7½" serving, round (closely resembles flat rim soup), 2¼" deep.................$15.00 – 20.00

    8½" serving, round, 2¼" deep...$18.00 – 25.00

    9" serving, angular ....$20.00 – 25.00

    9" serving, round, open (inner ridge for cover) ....$20.00 – 25.00

        covered ....$50.00 – 60.00

    9" serving, round, without ridge ....$20.00 – 25.00

    10" serving, oval...$20.00 – 25.00

    10" divided serving, oval ....$20.00 – 30.00

    *10½" salad, round..$40.00 – 65.00

    13" salad, round..$40.00 – 65.00

    13" salad, angular..$40.00 – 65.00

    15" salad, angular..$45.00 – 70.00

    1-pint, angular or round, 5" diameter, 2¾" deep ....$20.00 – 30.00

    Mixing, 5-piece set (set was also sold as 4-piece set without 9" bowl) ....$135.00 – 195.00

        5" ....$18.00 – 20.00

        6" ....$20.00 – 25.00

        7" ....$22.00 – 30.00

        8" ....$25.00 – 35.00

        9" ....$30.00 – 45.00

* Note: 7¼" soup found in Early California and Modern California.

Buffet Server, trio ....$50.00 – 80.00

*Butter pat, 2½", individual..$15.00 – 25.00

Butter tray, covered, oblong, "rippled," knob finial.............................$35.00 – 65.00

       plain, rectangular finial ....$35.00 – 65.00

Candleholder, saucer, metal fitting, chamberstick type ....$30.00 – 40.00

       teacups, pair ....$65.00 – 75.00

Casserole, two-handled, covered, angular, 7½" diameter........................$45.00 – 65.00

       round, 8" (11" including handles) ....$35.00 – 70.00

        *4" individual, covered. ....$15.00 – 25.00

        *4" chicken pie, stick handle, covered.....................................$18.00 – 28.00

*Casserole Hot, complete with metal stand ....$65.00 – 85.00

*Casserole Round-Up, black metal stand w/candle warmer ....$150.00 – 250.00

Coaster or cup warmer, 4½" ....$20.00 – 25.00

*Coaster, 3¾", ridged ....$18.00 – 22.00

Coffee Pot, 2-cup, after dinner, scarce ....$75.00 – 125.00

Coffee Server (carafe) and stopper, 10-cup, angular or round ....$40.00 – 75.00

       stopper only ....$15.00 – 20.00

*Coffee Hot, black metal stand with candle warmer............................$20.00 – 25.00

Comport, footed, 9½" diameter, early, scarce. ....$50.00 – 75.00

Creamer, individual, angular or round, open ....$15.00 – 20.00

       regular, angular or round, open..$15.00 – 20.00

       regular, round, covered, doubled as individual teapot..................$25.00 – 30.00

*Cups, custard, 3", scarce..$20.00 – 30.00

Cups and saucers, after dinner (demitasse), 2⅞",

       angular or round, 5¼" saucer..$18.00 – 25.00

       teacup, 4", angular or round, 6½" saucer ....$12.00 – 20.00

       *jumbo cup, 4¼", 12 oz. 6¾" saucer ....$30.00 – 40.00

       *colossal cup, 9⅜", 4 quart, 15" saucer ....$125.00 – 195.00

Egg cup, double, cupped or straight sides ....$18.00 – 25.00

*Flower Pots, 3" ....$25.00 – 30.00

       saucer ....$10.00 – 15.00

       *4"...$30.00 – 35.00

       saucer ....$10.00 – 15.00

       *5"...$35.00 – 45.00

       saucer ....$10.00 – 15.00

Jam jar, 5", notched lid...$65.00 – 95.00

    lid only ....$15.00 – 20.00

Lemon server, 6", center brass handle ....$25.00 – 35.00

    center pottery handle ....$45.00 – 65.00

Muffin tray, 9", tab handles, dome cover...$75.00 – 95.00

    cover only ....$45.00 – 65.00

Mugs, 3¾" bulb bottom, 8 oz., clip handle......................................$18.00 – 25.00

    3¾" bulb bottom, 8 oz., applied handle...........................$20.00 – 30.00

    3½" straight sides, 9 oz., later style ....$15.00 – 35.00

Pitchers, disk, 2 quart, plain or decorated......................................$65.00 –100.00

    jug, 1 pint, bulb bottom..$25.00 – 50.00

    jug, 1 quart, bulb bottom ....$45.00 – 65.00

    streamlined, *¼ pint, 4"...$20.00 – 30.00

        *½ pint, 5"...$20.00 – 30.00

        1-pint, 6"...$25.00 – 35.00

        1-quart, 8½"..$28.00 – 38.00

        2-quart, 11"...$35.00 – 60.00

    tankard, 1½-quart (also in smaller size)........................$60.00 – 70.00

    *syrup, drip-cut top ....$45.00 – 75.00

Plates, *2½" lapel plate with pin ....$20.00 – 25.00

    4½" coaster or cup warmer...$18.00 – 25.00

    6½" bread and butter ....$5.00 – 10.00

    7½" salad ....$8.00 – 15.00

    8½" luncheon ....$15.00 – 20.00

    9½" luncheon ....$12.00 – 20.00

    10½" dinner ....$15.00 – 25.00

    11" grill..$15.00 – 25.00

    13½" x 10½" indented grill (rare) ....$40.00 – 50.00

    12" chop...$20.00 – 35.00

    14" chop...$35.00 – 50.00

    17" chop...$50.00 – 95.00

Platters, 8½" – 9" (relish or pickle) ....$20.00 – 30.00

    10½" ....$18.00 – 25.00

    12"...$20.00 – 30.00

14" ....$30.00 – 45.00

16" ....$50.00 – 95.00

Relish, 7" x 10", clover shape, 3-part ("3-way" in company literature) ....$35.00 – 65.00

Sauce (gravy) boat, angular or round ....$20.00 – 25.00

     fast stand, double spout ....$35.00 – 50.00

Shakers, salt, regular ....$7.50 – 12.50

     *salt, large ....$20.00 – 25.00

     *salt, wood encased, 4½" ....$35.00 – 45.00

     pepper, regular ....$7.50 – 12.50

     *pepper, large...$20.00 – 25.00

     *pepper mill (large, metal fitting) ....$40.00 – 50.00

     *pepper mill, wood encased, 4½" ....$45.00 – 55.00

*Spoon holder ....$45.00 – 65.00

Sugar, individual, angular, open ....$18.00 – 20.00

     individual, round, open ....$15.00 – 18.00

          covered ....$20.00 – 25.00

     regular, angular or round, open..$10.00 – 15.00

          covered ....$15.00 – 22.00

Teapot, covered, angular or round..$45.00 – 95.00

Tidbit server, two-tier, wooden fixture...$20.00 – 30.00

Tidbit server, three-tier , wooden fixture ....$25.00 – 45.00

Tumblers, #1, 4½", banded rim and base...$20.00 – 25.00

     #2, 4½" rings midway, bulge top..$20.00 – 25.00

     #3, 3¾", bulb bottom ....$20.00 – 25.00

     #4, 5", flared top, 13 oz. (iced tea) interchangeable with Ultra ....$25.00 – 40.00

     #5, 5", straight sides, 14 oz., interchangeable with San Marino and R.F.D ....$20.00 – 30.00

     Coronado, cubist top rim ....$20.00 – 25.00

Values for artist patterns: Bird, Turnbull, and Winchester '73/Frontier Days, are worth two to four times more than other items of the same kind. Disney pieces are seven to eight times higher, with hand-tinted patterns at the upper end of the value range, blue being the rarest.

Additional notes:

1. For easier identification, tumblers are numbered chronologically.

2. The Plaids and Brown Eyed Susan starter sets were sold with 9½" plates, thus 9½" plates may be more plentiful. The 10½" plates were available as open stock.

*These are 1950s items found in popular patterns; e.g., Plaids, Brown Eyed Susan, Frontier Days, Winchester '73.

Ultra ∞

The overall shape of Ultra is credited to Gale Turnbull, and the "upside down" handles of the hollow ware to Jane Bennison. The shape was used chiefly for the designer patterns of Rockwell Kent, Don Blanding, Disney (though some Disney patterns were executed on a combination of Ultra flatware and Montecito hollow ware), and Turnbull's own designs. The ware is distinctive for both the narrow "dipped" rims on coupe-shaped flatware and the upside down handles. It is believed that the shape was discontinued in the early 1940s. The photographs show all available examples of items and patterns in the Ultra shape, beginning with the Ultra California solid-color pattern.

Ultra California was the pattern name; the name "Ultra" was assigned by the author to identify the shape because the company name for it is unknown. A November 1939 *House Beautiful* ad described the colors as rich half-tones in Buttercup (yellow), Gardenia (ivory), Carnation (pink), and Aster (blue). Other colors that have been found are maroon (scarce) and Ice Green. All items pictured have mark 15.

TOP: 2-quart disk jug (interchangeable with other shapes); 8½" plate; 13 oz. iced tea, no. 4 style (also interchangeable); 12½" chop plate; 9½" plate; 6½" plate; 2-cup coffee pot (note longer spout); 2-quart open pitcher.
CENTER: 2-handled covered 8" casserole; sauce boat; tea cup and saucer; demitasse cup and saucer; jam jar with notched lid; single egg cup.
BOTTOM: Salt shaker; short creamer; 5½" fruit, tall creamer. It is assumed that the short creamer and sugar were made to accompany the teapot and that the tall version was made for the coffee pot.

TOP: Nest of five mixing bowls, shown individually.
BOTTOM: Muffin cover; footed comport (interchangeable shape); tab-handled pickle dish.

The same basic Ultra shape items shown above will be seen in the next photographs in the elaborate and beautiful hand-painted designs of Gale Turnbull. All have mark 33 except where noted.

TOP: Vera 6-cup coffee pot; Flora 13½" chop plate; Harvest 1-pint open pitcher, mark 19.
CENTER: Bouquet 12½" chop plate; Five Fingers 7½" plate; Flora 13 oz. tumbler, no. 4 style; Harvest 8½" plate, mark 19.
BOTTOM: Flora 2-cup coffee pot; Harvest salt shaker; Vera butter cover only.

Rosalie coffee pot. Mark 33 and the initials "G.T." Another example of Turnbull hand-painted florals.
Kay Bernhard photo.

No. 769, hand-painted floral decoration cup and saucer, after dinner size. Mark 19. Pattern name is unknown.
Brent and Sandra Purdom photo.

Simpler hand-painted patterns are illustrated here. The Rio group and its counterpart, Sierra Madre, are featured, along with Yellow Rose No. 1 and No. 2 and Orchard. All have mark 19 with respective pattern name, unless noted. Note that the individual sugar is handleless in the Ultra shape. The difference in the three Rio patterns is in the color of the wide band. Sierra Madre has the same color border but without a floral. The patterns can be mixed or matched. The difference in T-742, T-743, and T-744 (seen on page 228, bottom photo) is in the leaf and rim color.

TOP: T-743 Yellow Rose No. 2 teapot (mark 33); Rio Vista 4½" jam jar with notched lid; Rio Chico 12½" chop plate; Sierra Madre 10½" plate.

CENTER: T-742 Yellow Rose No. 1 sugar bowl (mark 33); Orchard 9½" plate; Rio Vista 8½" vegetable bowl; T-742 creamer (mark 33); Rio Verde 7½" plate.

BOTTOM: Rio Chico chowder; Rio Vista salt shaker; individual creamer and sugar.

Pictured is an unusual Turnbull sugar bowl. Tropical beach scene, sail boats on the horizon. Hand-painted underglaze. Mark 33. Unknown pattern name.

Chintz-type ⬚ Always a pacesetter and leader in dinnerware design and trends, in the late 1930s Vernon Kilns again met the challenge of English chintz patterns with the introduction of its colorful and dainty all-over chintz-type patterns. Seen in the next pictures are the company's versions of the collectible chintz patterns of that period, perennial favorites more than half a century later. Vernon's chintz patterns executed on the Ultra shape include Santa Barbara, Santa Clara, Santa Maria, Santa Paula, Santa Rosa, Bellflower, Choice, Colleen, Floret, and Grace. Blanding's exotic all-over Hawaiian floral patterns might also be classified as chintz. In the Montecito shape there were counterpart patterns — Dainty, Dame, Victoria, and Trailing Rose. Later, in the early 1940s, the company introduced its English look-alike patterns to fill the demand for English dinnerware unavailable because of the war effort (see Melinda and San Fernando sections for patterns).

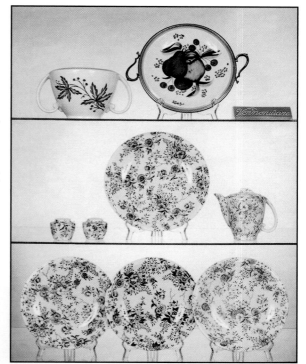

Vernon's chintz-style transfer and hand-painted patterns are seen in this picture. Some have Turnbull's mark (33).
TOP: Five Fingers tureenette without the notched lid; Harvest 9½" plate mounted in pewter holder; Vernonware display sign.
CENTER: Santa Clara blue salt and pepper shakers; Santa Rosa 10½" plate; Santa Clara pink 2-cup coffee pot (note the longer spout on the coffee pot).
BOTTOM: Santa Maria, Santa Barbara, and Santa Paula 9½" plates (mark 16).

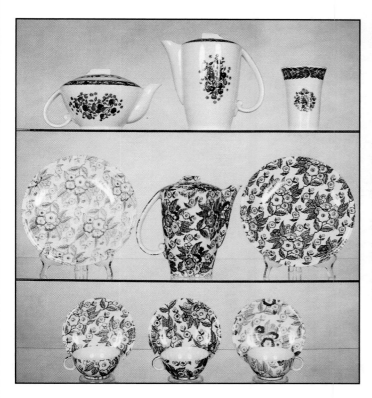

All examples in this photograph are transfer prints, both plain and hand filled.
TOP: Taste tea pot; Style coffee pot; Taste tumbler, mark 34. All of these are transfer patterns with hand-painted touches of raised enamel.
CENTER: Floret 9½" plate, unmarked except for a handwritten "765" under glaze; Grace coffee pot and 9½" plate, plate unmarked except for "163" under glaze and the initials "B.B."
BOTTOM: Bellflower, Colleen, and Choice cups and saucers. The center and bottom rows are counterpart patterns. Style was pictured in a 1954 Culinary Arts Institute *250 Delectable Dessert Recipes* booklet.

Two different table lamps decorated in Vernon's chintz are seen in these pictures. Both are considered rare.

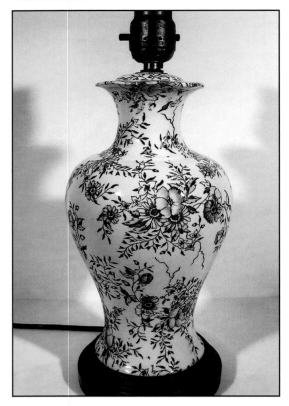

Vernon's Santa Rosa pattern. *Sean Meredith photo.*

Table lamp decorated in Santa Barbara all-over pattern, with gold touches on handles. A 10½" tall lamp base in Santa Paula has been found. Also, it has been reported that a late company price list had added a vase to the items available.

Taste muffin cover sitting on 7½" plate. In the Ultra shape, Vernon didn't design a plate to accompany the cover. Taste and counterpart patterns Abundance, Mode, and Style are more formal styles of dinnerware.

John and Joanne Barrett photo.

Included in this photograph is a Montecito pattern, Peppers. All are hand painted.
TOP: Peppers 9½" plate on ivory ground (Peppers in Montecito section is pictured on sand ground); Rosa 12½" chop plate; T-744 10½" plate.
BOTTOM: Rio Vista tumbler, no. 4 style. Note how the design was applied to this piece.

Full page ad from the November 1939 issue of *House Beautiful.*

Don Blanding ∞ Don Blanding's tropical designs were basically three transfer prints and one free handpainted pattern, all executed on Ultra. The colors in the transfer prints determine the pattern name. These designs are grouped according to design and known colors. All are on a cream background. There are possibly other colors.

Lotus Floral

Hawaiian Flower	Plain print in different colors of pink, blue, maroon, or light orange.
Honolulu	Hand-tinted yellow flowers on blue print. The same hand-tinted blue print has been found with the Hawaiian Flowers backstamp; it may have been mismarked.
Hilo	Hand-tinted light brown print.
Lei Lani	Hand-tinted maroon print. In 1947, the pattern was executed on the San Marino shape.
Hawaii	Listed here, but is Lei Lani on the Melinda shape (produced about 1942 – 1946).

Camellia* and Gardenia Floral

Glamour	A plain print in blue, brown, or maroon.
Joy	Hand-tinted yellow camellia on light brown print.
Delight	Hand-tinted yellow camellia on blue print.
Ecstasy	Hand-tinted pink camellia on light brown print.

Tropical Fish

Coral Reef	Plain print in blue, maroon, light orange, light pink, and medium pink on cream ground.
Aquarium	Hand painted Tropical Fish design, different on each item in brilliant colors.

* The author previously described this flower as a peony.

Blanding's mark (35) does not include "hand painted" for the hand-tinted prints, unlike the backstamp for Vernon Kilns' other hand-tinted prints. Hand-painted Aquarium has the words "hand painted under glaze" added to mark 35.

Examples of Lotus Floral design are pictured, all bearing mark 35 and the respective pattern name except where noted.
TOP: Hawaiian Flowers tureenette with notched lid, 7½" diameter excluding handles (scarce in any pattern); Hilo 9½" plate; Lei Lani coffee pot.
CENTER: Hawaiian Flowers individual sugar; Hawaiian Flowers 13 oz. iced tea tumbler, no. 4 style; Hawaiian Flowers 6½" plate; Lei Lani regular creamer; Honolulu cup and saucer.
BOTTOM: Hilo individual creamer; Lei Lani butter tray and cover; Lei Lani lug chowder; Lei Lani salt shaker; Hawaiian Flowers 8 oz. handled mug; Hawaiian Flowers demitasse cup and saucer. (The butter tray and salt shaker do not include the pattern name. The mug is marked only "Vernon Kilns, U.S.A.")

Some unusual examples of transfer and Aquarium patterns are shown in the next set of photographs. TOP: Coral Reef no. 4 style tumbler; Honolulu 1-pint covered (short spout) pitcher (Pitchers were sold with or without covers.); Lei Lani 2-cup covered coffee pot; Lei Lani 1-pint bowl.
CENTER: Ecstasy disk pitcher; Hawaiian Flowers tumbler in scarce light orange; Hawaiian Flowers disk pitcher. Both pitchers are decorated with Blanding patterns and are considered scarce.
BOTTOM: Bennison pottery with the Hawaiian Flowers pattern. No. 3 Ring Bowl (11¾" diameter); No. 3 Dayrae bowl (11½" diameter); Sphere 3" candlestick.

Two pieces are pictured to illustrate distinct differences between a 1-pint pitcher with cover and a 2-cup coffee pot. On the left is a Delight pitcher, with a short spout, wide opening for lid, and a lid inner rim ¼" deep. On the right is a Lei Lani 2-cup coffee pot with a long spout, more narrow opening for lid, and a lid inner rim that is ½" deep. Lids are tilted in order to see the difference.

TOP: Delight 6-cup tea pot; Joy 6½" plate.
CENTER: Aquarium 6½" plate; Coral Reef 7½" plate; Glamour 9½" plate; Aquarium tumbler, no. 4 style; Ecstasy 7½" plate.
BOTTOM: Aquarium chowder; Aquarium cup and saucer; Coral reef 5½" fruit; Aquarium 7½" plate.

Coral Reef and Hawaiian Flowers executed on Bennison's 10" Ring Bowl No. 2 and Triple candlestick. Candlestick is decorated in center and at either end. *John and Joanne Barrett photo.*

Coral Reef disk pitcher. *Sean Meredith photo.*

Unusual multi-colored Coral Reef chop plate.

TOP: Coral Reef sugar; Lei Lani muffin cover (a tray was not made for Ultra).
CENTER: Aquarium mug; 10½" plate; 1-pint covered pitcher.
BOTTOM: Coral Reef butter cover and tray; Hawaiian Flowers covered lug chowder.

It has been reported that Lei Lani in blue was featured on page 135 of a *Heinz Wartime Supplement Cookbook.*

More examples of rare Aquarium.
BACK ROW: Salt & pepper shakers.
FRONT ROW: 1 pint bowl, tureenette, and egg cup.

Rockwell Kent ~ Through the effort of Mr. Bennison, Rockwell Kent was the second major American artist to be hired by Vernon Kilns, and he worked from his New York studio. Mr. Bennison visited Rockwell Kent in that studio in the late 1930s, told him of Don Blanding's earlier success, and convinced him there was opportunity to be had working for Vernon Kilns.

This artist was already well known for his illustrated books as well as bookplates, bookjackets, posters, Christmas cards, and advertisements. Two books, *A Guide for Youth,* (1922) and *A Basket of Posies* (1924), both by George S. Chappel, were illustrated by Hogarth, Jr. — Kent, working under a pseudonym. *Moby Dick* (1930) by Herman Melville, which had 280 Kent illustrations, and Kent's classic *Salamina,* which he wrote and illustrated, both served as the basis for his dinnerware patterns of the same names. In addition, he designed Our America, for a total of three major dinnerware patterns all of which were executed on the Ultra shape.

For Our America, Kent drew over 30 designs to represent American locales and pastimes. These were transfer prints in one of four different colors on a cream background: Walnut Brown, dark blue, maroon, and green (colors according to company literature). Our America has neven been found in green. The key piece of the series is the 17¼" chop plate that features, at top center, the national eagle above the American shield, the eagle's wings outspread over a city to the left and farmland to the right. Below this grouping and covering most of the face of the plate, is an outline map of the United States that has small perspective drawings of items or activities common to each state or region.

Life magazine's September 9, 1940, issue featured an article entitled "American Dishes, Home Product Fills Gap Made by War and Boycott." In full color photography were prominent examples of Kent's Our America, Salamina, Harvest, and Bouquet. The 17" Our America chop plate was the lead photo; this plate was the same as the one pictured on page 236.

Seen recently in an Arizona department store was open stock dinnerware very reminiscent of Our America. Now, almost 70 years later, this new patriotic dinnerware — also in brown tones on ivory — is called "Slice of Life." The pictures on these pieces have been described as "dinnerware portraits of America."

Rockwell Kent divided America into eight geographic regions as follows. An original company brochure, "What You Will See in Our America," listed them as follows:

No. 1	New England states	Maine, New Hampshire, Vermont, Connecticut, Massachusetts, Rhode Island.
No. 2	Middle Atlantic States	New York, New Jersey, Pennsylvania, Maryland, Delaware.
No. 3	Southern Colonial States	Virginia, West Virginia, the Carolinas, Georgia.
No. 4	Mississippi River States	Louisiana, Mississippi, Arkansas, Tennessee, Kentucky, Missouri.
No. 5	Great Lakes States	Ohio, Indiana, Illinois, Michigan, Wisconsin, Minnesota.
No. 6	Plains and Mountain States	Texas, Oklahoma, Kansas, Nebraska, the Dakotas, Iowa, Montana, Wyoming, Colorado, New Mexico, Arizona, Utah, Idaho, Nevada.
No. 7	Gulf States	Florida, Alabama.
No. 8	Pacific States	California, Oregon, Washington.

Each piece of flatware was decorated, in addition to its star-spangled border, with a central drawing that illustrated one of these eight regions, as follows:

17" chop plate		Map of the United States (described on the preceding page).
14" Chop plate	Region No. 8	We see a dam across a lake bordered with big California trees; behind it rise mountain peaks.
12" Chop Plate	Region No. 6	The rich Middle West corn belt is represented by grain elevators and fields of grain; cattle are in the middle distance.
10½" Plate	Region No. 2	New York City is seen from the bay; its outflung piers radiate in the water, and its tall buildings reach into a twilight sky.
9½" Plate	Region No. 5	We are approaching Chicago on the river; the drawbridge rises before us, and we see in the distance the buildings of the city.
8½" Plate	Region No. 1	New England's fishing industries are depicted in a busy scene of its fishing banks.
7½" Plate	Region No. 3	In the Deep South we see cotton pickers before a gracious Colonial mansion.
8¼" Soups	Region No. 1	Same as 8½" plates.
6½" Plate (and Saucers)	Region No. 4	A stern-wheeler on the Mississippi, taking on a cargo of cotton.
Chowder Bowl	Region No. 7	Coconut palms in Florida, bordering the lagoon.
5½" Fruit	Region No. 7	Same as Chowder Bowl.

The hollow ware was decorated with stars on handles, shoulders, covers, and knobs. Illustrations on the sides of hollow ware pieces are as follows:

Tea Cups	Region No. 4	Incoming and outgoing freight crowds the wharves of New Orleans.
After Dinner Cups	Region No. 1	Yacht racing at Newport.
After Dinner Saucers		Same as After Dinner Cups.
Pickle Dish		Same as After Dinner Cups and Saucers.
Jumbo Cups	Region No. 1	Tapping trees for maple sugar in the snowy Vermont winter.
Jumbo Saucers		Same as Jumbo Cups.
Regular Sugar Bowl	Region No. 4	Workers cutting fields of waving sugar cane.
Regular Creamer	Region No. 7	The floating homes of houseboaters in Florida.
Individual Sugar	Region No. 4	Shrimp fisherman plying their trade in the Gulf of Mexico.
Individual Creamer	Region No. 7	The wilds of the Florida Everglades.
Casserole	Region No. 5	Steamers and yachts on the Great Lakes.
Tureenette	Region No. 8	The giant trees in the Northwest fall beneath the lumbermen's axes.
2 Quart Pitcher	Region No. 2	Skyscrapers rise to house the workers of "the great city."
Tea Pot	Region No. 6	Indians of the high Mesa are shown herding their sheep.
Regular Coffee Pot	Region No. 8	The building of one of our great suspension bridges.

Individual 2-cup Coffee Pot	Region No. 3	A gentleman's sport in a gentleman's state - riding to hounds in Virginia.
Pint Jug (4½" tall)	Region No. 8	Steamers on the Columbia River.
Mug	Region No. 3	The Blue Grass Country and its blue-blooded stock in the sport of kings.
Jam Jar	Region No. 6	Towering oil derricks salute the oil fields of Texas.
13 oz. Tumbler	Region No. 5	Speed boats racing on the Great Lakes.
Butter Dish and Cover	Region No. 4	Steamboat coming around the bend on the lower Mississippi.
Sauce boat	Region No. 6	Smelters in the mining country.
Egg cup	Region No. 1	Stately old buildings stand among the trees of a New England college campus.
Muffin Cover	Region No. 1	The fishing fleet puts out to sea.
Salt and pepper shakers	Region No. 4	Flat boats on a southern river.
Pint Bowl	Region No. 7	Sailfishing.

Hollow ware pieces that did not appear on the company list are:

Vegetable Bowl, 8"	Region No. 5	Same picture as on the 9½" plate.
Vegetable Bowl, 9"	Region No. 2	Same as on the 10½" plate.
Salad Bowl, 11"	Region No. 8	Same as 14" Chop plate.
Tea tile, square	Region No. 1	Church, New England style (may have been special order).

Pictured is the key piece of Our America, the 17" chop plate in rare hand-tinted color.

Company literature incorrectly listed illustrations for the 7½" soup bowls using the same illustration as is on the 7½" plates. This is being corrected in this edition to show the 8¼" soup bowls using the same illustration as is on the 8½" plates. Also incorrect was the listing for the 8" vegetable bowl using the illustration from the 8½" plates, which is being corrected to show that the illustration is the same as that on the 9½" plates. See the picture to follow; it shows the correct illustrations.

LEFT: 8" vegetable bowl illustrated with the Region No. 5 scene from the 9½" plate.
RIGHT: 8¼" soup bowl using the Region No. 1 illustration from the 8½" plate.
Bob Hutchins photo.

Unlike most Our America pieces, the shakers, although marked, do not bear the Kent mark. *Bob Hutchins photo.*

Our America brown disk pitcher. The design is featured on each side. Mark 36.

Multicolored Our America 14" chop plate featuring a Region no. 8 scene, made for the Bennison family. Plate has two pierced holes, for hanging. *Bill Stern photo.*

Examples of Our America dinnerware, each bearing the Rockwell Kent mark (36).
TOP: 6-cup coffee pot (Pacific States, bridge building); cup and saucer (Mississippi River States, New Orleans wharves); 2-quart pitcher (Middle Atlantic States, skyscraper building).
CENTER: Regular (short version) creamer (Gulf States, houseboaters).
BOTTOM: Sauce boat (Plains and Mountain States, mining country smelters); regular (short version) sugar bowl (Mississippi River States, sugar cane fields); salt and pepper shakers (Mississippi River States, flat boats on river); casserole (Great Lakes States, boating).

More examples of Our America dinnerware, each bearing the Rockwell Kent mark (36).
TOP: 12" chop plate (Plains and Mountain States, Middle West grain fields); jam jar base, lid missing (Plains and Mountain States, Texas oil derricks); 10½" plate (Middle Atlantic States, New York City); 5½" fruit (Gulf States, Florida coconut palms); 14" chop plate (Pacific States, big trees and lakes, the West).
BOTTOM: 8½" plate (New England States, fishing banks); 7½" plate (Southern Colonial States, cotton pickers, old South); pickle dish (New England States, yacht racing); 9½" plate (Great Lakes States, Chicago as seen from the river); 6½" plate (Mississippi River States, sternwheeler).

Moby Dick was the most popular of the Rockwell Kent patterns. The scenes of full-rigged whalers, leaping porpoises, and spouting whales were adapted from his illustrations for the Herman Melville classic. The pattern was available in four colors of plain print: dark blue, maroon, Walnut Brown and yellow (previously described as orange). Each piece bears Rockwell Kent's signature as part of mark 36. Salt and pepper shakers may be exceptions that do not have this mark.

Pictured are examples of Moby Dick.
LEFT TO RIGHT: Single egg cup; salt and pepper shakers; 9½" plate; 8 oz. handled mug; 1-pint bowl; demitasse cup and saucer; pair of 4" rectangular single candlesticks (rare, Bennison pottery adapted to Moby Dick pattern).

Some examples of rare Moby Dick are pictured in the next four photographs. Here, two 14" chop plates; the one on the right is a reverse transfer.

A rare pink 12" chop plate, and a rare, yellow 14" chop plate with reverse transfer.

15½" Bennison Dayrae bowl decorated in yellow Moby Dick, very rare.

14" Bennison fluted bowl decorated with Moby Dick. Note the missing seagull here and on the above Bennison Dayrae bowl.

As previously mentioned, Farber Brothers purchased, from many companies, pottery and china to which it added metal holders, rims, and bases. Vernon Kilns was one of the notable china and pottery firms that supplied Farber Brothers with goods. Several different sizes of Kent Moby Dick and Blanding Lei Lani plates were shipped to Farber Brothers during the late 1930s and early 1940s. It purchased Moby Dick blue hand-tinted plates; the hand-tinted ware was distinctly different from the Vernon Kilns ware with plain prints. The Farber Brothers used their own back-stamp for the blue tinted Moby Dick and the Lei Lani dishes, though some pieces have been reported as having the Vernon Kilns mark. The finished products were pictured in a 1941 Farber Brothers catalog.

Three tinted Moby Dick plates in Farber Brothers frames.
TOP: 9½" plate.
BOTTOM: 7½" and 6½" plates (sizes are excluding frames).

The Farber Brothers mark.

241

The Salamina pattern was also adapted from a best selling book. Kent's *Salamina*, named for his housekeeper, was the chronicle of his life in Greenland. Rockwell Kent stated in his book that Salamina was the most faithful, most noble, most beautiful, and most altogether captivating of all the women of North Greenland. This was the only Kent design that was hand-tinted, and it is considered the most valuable of all Kent dinnerware.

TOP: Salamina coffee pot; yellow Moby Dick creamer, tall size; Our America butter and cover; Moby Dick coffee pot.
BOTTOM: Our America muffin cover; Our America tureenette; Moby Dick covered lug chowder.

TOP: All Moby Dick items. Tea cup and saucer; decorated Bennison Ring Bowl; jumbo cup and saucer.
BOTTOM: All Our America items. Tumbler; tea pot; demitasse cup and saucer.

Two versions of Salamina 1-pint pitcher. The one on the left with a figure was designed as a souvenir, "Ketchikan" appears on the handle; the one on the right is a dinnerware pitcher. In the center is a rare Salamina disk pitcher.

Examples of Salamina dinnerware, all bearing mark 36 and pattern name: Tall sugar bowl with cover, iceberg scene; cup with same scene; 10½" plate, Salamina kneeling; 6½" plate, Salamina peering out over the arctic waters; tumbler featuring Salamina in native costume, she is holding a coffee pot and a cup.

Close-up view of Salamina butter dish and jam jar. *Dennis Donnal photo.*

Rockwell Kent's Salamina in a contemporary 2003 setting. *Dennis Donnal photo.*

THE "Salamina" pattern of Vernonware is individually hand-painted under the glaze in vivid colors on an ivory ground. Each piece bears the signature of Rockwell Kent. 20-piece "Starter Set"—Special price $10.75. Individual prices as follows:

VERNON KILNS "SALAMINA" PRICE LIST

Bowl, 1 Pint	$1.00	Pitcher, 2 Qt. Cover Only	1.00
Butter Tray, Oblong	1.50	Pitcher, 1 Pt. Open	1.35
Butter Cover, Oblong	1.75	Pitcher, 1 Pt. Cover Only	.45
8" Casserole, Covered	5.00	6" Pickles (Round)	1.25
6" Cereal	.70	6½" Plates	.45
12" Chop Plate	2.50	7½" Plates	.55
14" Chop Plate	4.50	8½" Plates	.75
17" Chop Plate	6.50	9½" Plates	.90
Chowder, Open	.85	10½" Plates	1.10
Chowder, Cover Only	.35	7¼" Coupe Soups	.90
Coffee Cup "Jumbo"	1.40	Pepper Shaker	.75
Coffee Saucer "Jumbo"	.70	Salt Shaker	.75
Coffee Cups A.D.	.65	11" Salad Bowl	4.50
Coffee Saucer A.D.	.35	Sauce Boat, Reg.	2.25
Coffee Pot—2 cup	2.75	Sugar, Covered	2.25
Coffee Pot—6 Cup	3.90	Sugars, Covered Ind.	1.65
Creamer, Open	1.50	Tea Cup	.75
Creamer, Ind. (Open)	1.10	Tea Saucer	.35
Egg Cups (Single)	.75	Tea Pot, 6 Cup	3.90
5½" Fruits	.35	7" Tureenette—	
Jam Jar, Notched Cover	1.95	Notched Cover	5.75
Muffin Cover Only	1.95	13 oz. Tumbler—Iced Tea	.85
Mug, 8 oz. Hdl.	.85	8" Vegetable Rd.	1.50
Pitcher, 2 Quart Open	3.75	9" Vegetable Rd.	1.95

20-Piece "Starter Set".... 10.75

J. R. WESTBROOK CO.
SUCCESSOR TO
FRANZEN HARDWARE CO.
PHONE 542
RIVERSIDE, CALIFORNIA

SALAMINA

BY
ROCKWELL KENT

─A NEW PATTERN OF AUTHENTIC CALIFORNIA
VERNONWARE

Company brochure describing Salamina.
Note: In this brochure, coupe soup is listed as 7¼". However, collectors report having the coupe soup in 8¼" only.

Reproductions on the Market!

Sets of Salamina reproductions were offered in limited numbers on eBay in late 2002. Wares listed for sale were the "Dinner set (four 8-piece place settings) consisting of 10½", 9½", 8½", 7½", 6½" plates, 5½" berry bowl, cup and saucer, 32 pieces in all." The price was $350.00, and the listing stated that only 195 sets were available. The breakfast set consisted of an individual creamer and individual sugar, a 2-cup coffee pot with lid, a jam jar with a notched lid and spoon, a muffin cover, two jumbo coffee cups with saucers, two 8" and two 6" plates, and two egg

SALAMINA
designed for
VERNON
by Rockwell Kent

A FEW years ago a man went on a lonely journey to Greenland. There he settled down among the native people, in the midst of their ice-bound wilderness, built himself a home, and lived. He had two purposes in his self-imposed exile from America: one, to paint; the other, to find beauty and peace and simple contentment away from a world suddenly become —to him— stale and senseless.

Out of this life in Greenland grew a book . . . a book that in words and pictures told of

the incredible glory of the Arctic wasteland, the glittering majesty of icebergs, and above all, the childlike friendliness and wisdom and happiness of the Greenlanders of Igdlorssuit.

The man was Rockwell Kent. The book was "Salamina." When it was published, the name of Rockwell Kent was sufficient introduction to a world who already knew the fame of this man as an artist. But soon the book became a best seller on its own merit . . . for it opened the eyes of all who read it to the unsuspected beauty lying in the land of sea and night.

It is with pride that Vernon Kilns present "Salamina" in a new form . . . as a design adapted by Mr. Kent from his own book especially for Vernonware. You will see Salamina herself of whom Rockwell Kent says: "Of all the women of North Greenland, it had been told to me, the most faithful, noble, and most beautiful, most altogether captivating, was she named Salamina." You will see the icebergs of the Arctic Circle, gleaming in all their prismatic splendor. You will see the flaming rainbows of the northern landscape.

Beautiful enough, these designs on dinnerware, for the walls of an art museum . . . yet the pieces on which they appear are so durable that you can have the thrill of using them daily. The exclusive process by which Vernonware is manufactured insures the utmost resistance to cracking and chipping. Vernonware's brilliant glaze is guaranteed proof against crazing.

"As I now look back upon that first meeting with Salamina, my thought is of light, of light so bright that I am dazzled by it."

Rockwell Kent,
SALAMINA.

Company brochure describing Salamina.

cups. Twenty sets were available at $295.00 each. The tea set consisted of a 6-cup teapot, a creamer and a sugar, six cups and saucers, and six 7½" plates. Twenty sets were offered, at $275.00 each. The beverage set had the 2-quart disk pitcher and six tumblers. Twenty sets were available, at $199.00 each. The mixing bowl set had 5", 6", 7", 8" and 9" bowls and cost $179.95. Of these, there were only 195 sets. Assorted 4-piece sets included covered chowder bowls for $79.95, jumbo coffee cups for $74.50, mugs for $62.50, coupe soup for $69.95, egg cups for $69.95, demitasse cups/saucers for $89.95, tumblers for $89.95, and cereal bowls for $57.50. There were 195 sets of this type available. There was a breakdown of single pieces, priced per piece. At this time, the author does not know how the dishes are marked or how true they are to the original Rockwell Kent Salamina.

Walt Disney ∽ Probably the scarcest of the designer dinnerware is Walt Disney's Fantasia line. Transfer prints, some hand tinted, had one of two basic floral designs, one an all-over pattern and the other a floral border. Different pattern names were given to each print based on color or hand tint. Patterns were executed on the Ultra shape, except all-over-patterned hollow ware, which was executed on the Montecito shape. A January 1941 article described Disney's Fantasia dinnerware patterns. It stated that there were "51 pieces in the open stock sets." All known patterns* are listed:

Border

Enchantment	Hand-tinted blue print.
Nutcracker	Hand-tinted brown print.
Flower Ballet	Hand-tinted maroon print.
Dewdrop Fairies	Plain blue print.

All Over

Autumn Ballet	Hand-tinted maroon print.
Fairyland	Hand-tinted blue print.
Milkweed Dance	Two colors have been found: plain blue and plain maroon prints.
Fantasia	Hand-tinted brown print.

*A pattern called Firefly has also been reported, but its description is unknown.

All examples of Walt Disney dinnerware that were available for photographing are pictured. All have the Disney backstamp (mark 37) along with the respective pattern name.

Original retail prices for dinnerware patterns Autumn Ballet, Enchantment, Fairyland, Flower Ballet, and Nutcracker were as follows: 14-piece breakfast set, $12.15; 20-piece set, $13.20; 32-piece set, $21.45; 45-piece set, $35.40.

Dewdrop Fairies and Milkweed Dance patterns originally sold for the following: 14-piece set, $9.15; 20-piece set, $10.00; 32-piece set, $16.45; 45-piece set, $26.90.

Price differences were due to the hand-tinted decorating on the first group of patterns listed above; Dewdrop Fairies and Milkweed Dance are plain prints on an ivory background.

TOP: Enchantment 10½" plate; Autumn Ballet 14" charger encased in pewter rim; Fairyland 8½" plate. Nymphs are found on the latter two.
BOTTOM: Nutcracker 6½" plate; Milkweed Dance sugar bowl; Fantasia salt and pepper shakers (sugar bowl and shakers were executed on the Montecito shape); Flower Ballet tea cup and saucer. On the saucer, the nymph is touching a flower with her wand. © *Disney Enterprises, Inc.*

Close-up view of Nutcracker tall creamer,
teapot, and tall sugar.
© *Disney Enterprises, Inc.*

TOP: Fantasia 1-quart pitcher (Montecito); 10½" Fantasia plate; Fairyland mug (Montecito).
BOTTOM: Autumn Ballet salt and pepper shakers (Montecito).
© *Disney Enterprises, Inc.*

TOP: Fantasia fruit, tumbler, sugar (Montecito); Flower Ballet 10½" plate, egg cup.
BOTTOM: Fantasia graduated dinnerware plates, 6½", 7½", 8½", 9½".
© *Disney Enterprises, Inc.*

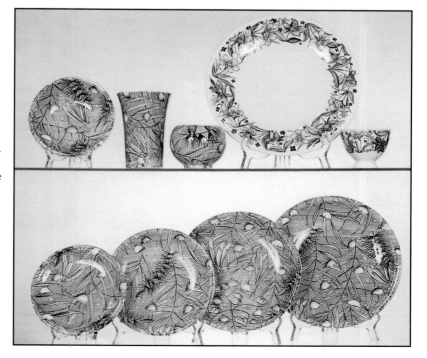

Ultra Pattern Index

The following are all known patterns for Ultra.

Name	Description	Approx. Period of Production	Artist
Abundance	Maroon plain transfer print. Tiny fruit and floral border and center spray. Counterpart patterns: Mode, Style, Taste.	1939	Turnbull
Aquarium	Hand-painted tropical fish.	1938	Blanding
Autumn Ballet	Maroon hand-tinted transfer print. All-over floral, leaf. Counterpart patterns: Fairyland, Milkweed Dance, Fantasia.	1940	Disney
Bellflower	Plain transfer print in red, blue, or green. All-over floral. Counterpart patterns: Choice, Colleen, Floret, Grace.	1939	Turnbull
Bouquet	Hand-painted elaborate floral, yellow rim.	1938	Turnbull
Brown Eyed Susan #838	Hand-painted yellow daisies, green leaves, ivory ground. Mostly found on Montecito.	1940	
"Calla Lily"	Author's name for Frederik Lunning, Inc., N.Y., 1940 unnamed pattern. Unmarked Vernon Kilns. Transfer print. Center design of single calla lily, green leaves, green-and-yellow-striped rim (cup in Montecito shape).	1940	
Choice	Blue hand-tinted transfer print, touches of yellow and rose. All-over floral. Counterpart patterns: Bellflower, Colleen, Floret, Grace.	1939	
Colleen	Green hand-tinted transfer print, touches of red and yellow. All-over floral. Counterpart patterns: Bellflower, Choice, Floret, Grace.	1939	
Coral Reef	Plain transfer print in blue, light orange, light pink, medium pink, or maroon on cream background. Tropical fish motif.	1940	Blanding
Delight	Blue hand-tinted transfer print, yellow flowers. Camellia and gardenia motif. Counterpart patterns: Ecstasy, Glamour, Joy.	1940	Blanding
Dewdrop Fairies	Blue plain transfer print, border on flatware, all-over on hollow ware. Counterpart patterns: Enchantment, Flower Ballet, Nutcracker.	1940	Disney
Ecstasy	Light brown hand-tinted transfer print. Camellia and gardenia motif. Counterpart patterns: Delight, Glamour, Joy.	1940	Blanding
Enchantment	Blue hand-tinted transfer print. Border on flatware, all-over on hollow ware. Counterpart patterns: Dewdrop Fairies, Flower Ballet, Nutcracker.	1940	Disney
Fairyland	Blue hand-tinted transfer print. All-over floral, leaf. Counterpart patterns: Autumn Ballet, Fantasia, Milkweed Dance.	1940	Disney
Fantasia	Brown hand-tinted transfer print. All-over floral, leaf. Counterpart patterns: Autumn Ballet, Fairyland, Milkweed Dance.	1940	Disney
Five Fingers	T-729. Hand-painted stylized autumn leaves and tendrils on ivory ground.	1938	Turnbull
Flora	Elaborate hand-painted floral spray, blue striped-rim.	1938	Turnbull

Name	Description	Approx. Period of Production	Artist
Floret	Red hand-tinted transfer print. All-over floral. Counterpart patterns: Bellflower, Choice, Colleen, Grace.	1939	Turnbull
Flower Ballet	Maroon hand-tinted transfer print. Border on flatware, all-over on hollow ware. Counterpart patterns: Dewdrop Fairies, Enchantment, Nutcracker.	1940	Disney
Glamour	Plain transfer print in blue, brown, or maroon. Camellia and gardenia motif. Counterpart patterns: Delight, Ecstasy, Joy.	1940	Blanding
Grace	Purple hand-tinted transfer print, touches of yellow, rose, and blue. All-over floral. Counterpart patterns: Bellflower, Choice, Colleen, Floret.	1939	
Harvest	Elaborate hand-painted design of fruit on ivory background, yellow striped rim.	1938	Turnbull
Hawaiian Flowers	Plain transfer print, pink, blue, maroon, or light orange. Lotus motif. Counterpart patterns: Honolulu, Hilo, Lei Lani (Hawaii).	1938 – 1942	Blanding
Hilo	Light brown hand-tinted transfer print. Lotus motif. Counterpart patterns: Hawaiian Flowers, Honolulu, Lei Lani (Hawaii).	1938	Blanding
Honolulu	Blue hand-tinted transfer print, yellow touches. Lotus motif. Counterpart patterns: Hawaiian Flowers, Hilo, Lei Lani (Hawaii).	1938	Blanding
Joy	Brown hand-tinted transfer print, yellow touches. Camellia and gardenia motif. Counterpart patterns: Delight, Ecstasy, Glamour.	1940	Blanding
Lei Lani	Maroon hand-tinted transfer print, Lotus motif. Hawaii is same pattern on Melinda shape. Counterpart patterns: Hawaiian Flowers, Honolulu, Hilo. Pattern continued on San Marino shape.	1938 – 1942	Blanding
Milkweed Dance	Plain transfer print in blue or maroon. All-over floral, leaf. Counterpart patterns: Autumn Ballet, Fairyland, Fantasia.	1940	Disney
Moby Dick	Plain transfer print in blue, brown, maroon, or yellow (rare). Whaling scenes.	1939 – 1942	Kent
Mode	Rust-green hand-tinted transfer print. Tiny fruit and floral border and center spray. Counterpart patterns: Abundance, Style, Taste.	1939	Turnbull
Nutcracker	Brown hand-tinted transfer print. Border on flatware, all-over on hollow ware. Counterpart patterns: Dewdrop Fairies, Enchantment, Flower Ballet.	1940	Disney
Orchard	Hand-painted simple fruit design.	1937	Turnbull
Our America	Plain transfer print in brown, blue, or maroon. Over 30 different scenes of America.	1940	Kent
Rio Chico	Hand painted, with wide pink border and small floral center. Counterpart patterns: Rio Verde, Rio Vista.	1938	
Rio Verde	Hand painted, with wide green border and small floral center. Counterpart patterns: Rio Chico, Rio Vista.	1938	
Rio Vista	Hand painted, with wide blue border and small floral center. Counterpart patterns: Rio Chico, Rio Verde.	1938	

Name	Description	Approx. Period of Production	Artist
Rosa	Hand painted, large single rose in center, border of small rosebuds, narrow rose band on rim.	1938	Turnbull
Rosalie	Hand painted, full blown rose and buds, green leaves floral spray. Rose-colored rim.	1938	Turnbull
Salamina	Hand-tinted transfer print. Greenland scenes and girl, Salamina.	1939	Kent
Santa Barbara	Brown hand-tinted transfer print, blue and yellow touches. All-over flower and leaf. Counterpart patterns: Santa Clara, Santa Maria, Santa Paula, Santa Rosa.	1939	
Santa Clara	Plain transfer print in pink or blue. All-over flower and leaf. Counterpart patterns: Santa Barbara, Santa Maria, Santa Paula, Santa Rosa.	1939	
Santa Maria	Purple hand-tinted transfer print, blue, and yellow touches. All-over flower and leaf. Counterpart patterns: Santa Barbara, Santa Clara, Santa Paula, Santa Rosa.	1939	
Santa Paula	Hand-tinted transfer with pink, blue, and yellow touches. All-over flower and leaf. Counterpart patterns: Santa Barbara, Santa Clara, Santa Maria, Santa Rosa.	1939	
Santa Rosa	Blue hand-tinted transfer print, blue and yellow touches. All-over flower and leaf. Counterpart patterns: Santa Barbara, Santa Clara, Santa Maria, Santa Paula.	1939	
Sierra Madre Two-Tone	Hand-painted wide colored border. Same as Rio patterns without the center flower. Colors of pink, blue, green, peach, maroon.	1941	
Style	Green hand-tinted transfer print, colors in raised enamel. Tiny fruit and floral border and center spray. Counterpart patterns: Abundance, Mode, Taste.	1939	Turnbull
Taste	Maroon hand-tinted transfer print, colors in raised enamel. Tiny fruit and floral border and center spray. Counterpart patterns: Abundance, Mode, Style.	1939	Turnbull
T-729	See Five Fingers.		
T-742	Hand-painted small yellow rose on cream background, blue rim. Has been named "Yellow Rose No. 1" by the author.	1938	Turnbull
T-743	Small hand-painted yellow rose on cream background, lime green rim. "Yellow Rose No. 2."	1938	Turnbull
T-744	Small hand-painted yellow rose on cream background, brown rim and leaf. "Yellow Rose No. 3."	1938	Turnbull
769	Hand-painted corsage-like spray pink flower. Rose-colored rim.	1938	Turnbull
Ultra California	Solid colors: Buttercup (yellow), Gardenia (ivory), Carnation (pink), Aster (blue). Other colors known are maroon, ice green.	1937 – 42	Turnbull
Vera	Elaborate hand-painted flora, blue-striped rim.	1938	Turnbull
#838	See Brown Eyed Susan	1940	

Ultra Values

Elaborate or hand-painted patterns will be worth more than simpler or solid-colored patterns. Values are based on mint condition. Dimensions will vary.

Bowls, 5½" fruit	$6.00 – 12.00
6" cereal	$10.00 – 15.00
6" chowder, open	$12.00 – 20.00
chowder, covered	$25.00 – 35.00
8¼" coupe soup	$12.00 – 20.00
8" serving, round	$18.00 – 25.00
9" serving, round	$18.00 – 30.00
11" salad	$45.00 – 85.00
1 pint	$20.00 – 30.00
Mixing, 5-piece set	
5"	$15.00 – 25.00
6"	$20.00 – 30.00
7"	$25.00 – 35.00
8"	$30.00 – 40.00
9"	$35.00 – 45.00
Butter tray and cover, oblong	$35.00 – 75.00
Casserole, 8" (inside diameter), covered.	$45.00 – 95.00
Coffee pots, after dinner, 2-cup	$65.00 –125.00
regular, 6-cup	$65.00 –125.00
*Comport, footed	$50.00 – 75.00
Creamers, open, individual	$12.00 – 20.00
open, regular, short or tall	$12.00 – 20.00
Cups and saucers, after dinner (demitasse)	$18.00 – 25.00
teacup	$12.00 – 20.00
jumbo cup	$35.00 – 40.00
Egg cup	$18.00 – 25.00
Jam Jar, notched lid	$65.00 – 95.00
lid only	$15.00 – 20.00
Muffin cover only (no matching tray)	$60.00 – 85.00
Mug, 3½", 8 oz.	$20.00 – 30.00
Pickle, 6" round, tab handle	$35.00 – 50.00
Pitchers, 4½", 1-pint jug, open	$35.00 – 50.00

1-pint jug, covered..$45.00 – 75.00

2-quart, open ....$45.00 – 75.00

2-quart, covered..$75.00 –125.00

    *disk..$65.00 –100.00

Plates, 6½" bread and butter..$6.00 – 10.00

    7½" salad...$8.00 – 12.00

    8½" luncheon...$15.00 – 20.00

    9½" luncheon...$10.00 – 20.00

    10½" dinner ....$12.00 – 20.00

    12" chop ....$20.00 – 30.00

    14" chop ....$40.00 – 60.00

    17" chop ....$65.00 – 95.00

Sauce boat ....$20.00 – 25.00

Shakers, set ....$20.00 – 30.00

Sugar, covered, individual ....$15.00 – 25.00

    covered, regular, short or tall ....$18.00 – 30.00

Teapot, 6-cup ....$45.00 –100.00

Tumbler, 5" (ice tea), 13 oz., Style #4 ....$25.00 – 40.00

Tureenette, 7", notched cover ....$95.00 –125.00

Values for artist patterns:

    Blanding: Three to four times higher; Aquarium is five to seven times higher.

    Kent: Moby Dick is two to four times higher; Our America is three to five times higher;
        Salamina is five to seven times higher. Moby dick and Blanding pieces in yellow, add 20%. Salamina is five to
        seven times higher.

    Disney: Five to seven times higher. Hand-tinted transfer patterns will be at the upper end of range, blue being the
        rarest. Border transfer are at the low end, ecept for covered items, mugs, tumblers, and pouring vessels.

    Turnbull: One to two times higher.

*Not found in all patterns.

Melinda ❦

The Melinda shape, a Royal Hickman design, was elaborate. Among its patterns were the traditional English pattern look-alikes. Introduced at the time of World War II, the patterns were particularly popular and filled the demand for similar English wares that were unavailable during the war.

The design of the flatware rim had an embossed leaf motif (described as a rope in earlier book editions). The bases of bowls, pitchers, and pots likewise had the same embossed leaf design. Handles were leaf-shaped and in relief, and finials were flower-like. Some serving pieces were leaf-shaped. An 8½" plate with squared-off corners was also made. According to an ad in the 1942 *Crockery and Glass Journal*, "10 different patterns were available, some hand-painted, some print-and-fill, all underglaze." There are two known, solid-colored patterns: Melinda (high glaze) and Native California (satin finish). Melinda is believed to be the earlier pattern and to have been in only two colors, aqua and ivory; Native California pastel colors were sapphire blue, emerald green, coral pink, and topaz yellow. There are more patterns than the ten mentioned in the ad.

Hand-tinted patterns include Chintz, Dolores, May Flower, Cosmos, Fruitdale, and Southern Rose. Rosedale and Wheat, made for Sears, are also hand tinted. Don Blanding's Hawaii on the Melinda shape is the same as Lei Lani on the Ultra shape. Plain prints include Blossom Time, Palm Brocade, and Lace Curtain (this last name, in lieu of unknown pattern name is author assigned). Hand-painted patterns include Carmel, Monterey, Philodendron, Arcadia, Santa Anita, Susan, and Beverly. Some designs are identical and the pattern name is determined by color; such is the case with Cosmos and Blossom Time, and with Monterey, Carmel, and Philodendron.

According to Michael Pratt, the Fruitdale pattern was created by Ed Botsford and was introduced in 1943. Botsford was also the artist for Vernon's 1860 and for Early Days (on the San Fernando shape).

The Beverly pattern was named after Harry Bird's granddaughter, Beverly. Bill Sterns, director of the Museum of California Design, discovered this while interviewing said Beverly.

Goes to Sea was a personalized, hand-painted yachting dinner pattern that had either the Philodendron or the Monterey-colored border; it was offered only through special order. The company brochure described it as "fine dinnerware… complete with the name of your yacht, copper-etched in rope design and house flag and yacht club burgee on each piece in full color under permanent glaze." It is rare, but fortunately, examples were available for photographing (pages 129 and 257). The company brochure described the Four Winds pattern as designed for the yacht that sailed the Transpacific Yacht Club Race from Los Angeles to Honolulu (year unknown to author). In addition to Four Winds, special order yacht names mentioned were Mary Clay, Flamingo, Goose B III, Hazel K., Jada, Kathleen-Newport, Kipajoge II, La Osa, Nan Jo, Pompano, Roaring Bessie, Sal Al III, Slip Away, and Tondeleyo. See page 91 for company brochure.

Other personalized special order items were Heraldry designs. These surnames and coat-of-arms plates can be seen on page 127; these are the only known examples at this time.

Name plates were still another special order item. Plates were described in an ad "as having the facsimile of your signature copper-etched" and as open stock available. No examples were available for photographing. A number of monogrammed pieces have been found. A few examples are seen on page 163 in the Montecito section.

Two patterns were designed for Sears, Roebuck & Co., Wheat and Rosedale (on pages 310 – 311). A set of Rotary Club dishes was also produced on the Melinda shape. The shape was used for serving pieces for Yosemite National Park dishes, and for other souvenirs. See pages 96, 100 – 103, and 127 – 128.

Pictured is the solid-color Native California. Colors known are aqua (both light and dark), blue, pink, yellow, ivory, and green. All have mark 18 unless otherwise noted. Some of the solid colors will be found with the Melinda mark (17).
TOP: 12½" salad bowl with footed base, 4½" deep (mark 12); 14" platter; 9½" plate (banner mark 20); 8½" rim soup.
CENTER: Salt and pepper shakers (unmarked); demitasse cup and saucer; 7½" plate; creamer.
BOTTOM: 5½" fruit; 6½" plate (mark 17), the only one in the group with the Melinda mark.

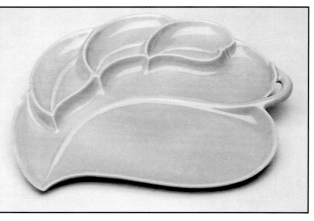

Pictured is the large 14" 4-part leaf shape server. Mark is a variation of 12.

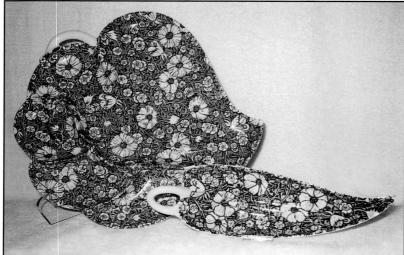

The 14" 4-part and the 12" single leaf-shaped relish servers in the Blossom time pattern.
Nancy Franz photo.

Jam jar, salad serving bowl, and 1-pint bowl in Monterey. *Bob Hutchins photo.*

Closeup view of Carmel (brown and yellow) pattern on the Melinda-shape jam jar with notched lid. Both pattern and jam jar are scarce. Carmel is the counterpart of Monterey (blue and red) and Philodendron (green and yellow). *Joanne and John Barrett photo.*

Some examples of the Melinda shape, not commonly seen.
TOP: Arcadia egg cup; Native California chowder; unmarked individual covered casserole, 4¾" dia. (scarce).
CENTER: 8½" square plates, in Arcadia, Cosmos, and Chintz.
BOTTOM: Blossom Time decorated #139 10" petal bowl; tea cup and saucer.
Note: No. 129 bowl (seen on page 77), has been found decorated with Cosmos.

Demitasse pieces: creamer, coffee pot, and covered sugar bowl. *Bob Hutchins photo.*

The small 1½-pint and large 2-quart pitchers in Monterey. *Bob Hutchins photo.*

TOP: Fruitdale 9½" plate; Chintz 13½" chop plate; Blossom Time covered casserole, 8" inside diameter, actual diameter including handles is 11", mark 19 without "hand painted under glaze." Note the embossed leaf handles and leaves on lid.

CENTER: Chintz butter tray and cover; Fruitdale 4" tall creamer and 4" tall sugar; May Flower 7½" plate, mark 21.

BOTTOM: Chintz 3" short creamer; Delores 3" short sugar, mark 20; Four Winds hand-painted cup with Monterey trim, marked "Made Especially for Don Carlos Heintz, Skipper of the Four Winds by Vernon Kilns"; Monterey saucer; Dolores 5½" fruit, mark 20; Southern Rose sauce boat (four-line mark giving pattern name, "hand painted underglazes, by Vernon Kilns, U.S.A.," in block letters, similar to mark 16).

Hand-painted and hand-tinted transfer patterns are shown. All have mark 19 except where noted.

TOP: Dolores 14" oval platter; Monterey 1½-pint pitcher; Chintz coffee pot.

CENTER: Arcadia 6-cup teapot; Fruitdale 2-tier server with brass fittings; Chintz salt shaker; May Flower pepper shaker (shaker marked only with pattern name and "Made in U.S.A."); May Flower 9½" oval vegetable.

BOTTOM: Monterey leaf-shaped 12" relish; Philodendron demitasse cup and saucer (mark 21); Southern Rose 2-part leaf-shaped serving dish (has same mark as the sauce boat in the above photo).

Chintz ad that appeared in a national magazine in 1942.

Susan coffee pot and tall creamer and sugar. Mark 19. *Linda and Jerry Lakomek photo.*

Arcadia after dinner 2-cup coffee pot, 6½" tall, with matching cup.

Note the similar color scheme and leaf design of the two patterns in the picture above and the one to the left. The names of the patterns are themselves related — The Santa Anita racetrack is in Arcadia in Southern California.

An example of the Santa Anita pattern. Mark 19.

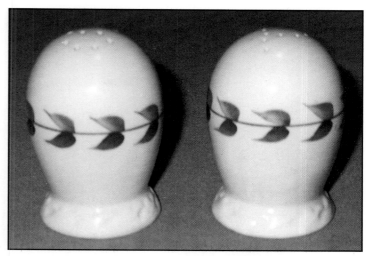

Pair of shakers in Laurel pattern. They have a similar leaf design to the Arcadia leaf. This is the only example in this pattern that was available. *Bob Hutchins photo.*

Examples of special order yachting dishes.
LEFT TO RIGHT: Kathleen-Newport 5½" fruit; Kipajoge II sugar bowl; Flamingo 5½" fruit; Kathleen-Newport 9" serving bowl.
Mark Smith photo.

Example of backstamp on sugar bowl.
Mark Smith photo.

Pictured are examples of Blanding's Hawaii, mark 35. Same as Lei Lani, but renamed for this Melinda shape.
TOP: Coffee pot flanked by tall creamer and sugar.
BOTTOM: 12½" chop plate (also marked "Made for Trojan"); teacup.

Some additional patterns are pictured, including two that were done for Sears & Roebuck with their Harmony House mark (see page 311, Miscellany, for picture of mark.)
TOP: Wheat demitasse cup and saucer; Rosedale 9½" plate. Both Harmony House.
CENTER: Lace Curtain* sugar, mark 22; Palm Brocade 10½" plate, unmarked and creamer (see mark 49 in Evolution of Marks).
BOTTOM: Beverly demitasse cup and saucer; 9½" plate; teacup and saucer, mark 19.

The Palm Brocade mark (49) is very similar in design to the Pan American Lei mark (44). It includes an artist name, Biondi.

In January of 1953, 16-piece May Flower starter sets sold for $14.95 each. A starter set consisted of four 10½" plates, four 6½" plates, and four tea cups and saucers.

*Author's name for this pattern.

1951 company photo of May Flower table setting.

Melinda Pattern Index

The following are all known patterns on the Melinda shape. "S.O." designates a special order, and quotation marks around a pattern name indicate that it is not an official company name, merely a lable provided by the author to aid reference.

Name	Description	Approx. Period of Production	Artist
Arcadia	Hand-painted brown and mustard laurel wreath border.	1942 – 1950 S.O. 1950 – 1955	
Beverly	Hand-painted rose blossoms, leaves encircle rims.	1942	
Blossom Time	Transfer. All-over blossoms, deep blue on ivory. Same as Cosmos except different color.	1942	
Carmel	Hand-painted embossed border, handles, and finials of brown and yellow. Same as Monterey and Philodendron except different colors.	1942 – 1948	
Chintz	Hand-tinted transfer. Traditional English-style floral.	1942 – 1950 S.O. 1950 – 1955	
Cosmos	Red hand-tinted transfer print. All-over blossoms. Same as Blossom Time except for color.	1942	
Dolores	Hand-tinted transfer. Traditional English-style floral.	1942 – 1950	
Fruitdale	Hand-tinted transfer. Colorful array of fruit. Traditional English-style.	1943 – 1950	Botsford
Hawaii	Maroon hand-tinted transfer print. Lotus motif. Same as Lei Lani except different shape.	1942 – 1950	Blanding
"Lace Curtain"	All-over transfer design resembling lace, pink color.	1950	
Laurel	Leaf border similar to Arcadia leaf pattern.		
May Flower	Hand-tinted transfer. Traditional English-style floral.	1942 – 1950 1953 – 1955 S.O. 1950 – 1953 and 1955 – 1956	
Melinda	Name of shape. Also, the name of an early pattern on this shape with high-glaze, solid colors of aqua and ivory.	1942	Hickman
Monterey	Hand-painted embossed border, handles, and finials in red and blue. Same as Carmel and Philodendron except different colors.	1942 – 1950 S.O. 1950 – 1955	
Native California	Satin-finish, solid pastel colors of sapphire blue, emerald green, coral pink, and topaz yellow.	1942 – 1950	Hickman
Palm Brocade	All-over transfer design of palm leaves, linen textured background, brown shades.	1950	Biondi
Philodendron	Hand-painted embossed border, handles and finials in green and yellow colors. Same as Carmel and Monterey except different colors.	1942 – 1950 S.O. 1950 – 1955	
Rosedale	Hand-tinted transfer. Spray of roses motif. Made for Sears under their name (in their 1950 catalog).	1950	
Rotary	Special order for Rotary Club of Vernon. Dishware decorated with Rotary Club emblem and members signatures.	1950	
Santa Anita	Hand-painted border, pink blossoms connected by brown wavy lines.	1942	
Southern Rose	Hand-tinted transfer. Floral bouquet.	1942	

Name	Description	Approx. Period of Production	Artist
Susan	Floral. Yellow, blue, and rose-colored blossoms, green pastel leaves. Touches of green pastel and rose on the handles and finials.	1942	
Wheat	Hand-tinted transfer. Large spray of blossoms and sheaths of wheat. Made for Sears under its name (in the 1950 catalog).	1950	
Yachting	Special order personalized yacht patterns that are known include: Mary Clay, Flamingo, Four Winds, Goose B III, Hazel K, Jada, Kathleen-Newport, Kipajoge II, La Osa, Nan Jo, Pompano, Roaring Bessie, Sal-Al III, Slip Away, Tondeleyo. Hand-painted border of maroon and blue on ivory ground, except for Goose B III, which has a green and yellow border.	1950	

Melinda Values

Elaborate patterns will have a higher value than simpler ones. All values are based on mint condition. Dimensions will vary.

Bowls, 5½" fruit ....$6.00 – 10.00

    6" lug chowder ....$12.00 – 18.00

    8" rim soup ....$12.00 – 18.00

    9" serving, round ....$18.00 – 25.00

    10" serving, oval ....$20.00 – 25.00

    10" petal (#139 bowl)..$35.00 – 45.00

    12" salad, footed base...$45.00 – 75.00

    1-pint ....$20.00 – 30.00

Butter tray and cover, oblong ....$35.00 – 75.00

*Casserole, covered, 8" (inside dia.) ....$45.00 – 75.00

    covered, individual, 4¾" dia. ....$25.00 – 35.00

Coffee pot, after dinner, 2-cup ....$65.00 – 75.00

    covered, 8-cup ....$55.00 – 85.00

Creamer, individual size ....$12.00 – 18.00

Creamer, short or tall ....$12.00 – 18.00

Cups and saucers, after dinner ....$15.00 – 20.00

    teacup ....$12.00 – 20.00

Egg cup...$18.00 – 25.00

Jam Jar ....$65.00 – 75.00

    lid only ....$15.00 – 20.00

Pitchers, 1½-pint ....$25.00 – 35.00

    2-quart...$35.00 – 50.00

* Called a covered dish in the Melinda shape.

Plates, 6½" bread and butter ....$6.00 – 10.00

    7½" salad ....$9.00 – 12.00

    8½" square luncheon ....$15.00 – 20.00

    9½" luncheon ....$12.00 – 15.00

    10½" dinner ....$12.00 – 18.00

    12" chop ....$20.00 – 30.00

    14" chop ....$35.00 – 50.00

    17" chop ....$50.00 – 75.00

Platters, 12" ....$20.00 – 30.00

    14" ....$35.00 – 50.00

    16" ....$55.00 – 85.00

Relish, single leaf shape, 12" ....$25.00 – 30.00

    two-part leaf shape, 11" ....$30.00 – 45.00

    four-part leaf shape, 14" ....$45.00 – 75.00

Sauce boat ....$20.00 – 30.00

Shakers, set ....$15.00 – 25.00

Sugar, covered, short or tall ....$15.00 – 25.00

    covered, individual size ....$18.00 – 22.00

Teapot, covered, 6-cup ....$45.00 – 85.00

Tidbit Server, two-tier, wooden fixture ....$20.00 – 30.00

    three-tier, wooden fixture ....$25.00 – 45.00

Values:

    Blanding pattern pieces are two times higher than the high end price of similar pieces.
    Sears & Roebuck pieces are in the high end of the price range.

San Fernando ⬳

Another elaborate shape (designer unknown) is believed to have been introduced during the same period as Melinda. The flatware has scalloped rims, and the hollow ware has fluted pedestal styled bases with fancy scrolled handles. The traditional patterns executed on the shape were extremely popular and again offered an English look. All patterns on this shape are transfer prints except for one, Flower Ballet (non-Disney pattern); there are no solid-color patterns. The plain prints were Early Days, Ariel, and R.F.D. The provincial R.F.D. (mark 45) included two different figural salt and pepper shakers (hurricane lamps and mail boxes) and a figural mail box butter tray and cover. The pattern artist was Paul Davidson.

Hand-tinted prints were Vernon's 1860, Hibiscus, Vernon Rose, Desert Bloom, Briar Rose, and Flower Ballet. (The 1860 print was simply the hand-tinted version of Botsford's Early Days print; some pieces and both patterns may be found signed.) A pattern called Good Earth has also been reported. For R.F.D. and Vernon's 1860, detailed backstamps were designed (see Evolution of Marks, numbers 45 and 40, respectively.) Vernon's Hibiscus is a dead ringer for Spode's Buttercup. The Vernon English – look-alike patterns helped to meet demand for English styles during the World War II years. This shape was also used for some of the Scenic America demitasse cups and saucers and 10½" picture plates.

TOP: Vernon's 1860 coffee pot and 10½" plate; Early Days 7½" plate. There may be an 1860 after dinner coffee pot, 2-cup size, and individual creamer and sugar, though none was listed on available company price lists. After dinner cups and saucers were listed.
CENTER: R.F.D. sauce boat with fast stand; Vernon's 1860 saucer; Early Days after dinner cup and saucer.
BOTTOM: R.F.D. 10" olive dish; Vernon's 1860 8" rim soup; R.F.D. butter tray and cover.

Vernon's 1860 Soup tureen, 13" diameter, with its 15" plate stand and eight chowder bowls. In July 1950, the hand-tinted pattern tureen sold for $21.00 and the plate stand for $9.00. Its counterpart was the untinted pink Early Days; the tureen in that pattern was $18.00 and the plate stand was $8.00.

Vernon's 1860 candlesticks and teapot kerosene lamp.

Company brochures for Vernon's Rose (right), Desert Bloom (top of next page), and Hibiscus (bottom of next page).

America's Finest Dinnerware

Two close-up views of R.F.D.'s unique salt and pepper shakers (mailboxes above and lanterns below). Both shapes are found only in the R.F.D. pattern. The salt and pepper shape used for the rest of the San Fernando patterns may be seen in the group picture on page 270.

Ariel pattern 10½" plate (banner mark 21). In addition to the backstamp, there was also crayoned information reading: "H-340, 6-6-52, Re Joe" (or Ro, this writing was hard to discern), which may indicate this was an experimental design. The *H* may be Elliott House's initial.

Coffee pot illustrating the non-Disney Flower Ballet pattern. At the present time, nothing is known about this pattern's production. Mark 21. *Tim and Linda Colling photo.*

TOP: Hibiscus 12" oval platter; Vernon Rose 14" chop plate; Hibiscus demitasse cup and saucer; Desert Bloom 10½" plate.
BOTTOM: Hibiscus 2-tier tidbit server, chowder, and salt shaker (unmarked); Desert Bloom salt shaker (unmarked); Hibiscus 10" oval vegetable, teacup and saucer, and 5½" fruit.

TOP: Briar Rose 10" olive dish (mark 21).
CENTER: Two 10½" plates (unmarked), with the Briar Rose design combined with the R.F.D. border in different colors.
BOTTOM: Two 10½" R.F.D. rooster-and-stove design plates with different color borders, back-stamp mark 45, Paul L. Davidson, 1951."

All items in these two photos have mark 21, except for R.F.D., Vernon's 1860, and where noted elsewhere.

In January of 1953, starter sets of 16 pieces, with four each of 10½" plates, 6½" plates, and tea cups and saucers, sold for the following: R.F.D., $13.95; Vernon's 1860, $15.95; and Desert Bloom and Hibiscus, $17.95. Since starter sets for these shapes were sold with 10½" plates, 9½" plates may be less plentiful today.

San Fernando Pattern Index

The following are all known patterns in the San Fernando shape.

Name	Description	Approx. Period of Production	Artist
Ariel	Spray of blue roses and butterflies, hand-tinted transfer. May not have been a production pattern.	1952	
Briar Rose	Hand-tinted transfer. Red and yellow roses on stem.	1950	
Desert Bloom	Rust hand-tinted transfer print. Tiny pink and blue flowers form wide border. Traditional English style.	1944 – 1954 S.O. 1955	
Early Days	Plain transfer print, deep rose color. Traditional English style, same scenes as Vernon's 1860.	1944 – 1950 S.O. 1950 – 1955	Ed Botsford
Flower Ballet	This is not the 1940 Disney pattern of the same name. At the present time, nothing is known about its production.		
Good Earth	Pumpkin and corn shock with farm building in background is the only known description of the pattern.		
Hibiscus	Hand-tinted transfer tiny yellow flowers on brown print. Traditional English style.	1944 – 1953 S.O. 1954	
R.F.D.	Transfer print, brown rooster, green plaid border.	1951 – 1953 S.O. 1954	P. L. Davidson
Vernon's 1860	Brown hand-tinted transfer print. Traditional English style, scenes of 1860 America.	1944 – 1953 S.O. 1954	Ed Botsford
Vernon Rose	Transfer print. Single large yellow rose and small blossoms, cream ground.	1944 – 1950 S.O. 1950-1954	

San Fernando Values

Bowls, 5½" fruit ....$6.00 – 10.00
   *5½" salad, individual...........................$12.00 – 18.00
   6" lug chowder...................................$12.00 – 18.00
   8" rim soup ....$12.00 – 20.00
   9" serving, round ....$18.00 – 25.00
   10" serving, oval ....$20.00 – 25.00
   *10½" salad......................................$45.00 – 65.00
*Bowls, 5-piece mixing set
   5" ....$15.00 – 19.00
   6" ....$19.00 – 24.00
   7" ....$22.00 – 29.00
   8" ....$25.00 – 32.00
   9" ....$30.00 – 35.00

*Butter tray and cover, mail box ....$40.00 – 45.00

**Candlesticks (converted teacups) ....$65.00 – 75.00

***Casserole, covered, 8" (inside dia.) ....$45.00 – 75.00

*Coaster, 3¾", ridged ....$15.00 – 20.00

Coffee pot, covered, 8-cup ....$35.00 – 75.00

Creamer, regular ....$12.00 – 15.00

Cups and saucer, after dinner ....$15.00 – 20.00

      teacup ....$12.00 – 18.00

*Egg cup, double ....$15.00 – 25.00

**Kerosene Lamp (converted teapot) ....$100.00 – 125.00

*Mug, 9 oz ....$20.00 – 25.00

Olive dish, 10" oval...$20.00 – 35.00

Pitcher, 1½ qt. ....$25.00 – 35.00

Plates, 6½" bread and butter..$6.00 – 10.00

      7½" salad..$8.00 – 12.00

      9½" luncheon (less plentiful) ....$10.00 – 15.00

      10½" dinner ....$12.00 – 18.00

      14" chop ....$35.00 – 50.00

Platters, 12" ....$20.00 – 30.00

      14" ....$35.00 – 50.00

      16" ....$50.00 – 75.00

Sauce boat, fast-stand ....$20.00 – 30.00

Shakers, salt ....$7.50 – 12.50

      pepper ....$7.50 – 12.50

      *figural mail box, pair ....$20.00 – 35.00

      *figural lanterns, pair..$15.00 – 25.00

*Spoon holder ....$40.00 – 50.00

Soup tureen, covered, 13", notched cover (none for R.F.D.) ....$250.00 – 300.00

      15" plate stand ....$40.00 – 50.00

Sugar, covered ....$15.00 – 20.00

Teapot, covered, 6-cup..$45.00 – 85.00

Tidbit, two-tier, wooden fixture ....$20.00 – 30.00

      three-tier, wooden fixture...$25.00 – 40.00

*Tumbler, 14 oz, Style #5...$20.00 – 25.00

*These items only in R.F.D.
**These items only in Vernon's 1860.
***Called a covered dish in this shape.

San Marino ∞

San Marino, an early 1950s shape, was a complete departure from the traditional. It had streamlined, elongated hollow ware and coupe flatware. Some lines were hand painted and some had print designs and interesting glazes. This shape had an exciting new look widely accepted by young housewives and it continued to be made until the company went out of business. Of known patterns, three are basic solid color lines: Casual California, California Shadows, and California Originals (also called California Heritage). Casual California was offered with the new color names of Snowhite, Acacia Yellow, Mocha Brown, Pine Green, Dawn Pink, Turquoise Blue, Lime Green, and Dusk Gray. California Originals were offered in the unusual colors of Raisin Purple, Redwood Brown, Almond Yellow, and Vineyard Green. California Shadows was only offered in Cocoa Brown and Antique Gray. Both California Shadows and California Originals have interesting drip glazes. A patent for the drip glaze technique used on California Originals (California Heritage) was applied for. The backstamp for this pattern includes the words "Cerametal-Process, Patent Applied for" and appears above the pattern name (this is a variation of mark 20).

Hand-painted San Marino patterns are Barkwood, Bel Air, Gayety, Mexicana, Mojave (unmarked Vernon Kilns), Raffia, Shantung, and Dreamtime (dā Bron). Transfer prints are Hawaiian Coral, Heyday, Lei Lani, Seven Seas, Shadow Leaf, Trade Winds, Sun Garden (artist Jean Ames), and Pan American Lei.

Four of a set of five mixing bowls of California Originals are pictured. A complete set is hard to find. 9" Vineyard Green, 6" Vineyard Green, 5" Raisin Purple, and 8" Almond Yellow. The 7" Redwood Brown is missing from the nested set. The Casual California nest of mixing bowls (not pictured) was made in 5" Dawn Pink, 6" Lime Green, 7" Pine Green, 8" Mocha Brown, and 9" Turquoise Blue.

In January 1953, 16-piece starter sets included four 10" plates, four 6" plates, and four teacups and saucers. Casual California sets sold for $7.50, and the 5-piece mixing bowl set sold for $6.95. California Originals (California Heritage) starter sets were listed at $11.95, and the 5-piece mixing bowl set at $8.95. A Lei Lani starter set was $20.95; a Lei Lani mixing bowl set was not listed.

Brilliant Colors...in the Modern Mood

Company brochure for Casual California.

All the color patterns of San Marino are pictured and have mark 20, except where noted.
TOP: California Originals Redwood Brown 10-cup coffee server, bakelite handle (mark 20, "cerametal" variation); California Shadows Cocoa Brown 13½" oval platter; California Originals Almond Yellow 8-cup teapot measuring 11" lengthwise (mark 20, "cerametal" variation).
TOP CENTER: Casual California Mahogany Brown 8-cup teapot measuring 14½" lengthwise; four 14 oz. tumblers, three are Casual California in Dusk Gray (mark 22), Mahogany Brown (mark 22), and Pine Green (unmarked), and one is a California Originals in Raisin Purple (unmarked).
BOTTOM CENTER: Casual California Lime Green butter tray and cover; Mocha Brown* creamer (mark 20); Dawn Pink sugar bowl; California Heritage Almond Yellow 9" vegetable (mark 20, "cerametal" variation); Casual California Lime Green 9 oz. mug (mark 22) and Mahogany Brown 9 oz. mug (marked only "Made in California," in block letters).
BOTTOM: Casual California Lime Green 4" coaster; California Originals Vineyard Green sugar bowl (mark 20, "cerametal" variation); Casual California Lime Green gourd-shaped salt shaker (unmarked) and ¼-pint pitcher.

*Mocha Brown serving pieces could also be combined with the Heyday pattern.

A 5½" fruit dish identical to the San Marino shape and backstamped "SUNSET POTTERY, MADE IN U.S.A." can be seen on page 313. A grill plate mentioned in the Montecito section on page 144 also sometimes bears the Sunset Pottery mark. Some collectors have long suspected a connection between Sunset Pottery and Vernon Kilns, although the author has no documentation to substantiate it. Monterey, another pottery, is also suspected of being a Vernon Kilns subsidiary (see pages 313 – 314 for further information and backstamp).

Pictured are patterns found in the San Marino shape, all have mark 21 except where noted.
TOP: Mojave* sugar bowl (mark 41); Hawaiian Coral 8-cup teapot; Raffia 5½" fruit; Sun Garden 6½" plate and creamer (mark 46, designer pattern).
CENTER: Seven Seas 11" platter; Shadow Leaf 10" plate; Barkwood ¼-pint pitcher; Hawaiian Coral 10" plate and double egg cup (unmarked).
BOTTOM: Raffia cup (unmarked) and saucer; Bel Air butter tray and cover (mark 22); Gayety cup (unmarked) and saucer; Trade Winds creamer (unmarked); Vernonware dealer sign; Hawaiian Coral individual casserole (mark 22) and butter pat; Casual California Dawn Pink 11" platter (mark 20); Heyday 6" plate.

*The Montgomery Ward 1952 – 1953 catalog showed the Mojave pattern and mentioned that it had been "made for Wards by a nationally known pottery in California." A 16-piece place setting for four was $9.50.

Company photo of the Seven Seas table setting.

Lei Lani is shown as it appears on the San Marino shape. Creamer; 10" plate; salt shaker.

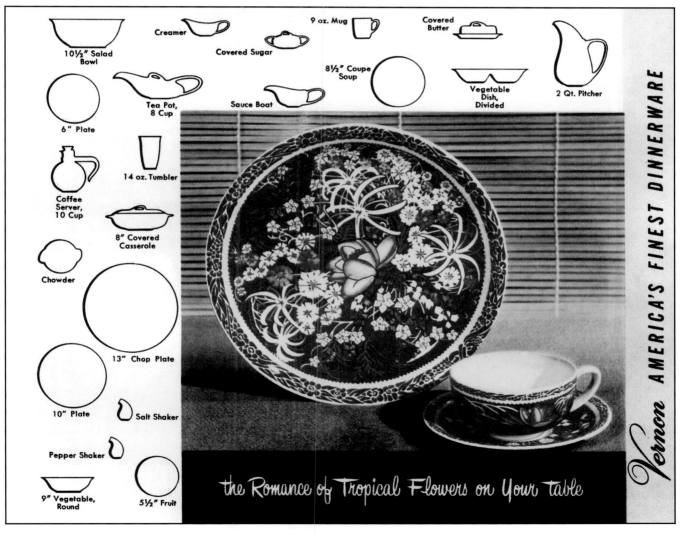

Company brochure showing Lei Lani on the San Marino shape.

277

TOP: Hawaiian Coral cup and saucer, drip-cut top syrup, and chowder. CENTER: Shantung 3" custard, mark 20; Casual California Acacia Yellow 10" plate, mark 20; Raffia mug (interchangeable with other shapes). BOTTOM: Barkwood 1-pint pitcher (one of five graduated sizes); covered casserole.

Two unusual Hawaiian Coral items are known to have been found. One is an umbrella stand and 20" tall, 11¾" diameter; the other is a large jar, 17" high and 17" across shoulders at the widest point. Neither one is marked.

Photograph of Heyday table setting, used for advertising purposes.

In 1953, complementary table accessories were added to the San Marino and the Montecito lines. These were black Coffee Hot and Casserole Hot wrought iron holders, complete with glass candle warmers. Company price lists do not indicate that the Casserole Round-Up stand was provided for the San Marino line; however, the stands were interchangeable.

Casual California Dusk Gray carafe and Coffee Hot stand.
Bob Hutchins photo.

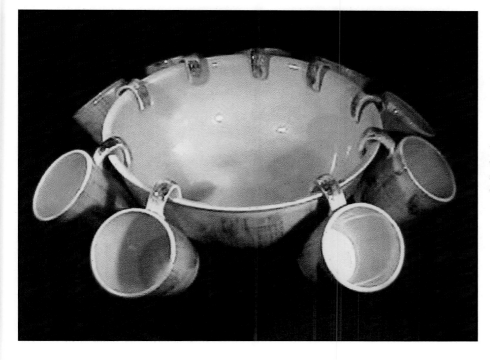

Unusual punch bowl set in Barkwood, consisting of a salad bowl and specially adapted mugs that can hang on rim of its bowl.
Tim and Linda Colling photo.

Spring Echo "Ceremetal-Process" backstamp. This mark also appears on California Originals (California Heritage) and the Royal Hawaiian after dinner cup and saucer. Also spelled Cer*a*metal. *Tim and Linda Colling photo.*

A rare pattern, Spring Echo, seen on this plate. Golden leaves on orange ground. *Tim and Linda Colling photo.*

An unmarked San Marino teacup in an unknown pattern somewhat reminiscent of Brown Eyed Susan. *Bob Hutchins photo.*

Mystery plate. Neither a number nor a mark.
Tim and Linda Colling photo.

San Marino Pattern Index

The following are all known patterns on the San Marino shape. "S.O." designates a special order.

Name	Description	Approx. Period of Production	Artist
*Barkwood	Warm brown on beige, hand painted and textured. Same as Raffia and Shantung except a different color.	1953 – 1958	
Bel Air	Hand-painted green and brown diagonal stripes on ivory ground. Same as Gayety except for color.	1950 S.O. 1955	
California Originals	Also called California Heritage. Drip glaze border in solid colors: Almond Yellow, Raisin Purple, Redwood Brown, Vineyard Green.	1950 S.O. 1954	
California Shadows	Solid color, streaked drip glaze border, mottled effect on lids. Cocoa Brown and Antique Gray in 1953. Cocoa Brown only in 1954.	1953 S.O. 1955	
Casual California	Solid Colors. 1950: Acacia Yellow, Lime Green, Mahogany Brown, and Pine Green; 1953 saw Dawn Pink, Dusk Gray, and Snowhite added. In 1954, Mahogany Brown and Snowhite were discontinued. Mocha Brown and Turquoise Blue were added. 1955 colors were Dawn Pink, Dusk Gray, Mocha Brown, and Turquoise Blue.	1950 – 1956 S.O. 1956	
Dreamtime	Hand-painted swirl pattern in green, rust, and yellow. Made for dà Bron.	1950	
Gayety	Hand-painted diagonal green and rose stripes on ivory ground. Same as Bel Air except for color.	1950 S.O. 1954	
Hawaiian Coral	Border in spattered blend of brown, yellow, and green on cream ground.	1952 S.O. 1956	
*Heyday	Geometric interlocking circles in deep green and brown, spattered beige background, mocha brown serving pieces. Spatter-decorated lids and knobs.	1954 – 1958	
Lei Lani	Maroon hand-tinted transfer print. Pattern was revived for a short time on this shape.	1953 – 1955 S.O. 1954	Blanding
Mexicana	1950 company price list showed the pattern as Montecito shape. 1951 company catalog showed the pattern as the San Marino shape. Border design of bands of rust, gold, and brown.	1950 – 1955 S.O. – 1954	
Mojave	Hand-painted bands of yellow, dark green, and brown on rim. Made for Montgomery Ward's 1952 – 1953 season.	1952 – 1953	
Pan American Lei	See pages 284 for description. Flatware, cups, mugs, pepper mills, and salt cellars were produced on this shape. Hollow ware and regular salt and pepper shakers were produced in the Lotus shape.	1950	
Raffia	Hand-painted textured pattern, henna on green ground. Same as Shantung and Barkwood except for color.	1953 – 1954	
Seven Seas	Stylized sailboats, brown and blue on ivory.	1954	
Shadow Leaf	Stylized red and green floral on green-tone swirl background. Same as Trade Winds except different colors.	1954 – 1955 S.O. 1956	
Shantung	Hand-painted textured pattern, dark brown on bright green ground. Same as Barkwood and Raffia except for color.		1953

Name	Description	Approx. Period of Production	Artist
Spring Echo	Golden leaves on orange ground. "Ceremetal process" in backstamp. Very scarce; nothing known about pattern.		
Sun Garden	Butterflies and flowers transfer, hand tinted on pale green ground.	1953	Jean Ames
Trade Winds	Rust and chartreuse floral on neutral swirl background. Same as Shadow Leaf except color.	1954 – 1955 S.O. 1956	
Wood Rose	Made for Belmar China Co.		
778	Evenly spaced red splashes on rim, white ground. Perhaps restaurant ware.	1950	

*Metlox continued this pattern for awhile.

San Marino Values

**Ashtray, 5½"	$12.00 – 20.00
Bowls, 5½" fruit	$5.00 – 8.00
*5½" salad, individual	$10.00 – 18.00
6" chowder	$10.00 – 15.00
7½" serving, round	$12.00 – 18.00
8½" coupe soup	$10.00 – 15.00
9" serving, round	$15.00 – 20.00
10" serving, divided.	$18.00 – 25.00
*10½" salad	$35.00 – 65.00
Mixing, 5"	$15.00 – 18.00
6"	$19.00 – 24.00
7"	$22.00 – 28.00
8"	$25.00 – 32.00
9"	$28.00 – 35.00
*Butter pat, individual, 2½" (Barkwood, Bel Air, Gayety and Hawaiian Coral)	$12.00 – 20.00
Butter tray and cover, oblong	$35.00 – 45.00
Casserole, covered, 8" (inside diameter)	$35.00 – 60.00
*covered, 4" individual	$13.00 – 18.00
*covered, chicken pie, 4" individual, stick handle	$15.00 – 20.00
*Casserole Hot, metal stand only with candle warmer	$20.00 – 25.00
*Casserole Round-Up, metal stand only with candle warmer	$35.00 – 50.00
Coaster, 3¾", ridged	$12.00 – 15.00

San Marino Values

Coffee server & stopper, 10-cup	$35.00 – 45.00
stopper only	$12.00 – 18.00
*Coffee Hot, metal stand with candle warmer	$15.00 – 20.00
Creamer, regular	$10.00 – 12.00
Cups and saucers, teacup	$8.00 – 15.00
*Jumbo cup	$25.00 – 35.00
*Colossal cup	$95.00 – 150.00
*Custard, 3"	$18.00 – 22.00
*Egg cup, double	$15.00 – 22.00
Flower Pot, *3"	$18.00 – 25.00
saucer	$10.00 – 15.00
*4"	$25.00 – 30.00
saucer	$10.00 – 15.00
*5"	$30.00 – 35.00
saucer	$10.00 – 15.00
Mug, 9 oz	$12.00 – 25.00
Pitchers, *¼ pint	$20.00 – 25.00
*½ pint	$20.00 – 25.00
1 pint	$22.00 – 30.00
1 quart	$25.00 – 32.00
2 quart	$30.00 – 40.00
*syrup, drip-cut top	$40.00 – 50.00
Plates, *2½" lapel plate with pin (Barkwood, Bel Air, Gayety, and Hawaiian Coral)	$18.00 – 22.00
6" bread and butter	$5.00 – 8.00
7½" salad	$7.00 – 12.00
10" dinner	$10.00 – 17.00
13" chop	$18.00 – 30.00
Platters, 9½"	$12.00 – 18.00
11"	$15.00 – 20.00
13"	$20.00 – 30.00
Sauce boat	$17.00 – 22.00
Shakers, gourd, set	$15.00 – 20.00
*salt, large (Montecito shape)	$20.00 – 25.00

San Marino Values

**salt cellar, wood encased, 4½"	$35.00 – 45.00
*pepper mill, metal fitting (Montecito shape)	$40.00 – 50.00
**pepper mill, wood encased, 4½"	$45.00 – 55.00
*Spoon holder	$30.00 – 45.00
Sugar, covered..	$12.00 – 17.00
Teapot, covered, 8-cup, 11" length	$35.00 – 50.00
14½" length	$50.00 – 65.00
Tidbit, two-tier, wooden fixture	$15.00 – 22.00
three-tier, wooden fixture	$20.00 – 30.00
Tumbler, 14 oz, Style #5	$20.00 – 25.00

Values:

In the Blanding and Pan American Lei patterns, most pieces are two to three times high end of value range.

*Made briefly in the 1950s.
**Known in Pan American Lei, California Heritage (California Originals).

Lotus and Pan American Lei ◈

In lieu of the company name (unknown), the Lotus pattern name was chosen by the author to identify this shape that was used for three different patterns. Coupe plates with offset rims and hollow ware with a bulky look characterize this line. Patterns were Lotus, Chinling, and Vintage (solid colors have also been reported, in lime green and bright yellow). The patterns were introduced in 1950 and were short-lived. A variation was Pan American Lei, which combined San Marino flatware with the Lotus hollow ware.

A Lotus-patterned plate has been found with the San Marino coupe shape; the flower color of this is lavender and yellow.

The October 1978 issue of the *Heisey Newsletter* offered the following information concerning the Pan American Lei pattern: Pan American Lei pattern was designed to coordinate with the Heisey etched stemware pattern No. 518. The Pan American Lei promotion was sponsored by Pan American Air Lines. The premiere showing was made in Honolulu on June 26, 1950; the mainland premiere showing was made in New York on July 10th, at the Plaza Hotel. The Lei promotion covered china, glass, Dirilyte flatware, draperies, and other kindred lines. Pan American Air Lines flew fresh leis to the various shows and to stores for their promotions.

According to Heisey's information, Vernon Kilns had considerable trouble working out decals for this pattern. The pattern has a designer backstamp (mark 44). A former employee thought Blanding may have designed the pattern, but since it is not signed by Blanding, this is unlikely. As mentioned before, the Pan American Lei mark is very similar to designer mark 49 by the artist Biondi.

A trade journal describing Vernon Kilns stated that Pan American Lei was the central campaign of one of the greatest coordinating home furnishings promotions to ever hit the retail field. Leading manufacturers in all home furnishing disciplines were tying their products in with the Lei pattern.

Seen in the picture are examples of the Lotus line. All have mark 21.
BACK ROW: Chinling 10½" plate; Lotus sugar bowl.
FRONT ROW: Vintage teapot (lid missing); Lotus creamer; Chinling sugar bowl.

TOP: 9 oz. mug; 10" plate; teapot.
BOTTOM: 8" covered casserole (13" outside diameter); 5½" fruit; teacup and saucer; salt and pepper shakers.

Vintage and Pan American Lei. Pan American Lei ashtray, Vintage 13½" chop plate. (Note the offset rim.)

America's Finest Dinnerware

Company brochure for Lotus pattern, which offered the following: "Starter Set (16 pcs.) List Price $16.50." Special Retail Price $12.95." Some prices for Lotus: butter tray and cover, $2.75; 13" chop plate, $3.50; chowder, $1.35; coffee pot, 8-cup, $4.80; 8" covered dish, $5.70; 5½" fruit, 80¢; shakers, $1.00 each; teapot, $4.80; 12 oz. tumbler, $1.35; double vegetable, $4.50.

Pan American Lei pepper mill and salt cellar, 4½". The metal working part of the Vernon Kilns pepper mills as seen in the Pan American Lei and Winchester '73 patterns was made in England, by Park Green & Co., Ltd. "Verity Southall, Altadena, CA" also appears on the base, probably the name of the distributor.

Lotus Pattern Index

The following are all known patterns on the Lotus shape. They are all hand-tinted transfer prints.

Name	Description	Approx. Period of Production
Chinling	Floral spray in Oriental style, ivory ground.	1950
Lotus	Large red and yellow lotus flower, buds, and leaf, ivory ground.	1950
Pan American Lei	Lotus variation. Flower lei design, pink ground. Hollowware.	1950
Vintage	Purple grapes, brown leaves, tendrils, ivory ground.	1950
Solid Color	Lime and yellow are known.	1950

None of these patterns were listed in the company's price lists by November of 1950.

Lotus and Pan American Lei Values

	Lotus	Pan American Lei
Ashtray, 5½"		$30.00 – 35.00
Butter tray and cover, oblong	$35.00 – 45.00	$60.00 – 65.00
Bowls, 5½" fruit	$6.00 – 10.00	$10.00 – 12.00
6" chowder	$10.00 – 15.00	$18.00 – 20.00
8½" soup, coupe		$18.00 – 25.00
9" vegetable, round	$18.00 – 22.00	$35.00 – 40.00
vegetable, divided	$20.00 – 25.00	$40.00 – 45.00
10½" salad		$75.00 – 85.00
12½" salad	$30.00 – 45.00	
Casserole, covered, 8" (inside diameter)	$35.00 – 45.00	$80.00 – 90.00
Coffee or tea pot, covered, 8-cup	$40.00 – 50.00	$85.00 – 95.00
Creamer	$12.00 – 15.00	$20.00 – 25.00
Cups and saucers, tea	$10.00 – 15.00	$20.00 – 30.00
Mug, 9 oz	$15.00 – 20.00	$30.00 – 35.00
Pitcher, 2 quart, jug	$25.00 – 35.00	$65.00 – 85.00
Plates, 6" coupe		$10.00 – 12.00
6½" offset	$6.00 – 8.00	
7½" coupe		$18.00 – 20.00
7½" offset	$8.00 – 10.00	
10" coupe		$20.00 – 30.00
10½" offset	$12.00 – 15.00	
13" chop, coupe		$50.00 – 60.00
13" chop, offset	$30.00 – 40.00	
Platter, 13½", coupe		$50.00 – 65.00
14", offset	$35.00 – 40.00	
Sauce boat	$18.00 – 22.00	$30.00 – 35.00
Shakers, salt	$7.50 – 10.00	$12.00 – 15.00
pepper	$7.50 – 10.00	$12.00 – 15.00
salt cellar, wooden encased, 4½"		$30.00 – 35.00
pepper mill, wooden encased, 4½"		$40.00 – 45.00
Sugar, covered	$15.00 – 18.00	$25.00 – 30.00
Tumbler, #5, 14 oz	$18.00 – 20.00	$30.00 – 35.00
Mixing bowls, 5-piece (Pan American only)		
5"		$20.00 – 30.00
6"		$25.00 – 35.00
7"		$30.00 – 40.00
8"		$35.00 – 45.00
9"		$40.00 – 50.00

In July 1950, a starter set of Pan American Lei sold for $15.95; a set of Lotus pattern sold for $12.95. Sets consisted of four each of 6½" plates, 10½" plates, and teacups and saucers.

Chatelaine ∞

Chatelaine was a designer shape and pattern created by Sharon Merrill. To read more about the artist, see page 75. This beautiful new line was promoted at nationwide gift shows in the spring of 1952. Square-shaped, with embossed leaf corners, leaf handles, and finials, it was produced in four solid colors, which gave the pattern its respective names: Bronze (light brown) and Topaz (creamy beige), both undecorated, Jade (celadon with subtly decorated leaf), and Platinum (cream-colored with boldly decorated leaf). Chatelaine did not sell well, apparently because of the impracticality of the shape.

Mark 47 illustrates how the dinnerware was marked, although not every piece will be found with the mark. Also, there may be slight variations; for instance, instead of a script "Vernonware, California" in the mark, the Vernon Kilns trademark 22 may be stamped and appear in combination with the incised "Chatelaine, a Sharon Merrill design."

Pictured are examples of Chatelaine. In Bronze are the 16" platter, the creamer, the teacup and saucer, and the salt and pepper shakers; in Topaz are the sugar bowl and the teacup and saucer; in Jade are the teacup and saucer, the chowders, the 14" chop plate, the 10½" plates (stacked), and the 12" salad bowl.

In Platinum: 10½" plate (note leaf decor in all four corners as opposed to only one corner as seen in preceding photo), 9" bowl (marks both 22 and 47), and creamer (unmarked). An example of the flat-bottomed coffee cup and saucer in Jade is shown.

Jade teapot and 10½" plates.
Daniel J. Trueblood photo.

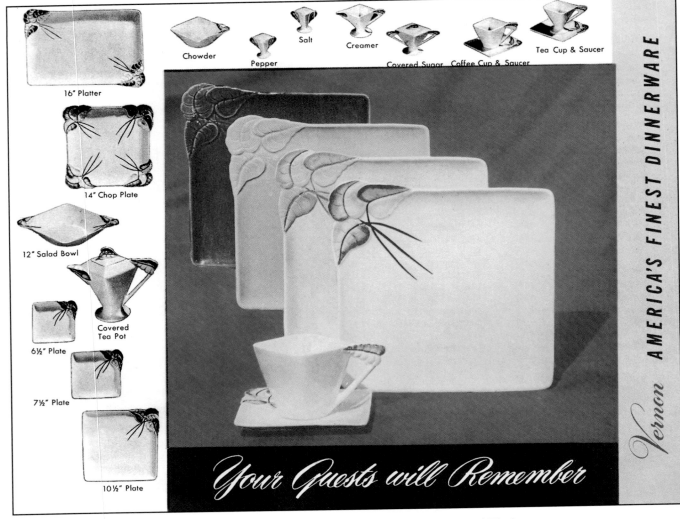

Company brochure illustrating Chatelaine's Bronze, Topaz, Jade, and Platinum patterns.

Chatelaine Pattern Index

The following are all known colors in the Chatelaine pattern.

Name	Description	Approx. Period of Production	Artist
Chatelaine	Bronze (brown), Topaz (beige), Decorated Jade (celadon), Decorated Platinum (beige).	1952 – 1953	Sharon Merrill

In January 1953, a five-piece place setting (6½" plate, 7½" plate, 10½" plate, teacup and saucer) in Bronze and Topaz sold for $6.75; in Jade and Platinum for $8.75.

Chatelaine Values

	Topaz & Bronze	Decorated Platinum & Jade
Bowls, 6" chowder	$12.00 – 15.00	$15.00 – 20.00
9" serving	$25.00 – 35.00	$35.00 – 45.00
12" salad	$45.00 – 55.00	$55.00 – 75.00
Cup and saucer, teacup, pedestal	$17.00 – 22.00	$22.00 – 25.00
coffee, flat base..	$15.00 – 20.00	$20.00 – 22.00
Creamer	$20.00 – 25.00	$30.00 – 35.00
Plates, 6½" bread and butter	$8.00 – 10.00	$10.00 – 12.00
7½" salad	$12.00 – 15.00	$15.00 – 18.00
10½" dinner (leaf one corner)	$15.00 – 17.00	$20.00 – 25.00
(leaf four corners)	$17.00 – 20.00	$25.00 – 30.00
14" chop	$40.00 – 45.00	$50.00 – 65.00
Platter, 16"	$50.00 – 65.00	$65.00 – 85.00
Shakers, set	$20.00 – 25.00	$25.00 – 30.00
Sugar, covered	$25.00 – 30.00	$35.00 – 40.00
Teapot, covered	$150.00 – 195.00	$250.00 – 295.00

San Clemente (Anytime) ⊗

Until recently, the company name for this shape was not known. Diligent research on the part of Michael Pratt, and his generous offer to share this information, has enabled the author to refer to this shape with its proper name. As were most of the preceding shapes, so too was this one named for a region of Southern California. It was named after the coastal city of San Clemente, a well-known Southern California locale. Throughout this book, both the proper name and the name previously assigned to this shape by the author will be shown together, as San Clemente (Anytime) in order to avoid confusion. The name Anytime is actually the name of one of the patterns executed on the San Clemente (Anytime), shape. According to Doug Bothwell, a former employee and son-in-law of Faye Bennison, the shape was designed by Elliott House, at that time the art director, and was introduced in about 1955. Flatware is coupe shaped, and hollow ware is somewhat barrel shaped, with ring handles and finials. Patterns are simple, with at least three having solid-color companion serving pieces that accent pattern color. Rose-A-Day has a satiny finish. Imperial, which was advertised as a "show stopper," was a designer pattern with a sgrafitto design carved with a penknife under the glaze.

Doug Bothwell mentioned that the production people did not like the pattern, since the color contaminated the kilns. Therefore, it was discontinued after a short time. The nine known patterns are Tickled Pink and Heavenly Days (identical except for their colors), Anytime, Imperial, Sherwood, Frolic, Young in Heart, Rose-A-Day, and Dis 'n Dot. Rose-A-Day was featured in the 1955 movie *Summer Love,* starring Jill St. John, in a patio scene of a teenage party.

In June 1955, a 16-piece starter set of Tickled Pink sold for $10.95; an Imperial 16-piece set was $16.95.

TOP: Heavenly Days 7½" plate, mark 27; Anytime 10" plate, mark 25 and 2-quart 10" pitcher, mark 23 Lollipop Tree gravy boat, although pictured here it belongs in the Transitional (Year 'Round) group.
CENTER: Tickled Pink butter tray and cover, mark 23, and solid-color pink companion salt and pepper shakers with wooden tops, unmarked; Heavenly Days aqua 9" vegetable bowl, mark 23, holding a Tickled Pink 6" chowder, unmarked; Tickled Pink gravy boat; Rose-A-Day 3-part relish, mark 27.
BOTTOM: Tickled Pink sugar and pink lid, mark 24; butter pat (became a lapel pin when fitted with a pin on the back); creamer, mark 24; pink teacup, unmarked; saucer, mark 24; mug, mark 27.

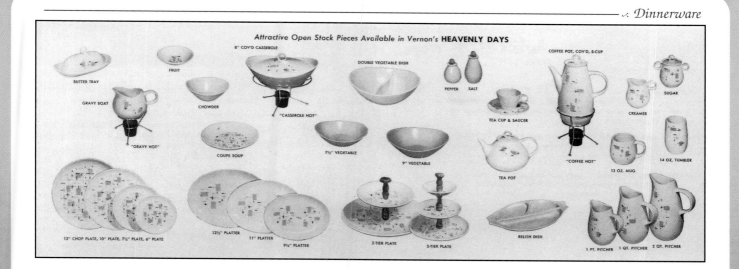

Attractive Open Stock Pieces Available in Vernon's **HEAVENLY DAYS**

A 1958 Metlox company brochure for Heavenly Days shows continued production of this pattern without change. Metlox added a wooden salad fork and spoon that had pottery handles to both Heavenly Days and Tickled Pink.

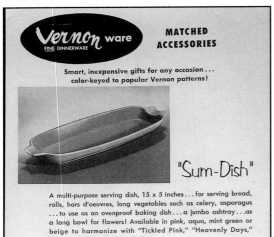

Pictured is a company ad from about 1956 that identifies a "Sum-Dish" and a "Cruet Set." The top item in the ad is the Sum-Dish, which was made in colors to harmonize with those of Tickled Pink, Heavenly Days, Anytime, and Sherwood. The lower item is the Cruet Set, which came with a ring-handled tray. The Sum-Dish and the Tray were made in pink, aqua, mint green, or beige, and the Oil and Vin cruets in a textured cream tone of the respective solid color. *Michael Pratt photo.*

Heavenly Days Cruet Set. *Devin Baker photo.*

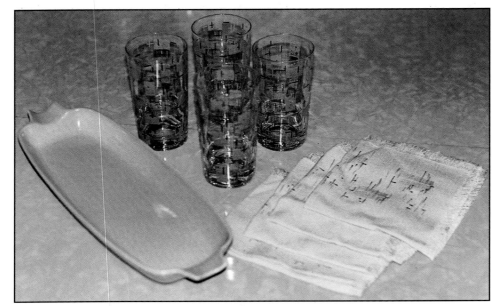

Heavenly Days Sum-Dish, 15" x 5", and matching decorated glass tumblers; Tickled Pink cloth napkins. *Devin Baker photo.*

TOP: Heavenly Days salt and pepper shakers and creamer; Rose-A-Day coffee pot; Heavenly Days sugar. BOTTOM: Tickled Pink 6" ring-handled oval Cruet Tray, designed to hold Cruet bottles (not a relish dish as previously identified); Dis 'N Dot tumbler; Anytime three section relish dish; Frolic cup and saucer. Most have mark 23 backstamp; salt and pepper shakers are unmarked.

Company photo with caption: "Julian Cale (left), western sales manager of the Cal-Kak Company and Doug Bothwell, Vernon Kilns vice president in charge of sales, pause for refreshments with star, Jill St. John, on the set of Summer Love... the new Universal-International picture about teenage romance. Cal-Dak tray tables and hostess carts in the Collector Items pattern and Vernon-ware Rose-A-Day dinnerware play important roles in the patio scene during a teenage party." The photo was dated August 13, 1956.
Photo given to the author by Zepha Bogert.

Company photo of Rose-A-Day pattern table setting; this was the pattern featured in the movie *Summer Love*. *Photo given to the author by Zepha Bogert.*

Company photo of Dis 'N Dot pattern table setting.

From Elliott House company files, loaned by Carol House.

Vernonware "DIS 'N DOT" Open Stock Newspaper Mats

Dinner Plate, 10" $1.50
Cup & Saucer $2.00

Vegetable Dishes
Divided—$5.95 9", Round—$2.50
7½", Round—$2.15

"Gravy Hot" $5.75
Incl. gravy boat & brass warmer stand
Gravy Boat $3.50

Salt & Pepper Shakers, each $1.20
Butter Tray & Cover $3.75

Relish Dish (3 section) $5.50

Platters
13½"—$4.25 11"—$3.25
9½"—$2.75

Sugar, Covered $3.25
Creamer $2.40

Tumbler, 14 oz. $1.45
Mug, 12 oz. $1.75

"Coffee Hot" $9.25
Incl. coffee server & brass warmer stand
Coffee Server, Cov'd. 8-cup $6.25

Pitchers
2-Qt.—$6.50 1-Qt.—$3.95
1-Pt.—$2.75

"Casserole Hot" $9.50
Incl. casserole & brass warmer stand
Casserole, Cov'd. 8" $6.50

Dis 'n Dot

Vernonware
FINE DINNERWARE

Ad Mat No. VK-7-140B

**SEE OTHER SIDE
FOR SUGGESTED LAYOUTS
USING THESE "OPEN STOCK" MATS**

Picture of a full-page Dis 'N Dot "open stock mat" used to suggest advertising layout.

From Elliott House company files, loaned by Carol House.

Company photo of an Anytime pattern table setting.
Photo given to the author by Zepha Bogert.

Company picture of a table setting of the Young in Heart pattern.

BACK: Imperial 10" plate, mark 48; Sherwood 13½" platter, mark 26. FRONT: Sherwood 10" server, brass handle, mark 25; 5½" fruit, mark 27; 14 oz. tumbler, mark 23; Seven Seas platter, although pictured here, it belongs in San Marino group.

All Imperial.
TOP: 1-pint pitcher; 1-quart pitcher; sugar and creamer.
CENTER: 9" serving bowl; 2-tier tidbit server; cup and saucer.
BOTTOM: 10" plate; salt and pepper shakers; 13" platter.

The following photos are all from 1955 company brochures, which stated of ware, "oven-proof, detergent proof (loves a dishwasher), guaranteed for 25 years against crazing or crackling, colors will not fade, mar or wash off with years of use."

Tickled Pink. Pink, aqua, and charcoal on a textured background.

Imperial. From brochure, "Shaded swirl pattern blending from an ebony border to soft grey center, highlighted by pure white-line abstract floral and a scattering of stars."

Sherwood. Gold, bronze, and brown in a leaf design on a beige textured background.

Frolic. Floral pattern in tones of gold, purple, and aqua on a textured spatter background.

13½" Heavenly Days platter with speckled aqua glaze, on the Transitional (Year 'Round) shape. *Bob Hutchins photo.*

San Clemente (Anytime) Pattern Index

The following are San Clemente (Anytime) shapes and patterns.

Name	Description	Approx. Period of Production
*Anytime	Abstract vertical bands of yellow, mocha, gray, and mint green. Creamy textured background. Serving pieces, lids mint green.	1956 – 1858
*Dis 'N Dot	Abstract off-center vertical lines and dots in blue, green, mustard, and ivory.	1957 – 1958
Frolic	Abstract floral, gold, purple, and aqua on a textured ivory background	1955
*Heavenly Days	Geometric design of small squares and crosses in aqua, pink, and mocha-charcoal. Solid aqua cups, serving pieces, and lids. Same as Tickled Pink except different color.	1956 – 1958
Imperial	Abstract sgraffito floral and scattered stars; ebony hollow ware, flatware has shaded swirl from ebony border to soft gray center.	1955 – 1956
*Rose-A-Day	Single pink rose, scattered leaves in soft colors. Satin ivory background.	1956 – 1958
*Sherwood	Leaves scattered in colors of gold, bronze, and brown, textured beige background.	1955 – 1958
*Tickled Pink	Geometric design of small squares and crosses in pink, aqua, and charcoal. Solid pink cups and serving pieces. Same as Heavenly Days except different color.	1955 – 1958
*Young in Heart	Dainty florals, subtle tones of yellow, aqua, charcoal, and mocha on creamy, textured background.	1956 – 1958

*When Vernon Kilns went out of business, they sold to Metlox the equipment and molds needed to produce these patterns. Metlox continued production for a while, without change, adding to the line a wooden salad fork and spoon that had pottery handles.

San Clemente (Anytime) Values

Bowls, 5½" fruit ....$5.00 – 8.00

    *6" chowder..$8.00 – 12.00

    7½" vegetable, round ....$10.00 – 15.00

    * 9" vegetable, round ....$12.00 – 18.00

    9" vegetable, divided ....$15.00 – 22.00

    soup, coupe ....$8.00 – 12.00

**Butter pat, 2½", individual..$15.00 – 20.00

Butter tray and cover..$30.00 – 40.00

*Casserole, covered, 8" diameter ....$30.00 – 50.00

*Casserole Hot, brass-colored metal stand........................$12.00 – 15.00

San Clemente (Anytime) Values

*Coffee pot, covered, 8-cup...$30.00 – 50.00

*Coffee Hot, brass color metal stand ....$12.00 – 15.00

*Creamer ....$8.00 – 12.00

***Cruet Set with Tray..$100.00 – 125.00

     Oil...$20.00 – 25.00

     Vin ....$20.00 – 25.00

     Tray, 6" oval, ring handled ....$40.00 – 50.00

*Cup and saucer, tea...$10.00 – 15.00

Gravy boat...$18.00 – 20.00

Gravy Hot, brass-colored metal stand..$12.00 – 15.00

Mug, 12 oz..$15.00 – 25.00

*Pitchers, 1-pint, 6 $\frac{1}{8}$" tall ....$18.00 – 22.00

     1-quart, 8" tall..$20.00 – 30.00

     *2-quart, 9$\frac{7}{8}$" tall..$22.00 – 35.00

Plates, *6" bread and butter...$4.00 – 6.00

     *7$\frac{1}{2}$" salad...$7.00 – 10.00

     *10" dinner ....$9.00 – 15.00

     *12" x 8" snack, indented for tumbler ....$40.00 – 50.00

     *13" chop..$18.00 – 25.00

     **Lapel pin plate, 2$\frac{1}{2}$" ....$18.00 – 22.00

Platters

     9$\frac{1}{2}$"...$10.00 – 15.00

     11" ....$12.00 – 20.00

     *13$\frac{1}{2}$"...$18.00 – 25.00

Relish dish, three section...$20.00 – 25.00

*Shakers, set ....$12.00 – 20.00

*Sugar, covered ....$12.00 – 20.00

*Syrup, drip-cut top..$45.00 – 65.00

*Teapot, covered..$35.00 – 65.00

***Sum-Dish, 15" x 5"...$25.00 – 30.00

*Tidbit, two-tier, wooden handle, also metal...$15.00 – 22.00

     three-tier, wooden handle, also metal ....$18.00 – 30.00

Tumbler, 14 oz. ....$15.00 – 25.00

---

* Imperial was a short set. These are the only pieces listed in the 1955 and 1956 price lists.
Nevertheless, there may be other pieces.

**Known in Tickled Pink

***Anytime, Heavenly Days, Sherwood, Tickled Pink only.

Transitional (Year 'Round) ⬥

Due to Michael Pratt's research, the company name for this shape is now known and is used throughout this book. The company name and the author-assigned name of previous books will be shown together, as Transitional (Year 'Round), to avoid confusion. The name Year 'Round is actually one of the patterns for this shape.

The shape is similar to the San Clemente (Anytime) shape, but the platters and vegetable bowls are rectangular instead of oval, the finials are button-shaped, the creamers and salt shakers are tall and slender, the sugar bowls are short, and the pepper shakers are ball-shaped, with slender necks. Teapots and coffee pots have pottery stands. Two patterns, Blueberry Hill and Lollipop Tree, have a satin finish, while two others, Country Cousin and Year 'Round, have textured backgrounds. These four are the only known Transitional (Year 'Round) patterns.

Metlox continued production of the Year 'Round pattern, but produced the pattern on the San Clemente (Anytime) shape, adding a 12" salad bowl and a salad serving fork and spoon set to the line.

TOP: Country Cousin sugar; Year 'Round 13½" platter; Country Cousin creamer.
BOTTOM: Lollipop Tree sugar, divided vegetable, creamer, and trio buffet server with brass handle.

An old company photo of a table setting of Lollipop Tree. Note the pottery stands. These accessories were made to hold the casserole, coffee pot, gravy boat (sometimes referred to as a batter bowl), and teapot.

Company ad showing Blueberry Hill.
Michael Pratt photo.

Blueberry Hill **Vernon ware** FINE DINNERWARE

Rich and luxurious in pattern and color...designed to blend with the new elegance in today's furnishings...BLUEBERRY HILL is gracefully traditional... modern in treatment...provincial in theme. You will find it equally at home with treasured family heirlooms or contemporary decor.
A decorative tulip and foliage pattern in tones of mocha-beige and aqua with highlights of rose and yellow.

Versatile Open Stock Items Available When You Want Them

The following pages (305 – 307) contain copies of material from Elliott House's company files and were loaned by Carol House, his widow, for this book.

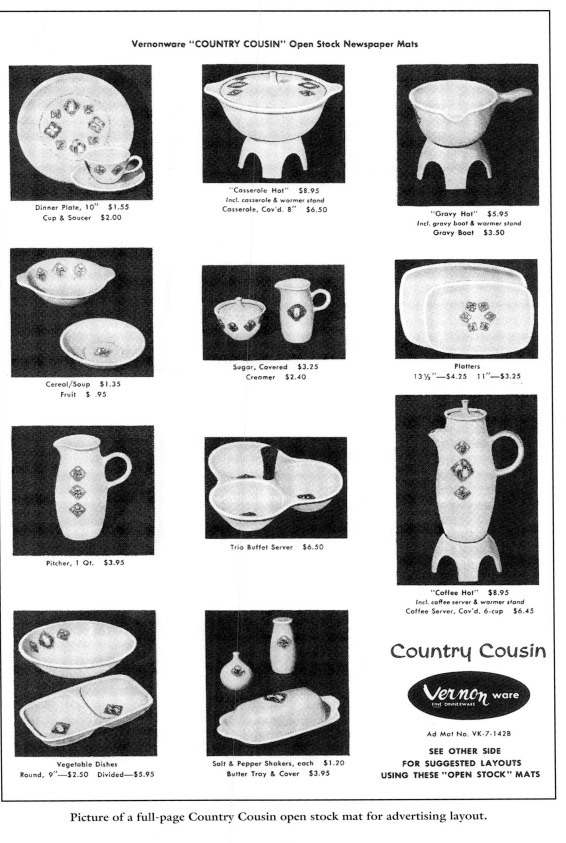

Vernonware "COUNTRY COUSIN" Open Stock Newspaper Mats

Dinner Plate, 10" $1.55
Cup & Saucer $2.00

"Casserole Hot" $8.95
Incl. casserole & warmer stand
Casserole, Cov'd. 8" $6.50

"Gravy Hot" $5.95
Incl. gravy boat & warmer stand
Gravy Boat $3.50

Cereal/Soup $1.35
Fruit $ .95

Sugar, Covered $3.25
Creamer $2.40

Platters
13½"—$4.25   11"—$3.25

Pitcher, 1 Qt. $3.95

Trio Buffet Server $6.50

"Coffee Hot" $8.95
Incl. coffee server & warmer stand
Coffee Server, Cov'd. 6-cup $6.45

Vegetable Dishes
Round, 9"—$2.50   Divided—$5.95

Salt & Pepper Shakers, each $1.20
Butter Tray & Cover $3.95

Country Cousin

Vernon ware
FINE DINNERWARE

Ad Mat No. VK-7-142B

**SEE OTHER SIDE
FOR SUGGESTED LAYOUTS
USING THESE "OPEN STOCK" MATS**

Picture of a full-page Country Cousin open stock mat for advertising layout.

305

Suggested One-Minute Radio or TV Spot

"COUNTRY COUSIN" Vernonware

If you like the warm glow of polished wood...the homey touch of a Grandma Moses painting...you'll love the friendly warmth and hospitality of Vernon's "COUNTRY COUSIN" dinnerware...now on display at (STORE NAME). It's a charming provincial pattern, quaint in design, modern in treatment...with boy and girl figures in rose, blue, green and yellow in gold patchwork squares on a cream background. Vernon's exclusive "Glaze-Lock" process makes "COUNTRY COUSIN" dishwasher-safe, wonderful for oven-to-table service. It's as durable and practical as it is smart...and surprisingly inexpensive. (STORE NAME) offers a 16-piece starter set, including four dinner plates, four salad plates, four cups and four saucers at just $12.95...and you can add colorful service pieces and extra place settings any time from open stock. Come in and see "COUNTRY COUSIN" and other delightful Vernonware patterns at (STORE NAME AND ADDRESS).

TO ADAPT THIS RADIO SPOT FOR TELEVISION...

Open VIDEO with a C.U. of Card reading:

(STORE NAME) Presents...

Country Cousin
Vernonware

Cut to table setting, showing place settings and open stock serving pieces (or a matte photograph of table setting, available from Vernon Kilns' Advertising Dept.) featuring the "COUNTRY COUSIN" pattern.

Close with a C.U. of Card reading:

Country Cousin
Vernonware
**16-pc. Starter Set
Service for four
Only $12.95**
at
(STORE NAME AND ADDRESS)

Suggested one-minute radio or TV spot advertising.

1957 VERNONWARE ADVERTISING SCHEDULE

PUBLICATION	JAN.	FEB.	MAR.	APR.	MAY	JUNE	JULY	AUG.	SEPT.	OCT.	NOV.	DEC.
BRIDE'S MAGAZINE	I Pg. 4-col T.P.			I Pg. 2-col H.D.			I Pg. 4-col New			I Pg. 4-col Any.		
MODERN BRIDE	I Pg. 4-col Any.			I Pg. 4-col T.P.			I Pg. 2-col H.D.			I Pg. 4-col New		
LIVING FOR YOUNG HOMEMAKERS			½ Pg. 2-col T.P.							½ Pg. 4-col New	½ Pg. 4-col New	
SEVENTEEN		¼ Pg. 2-col T.P.		¼ Pg. 2-col H.D.						¼ Pg. 2-col T.P.		
RETAILING DAILY	x x	x	x	x	x	x	x x	x	x	x	x	x
CROCKERY & GLASS	I Pg. B&W		I Pg. B&W				I Pg. B&W			I Pg. B&W		
CHINA GLASS DIRECTORY					I Pg. B&W							

VK–670

Copy of a 1957 Vernonware advertising schedule.

Transitional (Year 'Round) Pattern Index

Listed are Transitional (Year 'Round) shape patterns. Approximate production of this shape was between 1957 and 1958.

Name	Description
Blueberry Hill	Tulip and foliage pattern in tones of mocha-beige and aqua, with highlights of rose and yellow on a creamy satin background.
Country Cousin	Provincial pattern of boy and girl figures in rose, blue, green, and yellow, in gold patchwork squares on a creamy background.
Lollipop Tree	Freeform pattern in brilliant tones of blue, green, red, and gold on a creamy satin background.
Year 'Round	Geometric circle design in yellow, Mocha, and gray on creamy, textured background. Serving pieces, lids, and stands in Mocha. Metlox continued production of this pattern on the San Clemente (Anytime) shape.

Transitional (Year 'Round) Values

Bowls, 5½" fruit ....$5.00 – 7.00

     cereal/soup ....$8.00 – 10.00

     9" vegetable, round ....$12.00 – 17.00

     9" vegetable, divided ....$15.00 – 20.00

Buffet server, trio ....$35.00 – 50.00

Butter tray and cover...$25.00 – 35.00

Casserole, covered, 8"...$25.00 – 45.00

Casserole Hot, pottery stand...$20.00 – 22.00

Coffee pot, covered, 6-cup...$25.00 – 45.00

Coffee Hot, pottery stand ....$20.00 – 22.00

Creamer ....$8.00 – 10.00

Cup and saucer, tea...$8.00 – 12.00

Gravy boat...$18.00 – 25.00

Gravy Hot, pottery stand ....$20.00 – 22.00

Mug, 12 oz...$12.00 – 20.00

Pitcher, 1-quart ....$20.00 – 25.00

Plates, 6" bread and butter ....$4.00 – 6.00

     7½" salad..$6.00 – 10.00

     10" dinner ....$9.00 – 13.00

Platters, 11"...$12.00 – 20.00

     13½" ....$18.00 – 25.00

Shakers, salt and pepper...$12.00 – 15.00

Sugar, covered ....$10.00 – 15.00

Tea Hot, pottery stand..$20.00 – 22.00

Teapot, covered...$25.00 – 50.00

Miscellany ∞

Over the years and since the author's first book was published in 1978, a number of pottery items have been found which are Vernon products but which were backstamped with the trademarks of other companies. Although there are no company records to substantiate the claim, it has become quite evident that Vernon Kilns did produce pottery for other companies. Wherever possible, known examples of Vernon products that carry another company's trademark are pictured with the company backstamps.

In the group picture on the next page, examples are shown of dā Bron's Countryside, Spice Island, and Dreamtime, Frederick Lunning's Calla Lily and Floral Wreath (both author-assigned names), and Sears' Harmony House Rosedale. Another pattern, Wheat, was produced for Sears and is pictured. Photos of the three company backstamps are shown (see pages 314 – 315).

For Montgomery Ward's, Vernon produced the Mojave pattern on the San Marino shape (see page 276 for picture and information).

A pair of 7½" test plates are pictured, both with unusual abstract designs. Described are all marks on the backs of the plates. LEFT TO RIGHT: Montecito shape, marked on the back "3rd 3-color New Transfer Process Test, Pistachio Matt," dated 11-7-50, artist's initials in a circle; San Marino coupe, marked "2nd Series, New Transfer test," dated 5-7-51, "W. M." (artist's initials in circle), colors are B-Green #1, D-Brown #1, B1-Gray #1, and Pistachio.

Patterns made for other companies under their trade names are pictured. See shape sections for values.

TOP: dā Bron's Countryside, Montecito shape (P. L. Davidson, artist); Sears, Roebuck and Company, Harmony House Rosedale, Melinda shaped. Both 9½" plates are transfers and are hand tinted.

CENTER: dā Bron's Dreamtime 10" plate, San Marino shape; Frederik Lunning, Inc., N. Y., 12" plate, Floral Wreath* pattern, matching creamer and sugar; Lunning Calla Lily demitasse cup and saucer; all are on Montecito except demitasse saucer, it is on the Ultra shape. All except Calla Lily* are hand painted; it is a tinted transfer.

BOTTOM: dā Bron's Spice Islands, Montecito (P. L. Davidson, artist), 6½" and 9½" plates and cup and saucer. Hand-tinted transfer.

*Author's name for pattern.

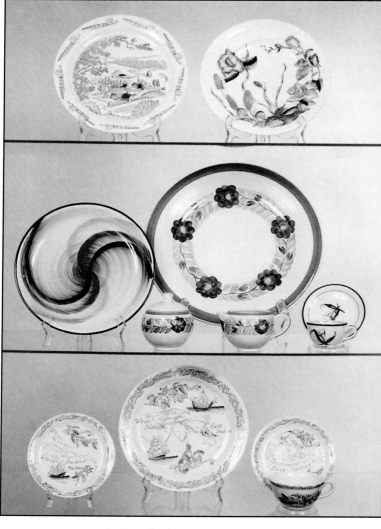

Hand-painted in California

ROSEDALE

Rosedale $13.95 16 pieces

Harmony House EXCLUSIVE . . .
Guaranteed against crazing and discoloration. Fetching floral pattern created for your own settings by one of the outstanding California potteries. Artistic floral design is painted by hand *under the glaze* so the true colors won't wear off. Semi-porcelain.
35 D 04679—16 pcs. . . . same as 20 pcs. without sauce dishes. Wt. 17 lbs. $13.95

WHEAT

Wheat $13.95 16 pieces

Harmony House EXCLUSIVE . . .
Guaranteed against crazing and discoloration. Charming pattern created just for you by one of the outstanding California potteries. Lovely flowers accented by graceful wheat sprays are hand-painted *under the glaze* so the glorious colors won't wear off. Semi-porcelain.
35 D 04680—16 pcs. . . . same as 20 pcs. without sauce dishes. Wt. 17 lbs. $13.95

Sears Harmony House patterns Rosedale and Wheat. From a page in a Sears catalog, 1950, spring/summer issue.

Wheat casserole, Melinda shape.
Phil Shurley photo.

Sears, Roebuck & Co. mark.

dā Bron mark.

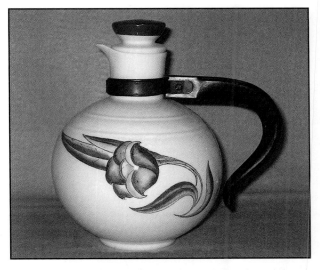

Wood Rose carafe. *Tim and Linda Colling photo.*

FREDERIK
LUNNING, INC.
NEW YORK

Frederik Lunning, Inc., mark.

Vernon Kilns wares were used for Belmar China Company's Wood Rose, executed on the San Marino shape. A carafe, plate, and backstamp are shown. A striking, elongated 14" teapot has been reported in the pattern. An example of the 14" teapot shape can be seen in the Casual California teapot in Mahogany Brown on page 275.

Backstamp for Wood Rose.
Tim and Linda Colling photo.

Wood Rose carafe. *Tim and Linda Colling photo.*

Still another Vernon Kilns product, a Montecito plate, was decorated by J. Lafayette & Co., Ltd., of Los Angeles. The label reads, "'THE DON' AGUA CALIENTE SET 'HANDPAINTED.'" This company is known for having purchased glazed Bauer blanks for decorating its copyrighted "Californio" design. This plate was one of a set of four purchased by Steve Soukup, who furnished this information and photo.

J. Lafayette & Co. decorated plate and label. Believed to be a Vernon Kilns Montecito blank. *Steve and Debra Soukup photo.*

Among some Vernon Kilns collectors, Sunset Pottery is believed to have been another line of the company. Padraig MacRauiri furnished the information and pictures for Sunset line. He states, "There is no Sunset Pottery listed in California's industrial record, the Directory of California Manufacturers (later named The California Manufacturer's Annual Register). Sunset Pottery is not listed in *Crockery and Glass Journal's* 'Red Books.'" There is little to substantiate Vernon Kilns' manufacture of Sunset other than observation, according to MacRauiri. The Sunset Pottery mark is found on more than one line of dinnerware, and these are not necessarily lines manufactured by Vernon Kilns. He observes that "the glazes and heft of the ware strongly compel one to speculate these are Vernon Kilns," and he further states that Vernon's Early California pattern glazes are identical to those of Sunset Pottery. The photo submitted for this book by MacRauiri shows the glazes on both Early California cups and Sunset Pottery cups. Early California grill plates have been found with the Sunset Pottery mark. Also San Marino shapes have been found with the Sunset Pottery mark, as seen in the fruit bowl pictured on the next page.

This picture shows the likeness of Sunset to Vernon Kilns' Early California. *Padrag MacRauiri photo.*

Backstamp. *Padraig MacRauiri photo.*

Backstamp on the bottom of a San Marino fruit bowl.
Bob Hutchins photo.

Some collectors believe that the Monterey line of pottery was also a Vernon Kilns line, and more and more evidence is pointing in this direction. Others believe that Monterey was more likely a Metlox line. It is possible that Vernon Kilns introduced Monterey, and Metlox continued its production.

From information based on by Padraig MacRauiri's intensive research and collection of pottery, we have the following support for the theory that Vernon Kilns originated the Monterey of California line of pottery.

In his contact with Carol House (the widow of Elliott House), MacRauiri states that she confirmed that "Elliott worked with a small team of three men who designed Vernon's patterns." She recalled that they created Monterey in several shapes. Monterey came in six colors: pink and turquoise (identical to those used on Tickled Pink and Heavenly Days), and tan, celery green, yellow, and charcoal black. All except for black were speckled. Hollow ware shapes were changed, but the bowls had the "fish tail" handle of San Clemente (Anytime). The flatware had identical flatware as other Vernon shapes and glazes. Specific shapes shared by the two lines are found in the 13" chop plate, the 10", 7½", and 6¼" plates, the saucer (cup differs), the 8¼" shallow soup bowl, the 5⅝" fruit, and the 11" platter. One other bit of evidence pointing to Vernon as the manufacturer is the backstamped Monterey mug pictured on the following page. This mug has the Vernon Kilns Montecito (late) and San Marino shape, not a Metlox shape.

MacRauiri has had contact with a lady who, in 1956, worked at Eagles, a chain store in Moline, Illinois. The store offered the Monterey line as a promotional line; receipts could be traded in exchange for the pottery. By saving the grocery store receipts of the customers who had neglected to take them, she traded them for the dishes she was collecting.

Other information from MacRauiri mentions the existence of an 11" platter, marked "Vernon Ware – USA – safe in the oven and dishwasher," with mark 27 without the Metlox stamp. It was in a box purchased along with 25 pieces of tan Monterey dishes, with marks varying from no mark to the blue California map outline mark. The Vernon platter is identical in color, size, and shape to the Monterey. Further, MacRauiri says that he has seen the celery green Monterey glaze on a San Clemente (Anytime) bowl marked Vernonware.

Pictured is the California map outline backstamp that was predominantly used. There are two versions, one with "Monterey" in script or a similar backstamp with "Monterey" in print.

Monterey bowls with "fish tail" handles.
Padraig MacRauiri photo.

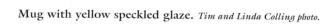

Backstamp of Monterey. *Padrag MacRauiri photo.*

Mug with yellow speckled glaze. *Tim and Linda Colling photo.*

Backstamp on mug. *Tim and Linda Colling photo.*

∞ *The Last Years* ∞

After World War II, the United States government encouraged trade with countries whose economies had suffered during the war. Consequently, our country was flooded with imports from Japan, England, and Scandinavia.

To offset this competition, an efficient Vernon sales department was organized with agents in Alaska, Hawaii, South America, the Canadian provinces of British Columbia and Ontario, and all major cities in the United States. Doug Bothwell, son-in-law of Faye Bennison, was persuaded to join Vernon Kilns in 1952 as the vice president in charge of sales. Major sales campaigns were conducted by Zepha Bogert and her husband, E. V. Bogert, who were the advertising agents for Vernon Kilns.

One of their most successful promotional techniques was the creation of the "Vernon Girls," a group of young ladies who arranged table displays in major department stores all over the country. Each girl was fictitiously known as "Ruth Vernon." Orders poured in from this campaign.

Other sales aids were developed by the Bogerts and made available to stores. The ceramic dealer sign pictured in dinnerware photos was designed especially to hold price cards for starter sets. Other sales aids available were brochures or price cards for display on store counters or shelves; a sales training 78 rpm record at $1.50 postpaid, recorded by "Ruth Vernon"; television slides and copy to provide stores with interesting television spots; a 16 mm motion picture entitled *A Date with a Vernon Dish,* in full color and with sound track available in 20 or 30 minute lengths, for schools, clubs, churches, and department store promotions (it featured table settings and a trip through the factory); and a series of 35 mm slides along with a 20-minute speech available to anyone wanting to give a talk.

In 1955, Mr. Bennison retired as the president to become the chairman of the board and was succeeded by Edward Fischer. With Mr. Bennison no longer active, much of the old spirit was gone. Finally, because the foreign competition and labor costs were becoming increasingly burdensome, and in spite of the successful sales campaigns, the unexpected decision to close the business was announced in January 1958. It was a sad day, and came as a shock for the many faithful employees, some of whom had been with the company since its inception. In Mr. Bennison's words, "I was heartbroken to close the plant, a wonderful skilled loyal bunch of people who had worked with us." It took most of the year to wind up the manufacturing operations. Some surplus pottery was sold to pottery yards.

Metlox Potteries, of Manhattan Beach, California (which went out of business in May 1989), bought the molds and, modifying some shapes, continued producing some patterns (mentioned earlier) for at least a year.

In 1958, manufacturing totally ceased and the company disbanded. Faye Bennison and Edward Fischer remained the active principals of the corporation until 1969, when Vernon Kilns was finally legally dissolved. Faye Bennison died five years later, on August 31, 1974, at the age of 91. Mr. Fischer passed away on November 19, 2002.

Because of ever-growing collector interest, Vernon Kilns has taken its rightful place as a major contributor to American pottery history.

Vernon Kilns Sales Representatives listed in a January 1956 company catalogue

Ken Angevine 1235 Wilson Drive West Covina, CA	Joseph S. Burrows 171 W. Cordova St. Vancouver, B.C., Can.	Collins, Groth & Johnson 1355 Market St. San Francisco, CA
Berni Brothers 1633 N.W. 21st Portland, OR	Joseph S. Burrows, Jr. 64 Wellington St., West Toronto, Ontario, Can.	Bill A. Cook P.O. Box 8175 Kansas City, MO
Harold B. Budd Convent P.O. Convent, NJ	Ray Cavanaugh 323 North Ey St. Tacoma, WA	Edward Cooper 4308 W. 87th Place Oaklawn, IL

Vernon Kilns Sales Representatives listed in a January 1956 company catalog

Robert S. Foster
1029 Summit Ave. N.
Seattle, WA

George Granville
29 Hurd Rd.
Belmont, MA

William J. Lee
566 Hickory Lane
Oshkosh, WI

Max May
P.O. Box 1425
Phoenix, AZ

Michael J. May
15 Bryan Place
Jersey City, NJ

Robert Reichardt
4119 Ovid Ave.
Des Moines, IA

Walter Songster
1601 Emerson St.
Denver, CO

Jay S. Sutton
4520 Reed St.
Wheatridge, CO

Thomas & Moore Co.
322 2nd Unit, Santa Fe Bldg.
Dallas, TX

Charles Weaver
4100 Peachtree Rd.
Atlanta, GA

The Weikels, Jim & Jay
P.O. Box1977
Greensboro, NC

Clar Worlds
P.O. Box 3264
Honolulu, HI

❧ Bibliography ❧

Ainsworth, Ed. *Painters of the Desert*. Palm Desert, CA: Desert Magazine Publisher, 1960.

Bennison, Faye G. *Our Story*. Los Angeles, CA: privately published, 1968.

Bredehoft, Neila. "Winchester '73." *Heisey Newsletter*, Vol. VI, No. 7. Newark, OH: July 25, 1977.

Christensen, Bess Gedney. "Vernon Kilns Souvenir Plates." *The Antique Trader*. June 3, 1992. Dubuque, IA.

Current Biographies. N.Y.: H. W. Wilson Co., 1942.

Eames, John Douglas. *The MGM Story*. London: Octopus Books Ltd., 1975.

Falk. *Who Was Who in American Art*. 1985.

Faux, Pat, editor. *Vernon Views* . Tempe/Scottsdale, AZ: Nancy Schadeberg, 1981 – 2002.

Gilbert, Dorothy B., ed. *Who's Who in American Art*. New York: R. R. Bowker Co. 1962.

Kent, Rockwell. *It's Me, O Lord*. New York: Dodd Mead & Co., 1955.

Kleinbeck, Allen. "About the Cover." *The Glaze*, February 1981. Springfield, Mo.

McClinton, Katherine Morrison. *Art Deco, A Guide for Collectors*. New York: Clarkson N. Potter, Inc., 1973.

Mebane, John. *Collecting Nostalgia*. New Rochelle, NY: Arlington House, 1972.

Nelson, Maxine Feek. *Versatile Vernon Kilns*. Costa Mesa, CA: Rainbow Publications, 1978.

_____. *Versatile Vernon Kilns, Book II*. Paducah, KY: Collector Books, 1983.

_____. *Collectible Vernon Kilns*. Paducah, KY: Collector Books, 1994.

Olmstead, Anna Wetherill. "American Ceramic Art Goes to Scandinavia." *Design*, vol. 38, no. 5, November 1936.

_____. *Contemporary American Ceramics Catalogue, 1937*. Syracuse, NY: Museum of Fine Arts.

Petteys, Chris. *Dictionary of Women Artists*. 1985.

Pickel, Susan E. "From Kiln to Kitchen." *American Design in Tableware Catalogue*. Springfield, IL 1980.

Sferrazza, Julie. *Farber Brothers Krome-Kraft*. Marietta, OH: Antique Publications, 1988.

Stiles, Helen E. *Pottery in the United States*. New York: E. P. Dutton & Co., Inc, 1941.

Swenson, James. "A Century of Progress." *The Antique Trader*. August 14, 1991 Dubuque, IA .

Index

Bold face numbers indicate photos or illustrations, plain face numbers indicate text.